RURAL PLANNING AND DEVELOPMENT
IN NORTHERN IRELAND

RURAL PLANNING AND DEVELOPMENT IN NORTHERN IRELAND

Edited by John Greer and Michael Murray

INSTITUTE OF PUBLIC
ADMINISTRATION

Published in 2003
by the Institute of Public Administration
57–61 Lansdowne Road
Dublin 4

British Library Cataloguing in Publication Data
A catalogue record for this book
is available from the British Library.

ISBN 1 902448 82 0

Cover design by M&J Graphics
Origination by Carole Lynch, Dublin
Printed by ColourBooks Ltd, Dublin

RURAL PLANNING AND DEVELOPMENT IN NORTHERN IRELAND

Edited by John Greer and Michael Murray

Accounts of planning and development in Northern Ireland tend to be dominated by Belfast as a case study. Less profile in published work exists for the smaller towns, villages and countryside that have moved during the 1990s to become a central concern of public policy. Rural affairs now command widespread popular interest, not least because of the many initiatives that have been brought forward in partnership with rural people. One such initiative is the Northern Ireland Regional Development Strategy adopted by Members of the Legislative Assembly in late 2001. This offers a consensus-driven framework to guide planning and development activities over the next twenty-five years and is at pains to highlight the inclusion of rural society, comprising its economies and communities, in this vision of the future. In *Rural Planning and Development in Northern Ireland*, the contributors unravel the personalities of, contemporary challenges for, and policy responses to rurality. The implications of this analysis are set against the promises and expectations of the Strategy and raise the provocative conclusion that its perceived transformational capacity may well be overstated. Rethinking rural planning and development in Northern Ireland remains an enduring quest.

CONTENTS

LIST OF ILLUSTRATIONS

LIST OF TABLES

LIST OF PHOTOGRAPHS

NOTES ON CONTRIBUTORS

Michael Anyadike-Danes is Director of the Northern Ireland Economic Research Centre, Belfast.

Michael Conway is Rural Co-ordinator at the Northern Ireland Housing Executive.

Niall Fitzduff is Director, Rural Community Network (Northern Ireland).

Brian Graham is Professor of Human Geography and Director of the Academy for Irish Cultural Heritages, University of Ulster at Magee.

Jonathan Greer is a Research Officer in the School of Policy Studies, University of Ulster at Jordanstown.

John Greer is a Senior Lecturer in the School of Environmental Planning, Queen's University, Belfast.

Mark Hart is Professor of Family Business Research, Small Business Research Unit, Kingston University.

Claire Jack is a Research Fellow in the Department of Agricultural and Food Economics, Queen's University, Belfast.

Nick Mack is Senior Research Officer with the Rural Development Council for Northern Ireland.

Seamus McErlean is a Lecturer in the Department of Agricultural and Food Economics, Queen's University, Belfast.

Alistair McKane is a Planner with the Department for Social Development, Northern Ireland.

Michael McSorley is a Planner with the Department for Social Development, Northern Ireland.

Joan Moss is a Senior Lecturer in the Department of Agricultural and Food Economics, Queen's University, Belfast.

Michael Murray is a Reader in the School of Environmental Planning, Queen's University, Belfast.

Brendan Murtagh is a Reader in the School of Environmental Planning, Queen's University, Belfast.

Rachel Naylor is a Lecturer in Sociology, University of Ulster at Magee.

Maureen O'Reilly is Head of Policy Evaluation at the Northern Ireland Economic Research Centre, Belfast.

Mark Scott is a Lecturer in the Department of Urban and Regional Planning, University College Dublin.

Ken Sterrett is a Senior Lecturer and Head of School in the School of Environmental Planning, Queen's University, Belfast.

Michael Wallace is a Lecturer in the Department of Agribusiness, Extension and Rural Development, University College Dublin.

ACKNOWLEDGMENTS

The financial support of Rural Innovation and Research Partnership (NI) Ltd, funded through the EU LEADER 2 programme, is gratefully acknowledged. The cover illustration *The Fox* by John Luke is reproduced with the kind permission of the Trustees of the Ulster Museum, Belfast. Photograph 1.1 *Mournes Harvest* is reproduced with the permission of the Northern Ireland Tourist Board, Belfast. Figure 5.1 is taken from the Department of the Environment for Northern Ireland (1994), *A Design Guide for Rural Northern Ireland* and is reproduced with the permission of Mr Arthur Acheson, RIBA. Photographs 6.1 to 6.4 are reproduced with the permission of the Northern Ireland Housing Executive, Belfast. Photographs 10.1 to 10.3 are reproduced with the permission of the Department for Social Development, Belfast.

FOREWORD

Niall Fitzduff

Too little has been written on rural life in Northern Ireland. The term 'rural' and the images and realities it evokes cross so many disciplines that no single book can be definitive. The story of change in rural Northern Ireland, especially in relation to planning and development, has received scant attention and hence a book with this focus is very welcome. The past ten years have seen a significant policy emphasis on rural revitalisation, a notable feature of which has been the engagement of rural communities in planning and development processes at regional and local scales. It is now, thankfully, inconceivable that policies would be devised without a rural dimension. And yet it is not so long ago that the prevailing orthodoxy was marked by an indifference to rural issues outside of agriculture. It is worth reflecting briefly on how this transformation has come about. The poet John Hewitt in 'Oh Country People' provides an interesting starting point for this task, capturing the essence of the rural other:

> I recognise the limits, I can stretch;
> even a lifetime among you should leave me strange,
> for I could not change enough, and you will not change.[1]

The relationship of people to land, place and community is indeed special. This connectedness, along with a perceived sense of independence of spirit from public institutions and bureaucracy, are commonly hailed as deeply embedded features of the rural psyche. Longstanding cultural and political

---

1. See F. Ormaby (1990), *Poets from the North of Ireland*, Belfast: Blackstaff Press, 31.

differences have tended to reinforce this historic sense of separation from 'the system' while the reciprocal response of 'Let the hare sit' may well have been the view of government. But the reality today is that rural people are much more willing to give voice to their deep frustrations on how public policies impact on rural living and circumstance. The preparation of a new Regional Development Strategy for Northern Ireland over the period since 1997 has prompted, for example, the following observation:

> I hope it doesn't come as a shock, but rural people live integrated lives. We use houses, travel on roads, need local schools, want accessible hospitals / healthcare. Can *Shaping Our Future* have clout in terms of all these key aspects of our lives or will it opt out of all this, with Planning Service yet again just ending up focusing the full force of its planning might on would-be, one-off housebuilders in rural areas?[2]

In short, issues of rural development are very much linked to challenging the barriers and constraints set in place by external top down control. Within Northern Ireland this critical engagement is rooted in initiatives undertaken during the 1980s.

The background to the participation of rural communities in local planning and development activities has many strands, some of which are associated with the contribution of individuals working at that time in organisations such as Queen's University, Northern Ireland Voluntary Trust (NIVT) and the Northern Ireland Housing Executive. The Rural Awards Scheme of NIVT, for example, helped to stimulate community action in rural areas in the early 1980s. In 1985 the opportunity arose to draw down funding from the

---

2. Comments by Chairman of Rural Community Network, cited in M. Murray and J. Greer (2000), *Rural Settlement Patterns and Physical Planning Policy in Northern Ireland: A Discussion Paper*, Cookstown: Rural Community Network.

Second Anti-Poverty Programme of the European Union. This led to the operation of an action research project co-sponsored by the Department of Health and Social Services, NIVT, Northern Ireland Council for Voluntary Action, the Rural Association and Strabane Citizens' Advice Bureau. The initiative was targeted at four areas of Northern Ireland which had previously been identified[3] as suffering from serious rural deprivation. Known as the Rural Action Project, it successfully highlighted the hidden nature of poverty in rural Northern Ireland based on the combined impact of local services withdrawal, unemployment, an age-ing population and the higher costs of living in remote com-munities. The effectiveness of a community development approach in tackling these serious problems was promoted as the necessary policy response. More precisely, it was rec-ommended[4] that:

- a rural community development agency be funded as a matter of urgency to undertake support, training, develop-ment, information sharing and the provision of expertise to locally based rural groups; and
- a policy of integrated rural planning and development be formulated and resourced through a process of commu-nity development and consultation as well as by means of the coordination of relevant statutory agencies.

The policy climate was appropriate for serious consideration to be given to these proposals. In 1988 the European Commission published *The Future of Rural Society,* and its President, Jacques Delors, emerged as a powerful advocate for policy adjustment. Within the United Kingdom, the House of Lords Select Committee on the European Communities was also active in the rural debate arena. Government in

3. See J. Armstrong, D. McClelland, and T. O'Brien (1980), *A Policy for Rural Problem Areas in Northern Ireland*, Belfast: Ulster Polytechnic.
4. Rural Action Project (1989), *Rural Development: A Challenge for the 1990s*, Londonderry: Rural Action Project (NI).

Northern Ireland responded by establishing an inter-
departmental committee in 1989 to provide advice on the
best way of carrying forward action to tackle the social and
economic problems in the most deprived rural areas of
Northern Ireland. The committee reported to ministers in
December 1990 with recommendations which included the
establishment of a formal hierarchy of responsibility for
rural development, the setting up of a Rural Development
Division within the Department of Agriculture, and the creation of an agency outside government — the Rural
Development Council. These recommendations were accepted
and put into practice. The need for the rural community
movement itself to have a voice so that it could influence
policy content resulted in the creation of Rural Community
Network (RCN) in February 1991, with an initial base of
some sixty community groups.

RCN largely inherited the mantle of the Rural Action
Project and took on the remit of networking community
groups in rural areas, giving a voice to rural communities in
relation to poverty and disadvantage, and seeking support
for community development. It also asssisted the Rural
Development Council in implementing its community
support programme in the most disadvantaged rural areas
of Northern Ireland. Grant aid from the Department of
Agriculture to RCN as a voluntary organisation facilitated
involvement in these activities, although with just one
development staff member and an administrator at that
time, RCN could only achieve its objectives by working
closely with others.

Throughout the 1990s, RCN was to the forefront of important policy debates relating to rural Northern Ireland.
The linkages between building community organisational
infrastructure, networking at the sub-regional scale, and
region-wide consultations on policy themes prompted wider
and deeper participation. Collaboration with the Rural
Development Council, government departments, other
agencies and voluntary sector organisations helped RCN to

respond better to a plethora of rural issues. These included rural services, water and electricity supplies, post office closures, community care, town and country planning, housing, future EU programmes and the Northern Ireland Rural Development Programme. Submissions on welfare benefits, advice and community services ensured that the central theme of poverty in rural areas was kept to the fore. Rural society in Northern Ireland does not exist in isolation from its neighbours and thus a further dimension of RCN's work has been the nurturing of networking relationships with similar organisations in England, Scotland, Wales and the Republic of Ireland. Within the latter cross-border context RCN and Irish Rural Link have organised joint Information Technology projects and have shared perspectives on rural and community development. But in the context of this book, the sheer breadth of issues covered over the past decade should be seen as a powerful illustration of the scale of the challenges being confronted by all those whose brief and interest is rural planning and development.

Dealing effectively with these challenges requires, however, more than a consultative and lobbying agenda built around meetings, clinics, conferences and publications. From the mid-1990s, RCN began to take on project and programme administration responsibilities in order to better achieve its strategic objectives. Thus, for example, it received funding for a Sperrins Community Tourism Initiative over a period of three years and for additional programmes related to arts and the environment. The EU Special Support Programme for Peace and Reconciliation in Northern Ireland and the Border Counties of Ireland provided a new opportunity to consolidate networking activity at the sub-regional level, to address some of the underlying divisions in rural areas, and to specifically target localities with a weak community infrastructure. Small grants to individual community groups stimulated local initiatives on social inclusion and reconciliation. A Millennium Halls Programme funded fifty-four community halls as open and shared venues for community development in rural areas. This focus on diversity and inclusion was subsequently extended during the second tranche of 'Peace' funding to engage women, farmers, people with disability and young people. Again, what this experience signifies is the reality that rural planning and development is action-oriented. Its integrity lies in the fact that it delivers a material difference to the lives of rural people. The research-based essays in this book demonstrate that this effort is necessary in a society now firmly committed to equality.

And so, after more than ten years of commitment by government to rural planning and development initiatives, there is much to celebrate. The positive engagement of rural communities, area-based partnerships and sub-regional networks is evidence of a stronger civil society. Devolution has created a new dynamic in policy responsiveness and rural proofing has now appeared as a formal requirement in the Northern Ireland Programme for Government. But there is still much to be done. The analysis and recommendations set out in this book are important reminders that there is still a significant agenda ahead. In this vein the unyielding complexity and persistence of the rural planning and development challenge is perhaps no better portrayed than by Seamus Heaney in his poem 'Bogland':

Every layer they stripped
Seems camped on before.
The bog holes might be Atlantic seepage.
The wet centre is bottomless.[5]

These are appropriate words with which to conclude this Foreword and to invite reflection on the pages that follow. Given the prominent focus on the welfare of rural society and the management of rural spaces across the island, as evidenced by the content of the Regional Development Strategy

---

5. S. Heaney (1972), 'Bogland', in *Door into the Dark*, London: Faber and Faber, 56.

for Northern Ireland and the thrust of the debate around the National Spatial Strategy for the Republic of Ireland, this exploration of what has worked well and what could be done differently and better should provide useful insights and encouragement to those who champion rural planning and development.

SECTION ONE:
INTRODUCTION

CHAPTER 1

Unravelling the Rural in Northern Ireland: A Planning and Development Perspective

John Greer and Michael Murray

INTRODUCTION

While Northern Ireland is synonymous with particular societal divisions, its experience of a longstanding rural-urban dialectic is shared in common with other parts of Europe and North America. In part, this is a problem born out of definitional uncertainty which categorises the rural as either open countryside or a combination of nucleated and dispersed settlement at the sub-regional scale. In each case, however, the spatial baseline remains the pattern of major urban locales and, as a classification (Cloke, 1978) of rural areas illustrates, using distance as a key variable, the hegemony of the urban is difficult to undo. The identification of pressured rural areas, accessible rural areas and remote rural areas mirrors the conventional codification of core and periphery in regional planning practice and takes the urban as the essential departure point for analysis.

But the rural-urban dialectic can also be traced back to the now discredited orthodoxy of what constitutes good planning.

This view supports the dominant role of planning experts embedded in the technocracy of government, whose toolkit of procedure and method is applied in a manner which is largely independent of the planned for. In a context where the rural has been perceived as residual, planners have sought to minimise wasted public effort by grasping the economies of scale offered by urban concentration. Northern Ireland is no stranger to that mode of policy prescription where a strong urban bias in planning and development has been conjoined with a protectionist imperative for the countryside over the period since the 1960s. This chapter begins, therefore, by interpreting more fully the rural dimension in Northern Ireland and its relationship with land use planning policy.

Arguments of equity, capacity and empowerment as expressed through community-led local development and area-based partnership governance have sought to challenge the marginalising of rural society. One effect has been that government policy makers have had to adjust their perceived wisdom on differential patterns of locational advantage and adopt a more interactive mode of planning and investment allocation. But harnessing the capacity of rural people to engage effectively and on a sustained basis with public officials requires the adoption of collaborative strategy building and initiative-based development processes. These lie at the heart of a social capital formation perspective on rural development. Accordingly this chapter, comprising the introductory section of the book, moves on to examine critically the progress of participatory rural development which has blossomed in Northern Ireland during the 1990s. This bottom up perspective on creating change, through nurtured bonding and bridging relationships, stands in stark contrast to the centrist, top down style of planning pursued earlier, though certainly the 'rules of the game' remain set from above.

Finally, the chapter concludes by introducing the contribution made by other essayists in this book to an analysis of rural planning and development in Northern Ireland. Essentially these narratives seek to explore aspects of the rural condition and key policy responses through the 1990s, as well as raising issues of contemporary relevance and wider interest.

INTERPRETING THE RURAL IN NORTHERN IRELAND

Rural scale

From the perspective of town and country planning, rural Northern Ireland has been defined by the Department of the Environment (1993) as everywhere within the region outside the Belfast Metropolitan Area and Derry/Londonderry. In 1991 some 60 per cent of the region's population (950,000) lived in the area defined as rural Northern Ireland, of which some 350,000, or 22 per cent, lived in the open countryside. This expansive definition of the rural comprises a combination of regional towns, small towns, villages, crossroads settlements and dwellings in open countryside and hints at an interpretation which is mindful of a strong functional interaction across settlement components. More recently, the Department of the Environment (1998a) has sought to sharpen that focus for regional planning purposes through its advocacy of the perspective of a family of settlements which distinguishes between the regional towns and what is labelled as 'the Rural Community'. For 1996 this redefined rural population was estimated at 652,250, amounting to 39 per cent of the population of Northern Ireland. The important point here is that, by either definition, the rural constituency is large, an observation which is underlined by the fact that the Belfast Metropolitan Area comprised 36 per cent of the Northern Ireland population, with Derry/ Londonderry, Craigavon and the other regional towns making up the balance of 25 per cent. The rural constituency, in short, contains a diversity of communities within which people live and work.

Physical planning policy at its most basic is concerned with helping to shape the future distribution of population across a territory by managing development pressures and processes. That policy may change over time, in line with regional strategies which seek to promote containment or expansion in urban areas and strict control or more relaxed stances on development in rural areas. Within Northern Ireland, the rural community, comprising a dispersed settlement pattern of small towns, villages, crossroads developments and dwellings in open countryside, has demonstrated an accelerating growth rate over three time periods since 1971. As illustrated in Table 1.1, significant growth has taken place in the small town, village and small rural settlement components of the rural community; over the period 1971 to 1996 the increase was 45 per cent whereas, in contrast, the equivalent for the open countryside was 3.4 per cent. This runs counter to a populist perception of the open countryside being swamped by housing development.

TABLE 1.1.
POPULATION TRENDS IN THE NORTHERN IRELAND RURAL COMMUNITY

The Rural Community Component	1971	1981	1991	1996
Small towns (under 10,000 pop)[1]	134,482	159,071	187,874	204,100
Villages and small settlements	68,417	76,034	83,646	89,300
Open countryside	346,954	344,274	349,667	358,850
Total	549,853	579,379	621,187	652,250

[1] Excludes the towns of Ballycastle, Ballymoney and Magherafelt, which are regional towns.
Source: Department of the Environment (1998b), *Shaping Our Future: The Family of Settlements Report,* p. 9.

However, the intensity of development activity implicit in this analysis of population change within the rural community does vary across Northern Ireland. Within the Belfast City Region, data from the Department of the Environment (1998b) highlight population growth for the rural community of some 32 per cent between 1971 and 1996, compared with 10 per cent in the rest of Northern Ireland over the same period. Whereas the population of the Belfast Metropolitan Area declined from 653,540 in 1971 to 591,950 in 1996, the small towns and villages within the Belfast City Region increased from 91,779 to 143,700 (+51,921) over the same period, with considerable impact on the scale and character of some of these settlements. Equally interesting is the recording of population growth of 13 per cent in the open countryside of the Belfast City Region, which increased from 118,760 in 1971 to 133,750 in 1996. This growth is all the more striking given the longstanding implementation of development restraint policies throughout much of this countryside (Murray, 1991). Within the remainder of rural Northern Ireland the population of the small towns and villages increased from 111,120 to 149,700 over the period 1971–1996, but the open countryside component actually fell by 2 per cent from 228,194 to 225,100 persons. In short, the trend-based evidence points to varying patterns of place-based population growth and stability across rural Northern Ireland.

Rural imagery

The rural in Northern Ireland, as elsewhere, is very much a social construction whose meaning varies across individuals and across interest groups. For some it is the simplistic essence of everything that is good in society — neighbourliness, fresh air or great scenery. It is thus the antithesis of everything that is perceived as less wholesome (and urban) — high density housing and anonymity, traffic congestion, poverty and violence. As a social construct, the rural comprises a complex melange of place, culture and identity, which, as suggested by Duffy (1997), may for most people be more myth than reality. Such representations, however, do serve to set it apart. The accompanying imagery, filtered from historical and contemporary realities, can invoke a romanticism and nostalgia, which at best is but a partial illustration of circumstance. Photographs can be an especially powerful influence on perception and behaviour, as portrayed by the branding of Northern Ireland for tourism promotion purposes as a place of bucolic harmony (see Photograph 1.1). But behind this gentle illusion of a normal society, alternative and unsaid interpretations of rural living are equally feasible: the isolation of the elderly, the marginal viability of the small farm, the depletion of community services.

PHOTOGRAPH 1.1 *MOURNES HARVEST*

PHOTOGRAPH COURTESY OF NORTHERN IRELAND TOURIST BOARD.

The cultural landscape, therefore, is a potent reservoir for informing analysis and policy prescription with a similar iconography capable of being used for different public agendas. The case of rural housing in Northern Ireland is a useful example of this multiple meaning. In a richly illustrated investigation into the constructional and typological aspects of rural houses, Gailey (1984) makes a genuine plea for the conservation and restoration of vernacular dwellings for their own sake. But a subsequent and again richly illustrated publication from the

Northern Ireland Housing Executive (1990), as part of its rural housing policy review, questions the picturesque postcard view of the thatched cottage which masks a lack of amenities and isolation. Its research identified a litany of rural housing problems at that time, for example, approximately one dwelling in twelve lacking basic amenities, more than 3,000 dwellings without mains electricity and a similar number not connected to a mains water supply, and some 68 per cent of all vacant rural dwellings regarded as unfit. In 1991, a policy statement *The Way Ahead* (Northern Ireland Housing Executive, 1991) argued not only for refurbishment aid, but also replacement grants. This differential commodification of rural housing into built heritage and unfit shelter is a depiction of broader debates about the nature of rurality in Northern Ireland which pitch environmental conservation against social deprivation. A deeply divided society provides an overlay of contested territory and relationships.

Rural planning and landscape protection

The environmental conservation ethic in Northern Ireland has a lineage extending back over fifty years. In 1946, the Planning Advisory Board published a report, *The Ulster Countryside*, which stated that the countryside was one of the region's most valuable assets, and in view of what was regarded as 'irreparable damage caused by thoughtless and careless development' recommended that: (1) public and private development should aim to preserve and improve amenities and rural architecture; (2) certain areas of particular beauty and interest should be protected and National Parks designated as appropriate; (3) the preservation of the coast should be a matter of national concern, with strict control of ribbon development; and (4) main roads should be protected from ribbon development. The subsequent passage of the Amenity Lands Act, 1965 provided the legislative base for the designation of National Parks and the appointment of an advisory body to government (the Ulster Countryside Committee) on these and related conservation matters. Proposals were made for National Parks during the late 1960s in Fermanagh, South Armagh and the Sperrins, but political

9

opposition deterred government follow-through. However, eight Areas of Outstanding Natural Beauty (AONBs) were confirmed, the Ulster Countryside Committee believing that strict development control would at least ensure a degree of landscape protection until National Parks were finally designated (Buchanan, 1982). In short, this formative period underlines an incomplete perception of the personality of rural Ulster which was weighted more towards a negative, regulatory concern for amenity and the preservation of the landscape (Caldwell and Greer, 1983).

These precepts, when linked with the adoption of growth centre principles, were carried forward in a series of regional planning frameworks extending from the Matthew Plan of 1964, through the Northern Ireland Development Programme 1970–1975, to the Regional Physical Development Strategy 1975–1995. A telling judgement from Evans (1970) was quietly ignored as physical and economic planning policy continued to shackle rural society with a relentless urban preference:

The personality of Ulster is too strong for solutions to its problems to be found in economic planning alone. However much its people are advised to forget the past and their entrenched myths and attitudes, the realities of social history and geography cannot be overlooked. Even at the level of economic planning these factors must be taken into account. Solutions for the highly urbanised and on the whole successfully urbanised English community are not likely to succeed in this environment.

Even though the number of country towns and larger villages selected for growth in subsequent local plans did increase, this expansion could only be achieved by considerable population movement from the smaller settlements and families living in the open countryside, a settlement pattern which personifies rural Northern Ireland. Development control policies exercised a presumption against new housing outside selected settlements, unless need could be proven, and became a necessary adjunct to achieving the targets set for these growth centres.

A short-term relaxation of strict control did occur in the aftermath of the 1978 review of rural planning policy by the Cockcroft Committee. But this so dismayed the conservation lobby that the Department of the Environment was prompted to introduce a further policy adjustment in the 1980s with an emphasis on the criteria of suitable location, siting and design of new development in the countryside. Housing availability and a freedom to build are at the centre of the rural debate, not least for the implications which arise for the sustainability of rural communities and their service infrastructure, and thus when government published *A Planning Strategy for Rural Northern Ireland* in 1993 it is not surprising that the language used was conciliatory to all interests. It is unfortunate that this document with its 117 policies, some quite detailed in nature, was quickly adopted for the framing of planning permission refusals, since perhaps for the first time there was an opportunity to give rural planning a new set of credentials. That document, unlike its predecessors, sought to reconcile the diverse and conflicting aspirations of different groups in society, abandoned a rigid hierarchy of settlements and the related direction of population and development, promised generous development limits around smaller settlements and promoted rural regeneration in circumstances of economic and social disadvantage. But with the emphasis in the *Rural Strategy* firmly on development control policies, it is scarcely surprising that strong opposition was spawned, which has received high-level support from the House of Commons Northern Ireland Affairs Committee (1996) in an authoritative review of planning in the region. Government has responded by indicating that the *Rural Strategy* will be progressively withdrawn and replaced by new guidance set out in a series of planning policy statements. The publication of the Northern Ireland Regional Development Strategy in late 2001, following its adoption by the Legislative Assembly, provides some preliminary insight into possible policy directions. While there is positive support for the creation of a living countryside with a high quality of life for all its residents, concerns are expressed about the cumulative visual impact of inappropriate single house development. There is little doubt, therefore, that this most wicked of planning problems will continue as a topic of contestation.

Rural landscapes and environmental stewardship

In recent years a different and, arguably, more enlightened policy agenda has sought to mediate the excesses of the protection ethic in rural areas by highlighting the benefits of good stewardship by land owners. The enactment of the Nature Conservation and Amenity Lands (Northern Ireland) Order 1985 has provided a new impetus for innovative landscape management which can bring benefit to farmers and visitors, not least through the funding of enhancement initiatives in redesignated AONBs (Figure 1.1). Moreover, a suite of Environmentally Sensitive Area (ESA) designations over the period since 1987 has provided incentive payments on an annual basis to landholders on the basis that farming operations are integrated with sympathetic landscape maintenance (Moss and Chilton, 1993). Five locales comprising the Mournes, Antrim Glens and Rathlin Island, the Sperrins, Fermanagh and Slieve Gullion have been designated, totalling 20 per cent of the land area of Northern Ireland. By December 1999 over 4,500 farmers had entered 145,000 hectares (65 per cent of the eligible land) into ten-year management agreements at a total annual cost of some £5 million (McWhinney, 2001). Outside the designated ESA, landowners are encouraged to adopt environmentally sensitive farming practices through the Countryside Management Scheme. This commenced in May 1999 and it is envisaged that over 4,000 farmers will have completed an agreement with the Department of Agriculture and Rural Development over the period to 2006.

The association of AONBs solely with planning control under the 1965 Act can be regarded as having been particularly unhelpful for environmental management. Thus the 1985 legislation was used to review the former designations and to introduce new powers for the Department of the Environment to make proposals for conservation, enjoyment and access. The designation procedures have required extensive consultation

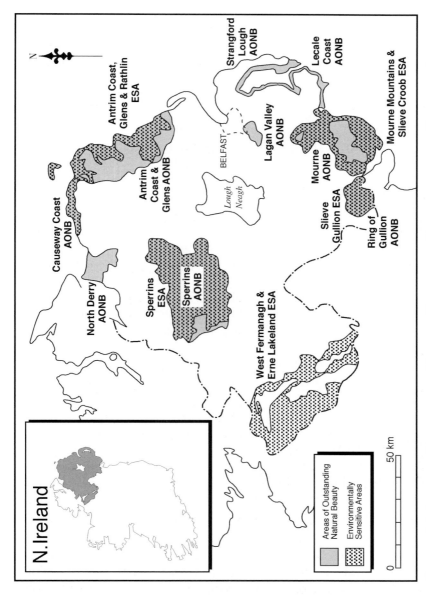

FIGURE 1.1 AREAS OF OUTSTANDING NATURAL BEAUTY AND ENVIRONMENTALLY SENSITIVE AREAS IN NORTHERN IRELAND

and, as observed by Faulkner (1999), this task 'has proved to be an exercise in balancing the interests of those who are concerned about the possible restrictive effects of designation and those who are enthusiastic about the accolade of designated status' (3). The policy emphasis of AONBs is clearly on positive management, and new multiple stakeholder structures have been established at a local level to facilitate this need and to involve communities where possible. Actions taken have included the preparation of strategies for recreation and access, for example, the introduction of identity and information measures (leaflets, logos and signage), the coordination of advice, and project-related grant aid in the Mournes (Greer and Murray, 1988) and along the Causeway Coast (Greer and Murray, 1992). What is important here in the context of rural planning and development is the recognition that prized landscapes place heavy reliance on the contribution of local people working in partnership with support agencies to maintain and enhance their identity and distinctiveness. A lived-in and active landscape is very much part of this sense of place.

Northern Ireland does not have any National Parks, with the preferred approach by policy makers, thus far, being to complete the designation of AONBs. Nevertheless, it is interesting to note that the new Regional Development Strategy suggests that the establishment of one or more National Parks will be considered 'where there is a high landscape quality, significant recreation and tourism use or potential, the local community is in favour and an acceptable model can be agreed'. There can be little doubt that areas such as the Mournes and the Causeway Coast will feature in this debate in the near future. Given the progress of environmental management policy and practice in Northern Ireland over the past decade, it would be unfortunate if discussions were unable to advance beyond the longstanding tensions associated with rural planning control.

Rural deprivation and Targeting Social Need

As an alternative discourse in the interpretation of rural Northern Ireland, social deprivation is not only more recent, but also represents a cultural iconography representative of more fundamental perceived power imbalances between Belfast with its hinterland and the rest of the region. This has been poignantly embodied in the slogan 'West of the Bann', which signifies a separation of the disadvantaged rural sub-region from its more prosperous and urban counterpart. Unravelling the spatial configuration and complexity of this disadvantage has moved on from days when the rural problem was solely aligned to the hardship of the small farmer, whose interests were represented by a union with credentials for entry into the policy community of government. A conventional analysis ran as follows:

> Finally, it should be borne in mind that while commercial farming and state regulation of agriculture have been the dominant trends in the last few decades, skills and attitudes that are far older have been by no means lost or abandoned. The small farmer inherits an indefinable quality of stock-manship which is perhaps his greatest asset, and even if he can no longer do what he likes he generally likes what he does. He is not given to spending money which is hard-won and it tends to be valued far more than the commodities that it can buy. There are many parts of the country where modesty and other peasant attributes are regarded as the highest virtues and ostentation is deplored. In the face of these attitudes capital investment and improvements are not readily undertaken... The problem of improving the quality of rural living and providing modern amenities is further increased by the extreme dispersion of the farm-steads. (Symons, 1963: 22)

The identification of rural diversity and the persistence of broader rural deprivation owes much to the seminal research of Armstrong et al (1980). Six categories of rurality were noted, ranging from the periphery of the Belfast Urban Area (Category 1) to wards which displayed a marked dependency on primary sector employment, contained the highest levels of over-crowding and unemployment, and had the lowest provision of household amenities (Category 6). The latter are defined in the report as 'rural problem areas', accounting for two-thirds of the land area of Northern Ireland and a 1971 population of 230,000. A subsequent reworking of this analysis by Caldwell and Greer (1983) which incorporated those Category 5 wards adjacent to Category 6 offered a more complete portrayal of 'peripheral rural areas', the principal effect being to form a monolithic block which stretches from North Antrim through to almost the entire west of the region, the Armagh/Monaghan borderlands, South Armagh and South Down (Figure 1.2). This equates with a population of 276,830 in 1981, almost 19 per cent of the population of Northern Ireland at that time. Apart from the already noted correlation of rural peripherality with scenic amenity, it is notable that these areas (with the exception of North Antrim) either directly abut, or run close to the Border between Northern Ireland and the Republic of Ireland. Its proximity in some cases creates peripherality, as in the north-west, or at the very least adds to it, with every peripheral rural area in Northern Ireland having its counterpart in Counties Donegal, Leitrim, Cavan, Monaghan and Louth (see Haase et al, 1996: 13).

While these analyses have been updated and refined during the interim by Robson et al (1994) using inter alia 1991 Census data, and most recently by Noble et al (2001), the recurrent pattern of deprivation remains the peripheral areas of the west, south and north-east of the region, together with a suite of wards in Belfast and Derry/Londonderry. At an aggregate scale, analysis of the 1991 Census also suggests an ethnic geography of Northern Ireland which has become more sharply demarcated, with Catholics forming a substantial majority in all of Counties Fermanagh, Tyrone, and Londonderry, north-east Antrim and parts of Down (Graham, 1997: 201–202). The success of Sinn Féin and the Social Democratic and Labour Party in winning parliamentary seats within this territory in the 2001 general election underlines the depth of the political transformation which has occurred across much of rural Northern Ireland.

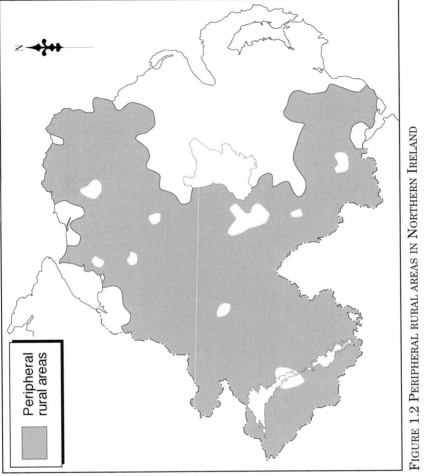

FIGURE 1.2 PERIPHERAL RURAL AREAS IN NORTHERN IRELAND
Source: J. Caldwell and J. Greer (1983), *Planning for Peripheral Rural Areas.*

The public discourse on rural disadvantage as conveyed by its spatial representation has become a powerful metaphor of key socio-economic differentials which have built up over time between the competing traditions of Northern Ireland. *Targeting Social Need* (TSN), announced in 1991 by the then Secretary of State, Peter Brooke, became one tool aimed at changing the policy-making process across the profile of public

17

expenditure in the pursuit of greater equality of opportunity and equity. The symbolism of TSN may, however, have outweighed its impact since, as reported by Quirk and McLaughlin (1996), there is little evidence that it had a substantial influence on the decision making and spending of government departments. Specifically in the case of the then Department of Agriculture (DANI), the lead department for rural development in Northern Ireland as discussed below, mainstream programmes were identified as having been untouched by TSN, with only rural development, at that time a small new area of activity, in any way related to this priority. Given, however, that this accounted for 6.5 per cent of DANI's expenditure and depended heavily (75 per cent) on European Union funding, it was concluded that this 'programme is clearly marginal and separate from the department's overall activities'(Quirk and McLaughlin, 1996: 166). It is within this context of rural circumstance and government performance that the progression of policy responsiveness beyond mere rhetoric should be located.

It is significant, therefore, that government announced the development of New TSN in 1998 as further commitment of its intention to respond more effectively to the needs of the most disadvantaged people in Northern Ireland. This has three complementary measures:

- a focus on tackling the problems of unemployment and on increasing employability;
- addressing inequalities in areas such as health, education and housing, and the problems of disadvantaged areas;
- promoting social inclusion through inter-departmental collaboration and wider partnership action.

New TSN is not an initiative with its own budget, but is seen as being a cross-cutting and targeting feature of existing spending programmes, not least related to the priorities set out in the annual Programme for Government. A commitment to publish New TSN Action Plans and Annual Reports on progress could arguably be regarded as an attempt to demonstrate performance and transparency in the face of that earlier criticism. At the same time there is scope for a more cautious interpretation of outcomes as observed by Ellis (2001). His assessment of the action plans of two government departments with a direct interest in land use planning suggests that only minor tinkering has taken place with existing policies, rather than the more fundamental realignment of objectives and expenditure required by the New TSN rhetoric:

> Any analysis of these documents can only conclude that they consist mainly of a reiteration of the conventional wisdom of modernist planning discourse clad in platitudes of achieving social inclusion. (403)

Dealing with diversity in rural society

The passage of the Northern Ireland Act, 1998 marked a significant effort by government to introduce provisions designed to secure deeper appreciation for diversity and to link this with the broader goal of inclusion. Section 75 of that legislation requires that listed public authorities in carrying out their functions have due regard to the need to promote equality of opportunity between:

- persons of different religious belief, political opinion, racial group, age, marital status or sexual orientation;
- men and women generally;
- persons with a disability and persons without;
- persons with dependents and persons without.

Public authorities are also obliged to have regard to the desirability of promoting good relations between persons of different religious belief, political opinion or racial group. The implications for rural development are that accepted spatial preferences for intervention based on deprivation are now complemented by the insistence that policy impacts are screened for equality of opportunity against the realities of difference in rural society. In carrying out this obligation the Equality Commission (1999) has suggested that it is necessary, for example, for consideration to be given to any evidence of higher or lower participation or uptake by different groups, evidence that different groups have varying needs or experiences of a particular policy, or whether there is an opportunity to promote better community relations by altering the policy, working with others in government or in the wider community.

Thus research commissioned by Rural Community Network (Shortall and Kelly, 2000) on gender-proofing the reforms of the Common Agricultural Policy (CAP) is located within this legislative context for diversity and provides a significant illustration of differential policy impacts on women and men. Key issues include: the underestimation of the work that women do on farms, an early retirement scheme for the two adults retiring rather than just the male 'farmer', training provisions for women due to changes brought about by the CAP reforms, stress levels linked to reduced incomes together with a combination of childcare and farm work responsibilities, and the under-representation of women in rural development. The central finding of this seminal research is that the broad social consequences of CAP reforms are not being sufficiently considered by policy makers.

A particular manifestation of the absence of respect for diversity in Northern Ireland is social prejudice, which all too often finds frequent expression as sectarianism. Rural Northern Ireland has suffered its share of sectarian tension and violence, thus creating a patchwork rural geography of inter- and intra-settlement apartheid. A divided society is characterised by villages and small towns cut off from their natural hinterlands by cross-border road closures, housing estates with emblem reminders of community territoriality, and central areas marked by property destruction and an aversion to private investment. Research by Murtagh (1996, 1998), reported in this book (Chapter 7), demonstrates that the social processes which have created 'peacelines' in Belfast do not stop at the greenbelt and that community attitudes in rural Northern Ireland need to be understood in the context of the political and ethno-religious group experiences of living through violence as well as perceptions of ethnic sustainability.

In short, the challenges facing many small towns, villages and dispersed rural communities in rural Northern Ireland are both complex and multidimensional. There are contested policy agendas and priorities, contested spaces and contested traditions which point to the existence of different rurals for different people. Moreover, rural society is itself highly differentiated across groups, and the groupings themselves need also to be disaggregated on the basis of diversity and inclusion. In other words, there are multiple and overlapping identities and conditions which impact on individuals. Thus, for example, the experience of women in rural life can be stratified on the basis of farming or non-farming background, age, race, sexual orientation, family/marital status, disability, religion, political opinion and so on. The inequalities, which express themselves as varying forms of prejudice, may be related, for example, to isolation, non-recognition, poverty and powerlessness. Social prejudice, in general, and sectarianism, in particular, are commonly acknowledged as being difficult issues to talk about because of sensitivity and as being difficult issues to quantify because of silence. The more local and the more personal conversations become, then the more problematic it is to confront the realities of diversity and exclusion. As discussed in the following section of this chapter, rural development policies have belatedly sought to make a contribution to the wider quest of restoring community confidence and building stability. Against a backcloth of contestation, it could be argued that the singular merit of rural development is its potential boundary-spanning inclusiveness based on participation.

PARTICIPATORY RURAL PLANNING AND
DEVELOPMENT IN NORTHERN IRELAND

Northern Ireland is marked by a large and vibrant community/ voluntary sector. Birrell and Murie (1980) have pointed to some 500 community groups and associations in existence in 1975, while more recently the Northern Ireland Council for Voluntary Action (1998) has estimated the current combined total of voluntary organisations, community groups and charitable bodies

21

at some 5,000. Their interests are wide-ranging and embrace planning, advocacy, service delivery and job creation in a manner which is complementary to the work of public bodies and the private sector. Community development processes have been central to these tasks, and in the difficult context of Northern Ireland these have sought additionally to construct necessary bridges across a deeply divided society.

As reported by Lovett et al (1994), the community development movement emerged during the 1970s out of a more radical, action-based ethos which proclaimed that people should have a greater say in the decisions affecting their everyday lives. In Belfast and Derry, for example, successful campaigns were mounted against housing redevelopment and road proposals. By the 1980s, many community groups had been absorbed as part of the broader state welfare system, with earlier oppositional stances to public policy tempered by a co-optive engagement based on responsibility and funding. While the initial locus of activity was essentially urban, this has been dramatically counterbalanced during the past decade by an increasingly organised rural constituency which has suffered equally from the worst effects of deprivation and violence. Herein, perhaps, is one of the paradoxes of Northern Ireland: the coexistence of a blossoming civil society in the mire of deep societal division. A defining characteristic of this participative democracy is that it involves people in decision making, thus nurturing a social ability to collaborate for shared interests. Robert Putnam, in his seminal 1993 book *Making Democracy Work,* expresses this concept in a more prosaic form: 'I'll do this for you now knowing that somewhere down the road you'll do something for me' (182). He argues that without these norms of local reciprocity and networks of engagement the outlook in any society is bleak. Outcomes include clientelism, lawlessness, economic stagnation and ineffective government. Strong participatory citizenship whereby people are involved in planning and in implementation, in facilitative leadership roles and in creating better futures for their own communities, is a necessary condition for avoidance of those ills. A benign institutional environment is, however, an overarching requirement. The recent experience of community-led local development and local partnership governance is illustrative of this linkage between rural development and civil society.

Community-led local development in rural Northern Ireland

Increased interest by the European Commission and lobbying at a local level, prompted by the recommendations from a pilot rural community action project, led the then Secretary of State for Northern Ireland, Peter Brooke, to appoint an Inter-Departmental Committee on Rural Development (IDCRD) in 1989. Its brief was to advise him on the best way of carrying forward action to tackle the social and economic problems in the most deprived rural areas in Northern Ireland. The committee reported in December 1990 with a panel of recommendations. In summary these were: (1) DANI should become the lead department with responsibility for promoting the development of the most deprived rural areas; (2) a permanent inter-agency forum should continue in operation to oversee progress; (3) an independent Rural Development Council (RDC) should be established, sponsored and funded, at least in its early years, by government. Its staff would be charged with responsibility for community-led rural development, and the organisation would also provide a forum for discussion between communities; (4) DANI should appoint a small team of local coordinators from across the public sector to bring together the responses from all public sector agencies to plans and projects located in the most deprived rural areas; and (5) a specific but relatively small fund for rural development should be set up to supplement mainline programme expenditure.

These recommendations were accepted in principle by government and formed the basis of its Rural Development Initiative launched in 1991. Thus from the outset, a new agency, outside government but dependent upon it for funding, assumed a pivotal role in facilitating community-based social and economic regeneration. The RDC determined that its entry to this field had to be through generic community development in the first instance and in late 1991 commenced the process of appointing a team of six community officers. The 1992–1995 Strategic Plan of the RDC defined their role as comprising: stimulating aware-ness of the value of collective action at local levels; building con-fidence in ability to bring about improvement; encouraging marginalised groups to participate; and promoting the adoption of good working practices. This community development sup-port was accompanied by financial assistance to facilitate group formation, to participate in training and education activities and to purchase technical services, for example, in regard to development strategies and project business plans. The RDC also articulated in its first Strategic Plan a commitment to providing a research and information service, and a willingness for cooperation and consultation with a wide range of rural interests. However, there is no mention in the documentation of the role identified by the IDCRD for RDC to provide a discus-sion forum between communities. This task, as noted by Fitzduff in the Foreword to this book, was addressed by the establishment in 1991 of Rural Community Network (RCN), a voluntary organisation which emerged out of the earlier Rural Action Project with a mission to identify and voice issues of con-cern to rural communities in relation to poverty, disadvantage and community development.

The achievements of the Rural Development Programme over the decade from 1991 have been identified by the Department of Agriculture and Rural Develpment (2001) as comprising the creation of over 1,000 jobs, the maintenance of over 900 existing jobs, support to 3,400 individual projects, 450 new rural busi-ness start-ups, 2,000 people completing training and further education courses, and 450 community groups involved in rural development. Notwithstanding the difficulties attached to the multiple counting of programme outputs on the basis of cocktail funding, the evidence is that an energised rural constituency has responded to the opportunities held before it. However, an annual departmental budget of over £6 billion in Northern Ireland sets the modest commitment of the rural development programme, as noted above, in context, albeit that other budget items do benefit rural society.

Partnership governance and rural development in Northern Ireland

Partnerships are increasingly being embraced in advanced capitalist societies as a service delivery mechanism. While not being a panacea for solving local development problems, partnerships can be effective mechanisms to improve relationships among multiple stakeholders and to bring together human and financial resources from a variety of funders to achieve common objectives. The concept implies a change in the nature of governance, not as an alternative to elected representation, but with the state taking a less pronounced role in dealing with complex problems such as urban and rural disadvantage or social exclusion. Moreover, the notion of partnerships converges easily with political pressures for a reduction in state activity and increased responsibility at the local level.

It is not surprising, therefore, that the corporate strategies, operational plans and annual reports of government departments and agencies within Northern Ireland should resound with approaches to creative collaboration. Indeed the rural development arena abounds with local partnerships. Elected representatives, public officials, the business and trade union sector, and community and voluntary interests have collectively engaged in a more grass roots approach to resolving local problems. The sheer scale of partnership governance for rural development is highlighted by the following structures which were operating during the 1990s:

- Under DANI's Rural Development Programme, in place through to 1999, there were eight Area-Based Strategy Action Groups, each of which was resourced with a budget of £1 million in order to lever in additional funding for regeneration projects within disadvantaged rural areas. The first Area-Based Strategy was launched in South Armagh in December 1995 within a border region which has suffered a negative image due to terrorism. The strategy covered small business development, agriculture, environmental management and tourism development and was implemented in

25

association with a locally based cross-community regeneration group.

- There were fifteen LEADER 2 local action groups in which District Councils played a prominent leadership role and whose brief comprised the giving of support to innovative, demonstrative and transferable rural development initiatives.
- Within each local authority area there was a District Partnership established under the EU Special Support Programme for Peace and Reconciliation, with a funding remit which comprised social inclusion, rural and urban development, productive investment and employment (for a further discussion see Hughes et al, 1998).
- Furthermore, District Councils have been able to establish local economic development partnerships which were concerned with the delivery of economic development measures contained within the EU Structural Funds Northern Ireland Single Programme for the period 1994–1999.
- The Department of the Environment in partnership with the International Fund for Ireland (IFI), District Councils and rural communities contributed to small town and village renewal through a portfolio of Community Regeneration and Improvement Special Programme (CRISP) projects. These comprise the blending of a core community business scheme, environmental improvements, and grant aid for private sector development.

Common to all these illustrations of partnership governance-in-action is (1) the critical involvement of local authorities in lead or support roles; (2) the preparation and implementation of locally prepared strategic plans; (3) a dependency upon public funding from EU, IFI and mainstream sources; (4) a high level of voluntary participation; (5) an appreciation that the rural development challenge is multidimensional, extending across economic, social, environmental and infrastructure needs; and (6) a policy preference, thus far, for a project-driven implementation approach in which community groups are a central delivery mechanism. There is, however, growing acceptance that this highly differentiated rural development arena has been rapidly 'crowding out', through the presence of multiple delivery agents which extend beyond the partnerships identified above, to include other organisations such as Local Enterprise Agencies, the Rural Development Council and Rural Community Network (Northern Ireland Economic Council, 2000; Hart and Murray, 2000; PricewaterhouseCoopers, 1999). Moreover, with the benefit of hindsight, serious questions have been posed about the wisdom of a policy imperative which almost exclusively has advocated large-scale capital support for community-led projects. Difficulties related to project management, profitability and the repayment of loan capital have surfaced in a number of instances and have prompted challenging scrutiny by the Northern Ireland Audit Office (2000) and the Public Accounts Committee of the Northern Ireland Assembly (2000). The bottom line questions to be debated after some ten years of activity are the sustainability of this local-scale participatory planning and development effort and its future effectiveness, if geared at this high level and when set against the prospect of a normal Northern Ireland, which increasingly will be driven by private sector investment and a reducing grant aid environment during the decade ahead.

In the latter part of the 1990s, government released a suite of prominent statements on regional physical and economic planning in Northern Ireland, which also included preliminary proposals for housing growth, transportation infrastructure and hospital services. In late 2001 a new Rural Development Programme to cover the period to 2006 was launched (DARD, 2001), and the Northern Ireland Assembly finally approved a new regional development strategy for Northern Ireland, *Shaping Our Future* (DRD, 2001). Their preparation and implementation is inextricably linked to a much more active, better organised and more astute rural constituency. This engagement spans the local and regional scales, and while community- and voluntary-led initiatives can assist with the reshaping of rural space at a micro level, rural constituencies acting collectively can also influence broader patterns of change.

BOOK STRUCTURE

This book has two main and related purposes. Firstly, it is designed to celebrate an involvement by rural people in creating better futures for themselves and to chart some new directions for policy and practice over the years ahead. But secondly, and inextricably linked to this, is the critical focus placed on the capacity of the Northern Ireland Regional Development Strategy to deliver a vision of the future relating to rural society. Accordingly, the analysis in this introductory chapter has sought to unravel the multiple threads of policy meaning which are wrapped around the concept of *the rural* in Northern Ireland. What is clear is that rurality has become a powerful metaphor for claims related to spatial equity, bottom up development processes, and intergenerational sustainability. An outside perception of rural areas as solely an environmental resource is being confronted by the internal reality of diverse and active community interests for whom place, culture and identity are increasingly powerful signifiers. Within this sphere of public policy there are disturbing tensions that pitch rural development against environmental protection, which surface, for example, within the contested arena of statutory town and country planning. This point may be underlined by the fact that many proposals related to rural development do require planning permission. Regional strategies, area plans, development control advice notes and planning policy statements thus become decision-making aids of first resort in this dialectic of approval versus refusal. But rural development is much more than statutory town and country planning and, as reflected in the content of this book, it encompasses broader themes of intervention and management.

The Northern Ireland Regional Development Strategy seeks to capture these dimensions, but in its analysis and prescription contains several explicit and implicit assumptions which deserve close scrutiny. Thus, for example, the Strategy conceives the existence of an almost monolithic and active rural community, portrays a future rural economy based on tourism and primary sector diversification, casts a dark shadow over the acceptability of single dwellings in the countryside, prioritises landscape protection and assumes the bliss of rural harmony in a society devoid of division and multiple identities. In contrast, the chapters in this book provide a more provocative analysis of rural realities and, through critical commentary, they signpost the deeper complexities associated with shaping that future. However, no book can claim comprehensiveness in regard to its coverage of rural planning and development. Accordingly, the chapters below have been selected to add new perspectives on contemporary debates in Northern Ireland and are complementary to an earlier set of research-based essays (Murray and Greer, 1993) which created some initial baselines of the rural situation.

Rural economies are the all-important bedrock upon which spatial and social realities are constructed. Thus Section Two of this book contains three chapters which examine contemporary challenges being faced by the rural economies of Northern Ireland. It is appropriate that the three chapters in this section should demonstrate a range of contemporary problems and potential across the sectors of agriculture, business enterprise and tourism. Collectively they demonstrate that there is no single rural economy in Northern Ireland, that economic activity in rural areas cannot be disentangled from economic activity in urban areas, and that rural economies do differ from area to area across the region.

In Chapter 2 Joan Moss, Claire Jack, Michael Wallace and Seamus McErlean investigate the sustainability of the small, family-run farms that dominate the Northern Ireland agricultural sector. They present analyses of rural (farm and non-farm) household decision making and the impact of policy scenarios on the small farm sector. In Chapter 3 Mark Hart, Maureen O'Reilly, and Michael Anyadike-Danes examine the performance of the small business sector in rural Northern Ireland during the 1990s. The popular view that Northern Ireland's economic engine is confined solely to the Belfast Region is challenged. Chapter 4, by Maureen O'Reilly and Mark Hart, reviews the contribution made by community-led rural tourism to local development in South Armagh and identifies a complexity of challenges imposed by place identity and multiple organisational relationships.

Section Three of this book comprises seven chapters which examine rural Northern Ireland through the lenses of place and community. The contributors assess the policies and behaviours which have helped to shape planning and development outcomes at different spatial scales. A recurrent theme in these narratives relates to the diversity of interactions among rural people and between rural people and those who are perceived to be 'in charge'.

Chapter 5 by Ken Sterrett revisits the enduring issue of single house development in the Northern Ireland countryside. The details of policy succession in this arena are examined and the tension between the state and the popular aesthetic in regard to house design is explored. In Chapter 6 Michael Conway traces the background to the rural housing policy of the Northern Ireland Housing Executive and looks at the impact of its Crossroads initiative in establishing new living places within the countryside. Brendan Murtagh examines the contested nature of rural places in Chapter 7 and, against the context of Targeting Social Need and equality imperatives, he identifies some important implications for planning practice within local arenas of ethno-spatial change. In Chapter 8 Mark Scott looks closely at the processes of social capital formation through collective participation in the LEADER 2 programme in Northern Ireland. He demonstrates the contribution made to increasingly shared understandings of local context on the basis of this collaborative engagement. This analysis is complemented by Nick Mack and Rachel Naylor in Chapter 9. The focus here, however, is on the creation of 'learning communities' through local level participatory and collaborative action, and thus the chapter outlines the deployment of a range of techniques to facilitate community planning. In contrast, the emphasis in Chapter 10 is more on development outcomes. Michael McSorley and Alistair McKane discuss the challenges faced by local community groups in undertaking village and small town renewal supported under the Community Regeneration and Improvement Special Programme (CRISP) of the International Fund for Ireland. Finally, while the geography of rural places, differentiated on the basis of scale and jurisdictional ownership, allows for the identification of sub-regional territories on either side of the Border between Northern Ireland and the Republic of Ireland, networks of joint engagement can also bring new perspectives to development problems. Thus in Chapter 11 Jonathan Greer assesses the potential of cross-border local authority coalitions as change agents within this extensive rural periphery.

Section 4, titled *Retrospect and Prospect,* seeks to critically reflect on how rurality has been interpreted in Northern Ireland, not least through the new Regional Development Strategy adopted by the Assembly in late 2001. In Chapter 12 Brian Graham considers why certain representations of the rural have dominated over others. He explores the resonances of these diverse interpretations against the backcloths of heritage and history and argues the need to rethink the rural in Northern Ireland in line with its progression into a post-productivist countryside. In Chapter 13 John Greer and Michael Murray critically review the future offered to rural Northern Ireland by the Regional Development Strategy. The discussion concludes by outlining the possibilities for further action by government and related organisations in relation to rural planning and development. While the empirical content of this book is derived from the Northern Ireland experience, it remains the case that these implications for policy and practice should command wider appreciation within the island of Ireland.

REFERENCES

Armstrong, J., D. McClelland and T. O'Brien (1980), *A Policy for Rural Problem Areas in Northern Ireland: A Discussion Document*, Belfast: Ulster Polytechnic.
Birrell, D. and A. Murie (1980), *Policy and Government in Northern Ireland: Lessons of Devolution*, Dublin: Gill and Macmillan.
Buchanan, R. (1982), 'The Ulster Society for the Preservation of the Countryside', in J. Forsyth and R. Buchanan (eds), *The Ulster Countryside in the 1980s*, Belfast: Institute of Irish Studies, Queen's University, Belfast.

Caldwell, J. and J. Greer (1983), *Planning for Peripheral Rural Areas: The Effects of Policy Change in Northern Ireland*, Belfast: Social Science Research Council Final Report, The Department of Town and Country Planning, Queen's University, Belfast.

Cloke, P. (1978), 'Changing Patterns of Urbanisation in the Rural Areas of England and Wales 1961–1971', *Regional Studies*, vol. 12: 603–617.

Department of Agriculture and Rural Development (2001), *The Northern Ireland Rural Development Programme Strategy 2001–2006.* Belfast: HMSO.

Department of the Environment for Northern Ireland (1993), *A Planning Strategy for Northern Ireland,* Belfast: HMSO.

Department of the Environment for Northern Ireland (1998a), *Draft Regional Strategic Framework for Northern Ireland,* Belfast: The Stationery Office.

Department of the Environment for Northern Ireland (1998b), *Shaping Our Future: The Family of Settlements Report,* Belfast: The Stationery Office.

Department for Regional Development (2001), *Shaping Our Future: Regional Development Strategy for Northern Ireland 2025*, Holywood: Corporate Document Services.

Duffy, P. (1997), 'Writing Ireland: Literature and Art in the Representation of Irish Place', in B. Graham (ed.), *In Search of Ireland*, London: Routledge.

Ellis, G. (2001), 'Social Exclusion, Equality and the Good Friday Peace Agreement: The Implications for Land Use Planning', *Policy and Politics*, vol. 29, no. 4: 393–411.

Equality Commission for Northern Ireland (1999), *Guide to Statutory Duties*, Belfast.

Evans, E. (1970), *The Personality of Ulster*, Belfast: Belfast Telegraph Centenary Edition, 1 September.

Faulkner, J. (1999), *Protected Landscapes: The Northern Ireland Experience*, paper presented at the conference 'Policies and Priorities for Ireland's Landscapes', The Heritage Council.

Gailey, A. (1984), *Rural Houses of the North of Ireland*, Edinburgh: John Donald Publishers Ltd.

Graham, B. (1997), 'The Imagining of Place', in B. Graham (ed.), *In Search of Ireland*, London: Routledge.

Greer, J. and M. Murray (1988), *A Recreation Strategy for Mourne Area of Outstanding Natural Beauty*, Belfast: The Sports Council for Northern Ireland.

Greer, J. and M. Murray (1992), *Access Strategy for the Causeway Coast Area of Outstanding Natural Beauty*, Belfast: Department of the Environment for Northern Ireland.

Haase, T., K. McKeown and S. Rourke (1996), *Local Development Strategies for Disadvantaged Areas*, Dublin: Area Development Management Ltd.

Hart, M. and M. Murray (2000), *Local Development in Northern Ireland: The Way Forward*, Belfast: Northern Ireland Economic Council.

House of Commons Northern Ireland Affairs Committee (1996), *The Planning System in Northern Ireland*, London: HMSO.

Hughes, J., C. Knox, M. Murray and J. Greer (1998), *Partnership Governance in Northern Ireland: The Path to Peace*, Dublin: Oak Tree Press.

Lovett, T., D. Gunn and T. Robson (1994), 'Education, Conflict and Community Development in Northern Ireland', *Community Development Journal*, vol. 29, no. 2: 11–18.

McWhinney, G. (2001), 'Agri-environment measures', *Northern Ireland Environment Link Environmental Fact Sheet*, vol. 2, no. 1: 39.

Moss, J.E. and S.M. Chilton (1993), 'Agriculture and the Environmentally Sensitive Area Scheme' in M. Murray and J. Greer (eds), *Rural Development in Ireland: A Challenge for the 1990s*, Aldershot: Avebury.

Murray, M. (1991), *The Politics and Pragmatism of Urban Containment: Belfast since 1940*, Aldershot: Avebury.

Murray, M. and J. Greer (1993), *Rural Development in Ireland*, Aldershot: Avebury.

Murtagh, B. (1996), *Community and Conflict in Rural Ulster*, Belfast: Northern Ireland Community Relations Council.

Murtagh, B. (1998), 'Community, Conflict and Rural Planning in Northern Ireland', *Journal of Rural Studies*, vol. 14, no. 2: 221–231.

M. Noble, G. Smith, G. Wright, C. Dibben, M. Lloyd and I. Shuttleworth (2001), *Measures of Deprivation in Northern Ireland*, Belfast: Northern Ireland Statistics and Research Agency.

Northern Ireland Audit Office (2000), *The Rural Development Programme*, Belfast: The Stationery Office.

Northern Ireland Assembly, Public Accounts Committee (2000), *Report on the Rural Development Programme*, Belfast: The Stationery Office.

Northern Ireland Council for Voluntary Action (1998), *The State of the Sector,* Belfast: Northern Ireland Council for Voluntary Action.

Northern Ireland Economic Council (2000), *Local Development: A Turning Point*, Belfast: Northern Ireland Economic Council.

Northern Ireland Housing Executive (1990), *Rural Housing Policy Review — Leading the Way*, Belfast: Northern Ireland Housing Executive.

Northern Ireland Housing Executive (1991), *Rural Housing Policy — The Way Ahead: A Policy Statement*, Belfast: Northern Ireland Housing Executive.

PricewaterhouseCoopers (1999), *Rural Development Programme Mid-Term Evaluation Synthesis Report*, Belfast: Department of Agriculture and Rural Development.

Putnam, R. (1993), *Making Democracy Work*, Princeton: Princeton University Press.

Quirk, P. and E. McLaughlin (1996), 'Targeting Social Need', in E. McLaughlin and P. Quirk (eds), *Policy Aspects of Employment Equality in Northern Ireland*, Belfast: The Standing Advisory Commission on Human Rights.

Robson, B., M. Bradford and I. Deas (1994), *Relative Deprivation in Northern Ireland*, Belfast: Occasional Paper no. 28, Policy Planning and Research Unit, Department of Finance and Personnel.

Shortall, S. and R. Kelly (2000), *Gender-Proofing CAP Reform*, Cookstown: Rural Community Network.

L. Symons (1963), *Land Use in Northern Ireland*, London: University of London Press.

SECTION TWO:
THE CHALLENGES
IN RURAL ECONOMIES

CHAPTER 2

AGRICULTURAL POLICY
AND THE VIABILITY OF THE
SMALL FARM SECTOR

Joan E. Moss, Claire G. Jack, Michael Wallace
and Seamus A. McErlean

INTRODUCTION

This chapter is located within the context of the current agricultural policy environment and investigates the sustainability of the small, family-run farms that dominate the Northern Ireland agricultural sector. An analysis of farmers' goals indicates that, even when farming incomes were at historically high levels in the mid-1990s, all but the largest beef, sheep and dairy farms were not able to finance modest levels of family consumption without running down the farms' capital base. The discussion illustrates that recent years have witnessed a collapse in farm incomes, and projections of future sectoral incomes do not indicate a return to the peak incomes of the mid-1990s. Farm diversification does not appear to be an option for most small farms. The chapter then considers the off-farm employment of both male and female members of farm households, which has become an essential source of income for the majority of farm households. The nature of this employment is examined and compared with non-farm household circumstances and behaviour in order to throw light on its future role and to help identify policy measures that can enhance the off-farm earning capability of farm household members.

POLICY BACKGROUND

Since its inception, the Common Agricultural Policy (CAP) has had two main elements: firstly, structural measures and secondly, price and market support. Structural measures were designed to tackle the fundamental structural problem of the agricultural sectors, i.e. too many small farm businesses in the European Community (EC), latterly the European Union (EU). The price and market support policies were concerned with the market alleviation of the adverse consequences of the structural problem, mainly low prices and incomes. Since the United Kingdom's accession to the EC in 1973, Northern Ireland's farming sector has operated subject to the CAP.

PRICE AND MARKET SUPPORT POLICY

Up until the early 1990s, the price and market policies of the CAP operated whereby a producer's income was determined principally by the price that produce fetched in the market, rather than by direct income supplements or allowances, determined by the area of crops grown or the number of livestock held. Prices were established, by the interaction of supply and demand in the EC market, within the framework of the various commodity regimes, at a level that was designed to ensure that even the relatively high-cost producers could earn a living. The onward march of technology and corresponding increases in agricultural productivity, however, steadily increased supply and the associated cost of support. Furthermore, it was recognised that most of the financial support went to the largest 20 per cent of farmers. There was also the negative impact on international trade caused by the disposal of subsidised exports onto the world market. This concern was articulated at the protracted GATT Uruguay Round of multilateral trade negotiations.

These problems were addressed, albeit in a partial fashion, by the 1992 MacSharry CAP reforms. The main element of these reforms was the reduction in cereal, beef and sheep meat price support and a significant move to direct payments. The direct (compensatory) payments were designed to compensate farmers for progressive reductions in intervention prices and the trigger prices for safety net intervention. The relentless expansion of agricultural production had to be curtailed. Farmers would be required to look beyond traditional farm enterprises for extra income. A set of accompanying measures was also introduced to promote the use of agricultural land for forestry and to grant aid the introduction or maintenance of production techniques that encouraged the protection of the environment, the landscape and natural resources (Commission of the European Communities, 1992).

Structural policy

Structural policy has also evolved since Northern Ireland farming came under the CAP. The two main elements of structural policy have been measures directed at decreasing the number of people employed in agriculture, and measures directed at increasing the size of farms. The early CAP structural instruments had the objectives of improving the structure of the agricultural sector by: modernising and enlarging farm holdings; training labour and encouraging the exit of excess (particularly elderly) labour from agriculture; strengthening the processing and marketing structures; reducing structural handicaps; and improving infrastructure in specific regions.

The main structural policy measures to impact on Northern Ireland agriculture have been the differentially larger capital grants and headage payments for breeding cattle and sheep in the designated Less Favoured Areas (LFA) that constitute over 70 per cent of the region's farmed land. Most farmers consider the headage payments (Hill Livestock Compensatory Allowances) to be derived from price support policy, but they have been an important regional element of structural policy. They were designed as direct income payments to help farmers remain in the LFA, despite the production and marketing disadvantages associated with their location.

The reasons for reforming the price support measures have already been mentioned. By the mid-1980s, it was recognised that structural policy was not having the desired effect. There still existed a serious low-income problem for smaller farmers, despite the expensive support measures and burgeoning surpluses. It could no longer be argued that supporting agricultural prices would guarantee all farmers an acceptable income, and it was accepted that the problems faced by the farming community could not be resolved solely within the agricultural sector. New economic activities were required, on and off the farms, to stimulate the economies of rural areas. The Single European Act of 1992 also placed the peripheral regions of the EU at a potential disadvantage. Consequently, it was agreed that these regions might require additional assistance.

The resultant reform of EU Structural Policy led to Northern Ireland being designated as an Objective 1 region, the highest priority category of disadvantaged regions. This resulted in initiatives that highlighted the improvement of the structure of the agricultural sector as being essential to the development of rural areas. Consequently there have been two Operational Programmes specifically relating to the agricultural sector: the Agricultural Development Operational Programme (ADOP), 1990–1994; and the Sub Programme for Agricultural and Rural Development (SPARD), 1995–1999. Both programmes provided capital grants to assist the agricultural sector and related industries take full advantage of market opportunities and to protect the natural environment. With regard to agricultural production, the emphasis has been on improving quality, as opposed to increasing agricultural outputs. Measures have also been funded to enhance the rural environment, reduce pollution incidents and conserve the ecological and amenity value of the rural landscape. In recognition of the failure of agriculture to generate a standard of living for farmers commensurate with that enjoyed by those employed in the non-farm sectors, funds have been made available to encourage farmers in Northern Ireland to diversify and develop alternative enterprises, both agricultural and non-agricultural.

The international pressure to further liberalise EU agricultural markets, i.e. open them up to imports and reduce the level of protection, continued unabated throughout the 1990s. An additional consideration has been the prospect of EU enlargement to encompass up to eleven transitional economy countries in central and eastern Europe. There has been a realisation that the existing CAP measures are inappropriate and too expensive to extend to the prospective new member states. But they cannot be treated differently from current member states because the Single Market legislation ensures that all member states are subject to the same policy measures in order that no country suffers a comparative market disadvantage.

Agenda 2000 reforms

The EU Commission's proposals for further reform of the CAP, the process of enlargement and the financial framework for the period 2000 to 2006 were presented in the Agenda 2000 Communication of July 1997 (European Commission, 1997). Rural development was given a higher priority and was described as the *'third pillar of the CAP'*. The Agenda 2000 proposals formed the basis of the political agreement reached at the Berlin summit in March 1999 (European Commission, 1999). Under the Berlin Agreement, the reforms initiated by MacSharry were further progressed, albeit to a lesser degree than in the original Agenda 2000 proposals, with further reductions in price support and corresponding increases in direct payments. Despite the emphasis on rural development, and recognition that rural development encompasses all rural dwellers, not just the farming community, the resources devoted to rural development initiatives, while increasing for the EU as a whole, would continue to be modest compared with agricultural support. This situation was reflected in the 1999 Northern Ireland agriculture funding which approximated £300 million, comprising £200m of direct payments (excluding BSE compensation) and an estimated further £100m of indirect market support (DARD, 2000a). By comparison, the total programme allocation for Northern Ireland over the period 1994–1999, explicitly for Rural Development initiatives, was £50m. The equivalent Northern Ireland Rural Development expenditure for the first programme period 1990–1994 was £9m (DARD, 2000b).

For the period 2000–2006, Northern Ireland did not qualify for Objective 1 status, which attracts maximum funding for the most seriously disadvantaged EU regions. Transitional Objective 1 status, which provides funding to assist with the necessary adjustment to the change in EU disadvantage status, was granted.

TRENDS IN FARMING INCOME

Throughout the 1990s, Northern Ireland farmers experienced an improvement followed by a dramatic decline in farming incomes (see Figure 2.1). The combination of declining sectoral income and the predominance of small-scale, family-run farms, is reflected in the average net dairy farm income of £24,578 in 1995, dropping to £3,489 in 1999/2000, and equivalent LFA beef and sheep farm incomes of £6,950 and -£196 respectively (DARD, 2000c).

FIGURE 2.1: NET FARM REAL INCOME INDICES
(AV. 1989/90 TO 1991/92=100)

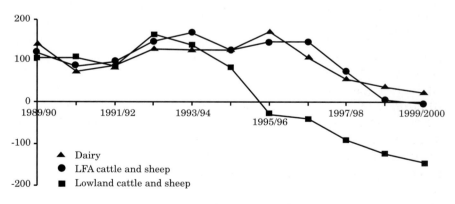

Source: DARD, Economics and Statistics Division

Farm family goals

The current very low levels of farm income call into question the sustainability of small family-run farm businesses. It has long been observed (Heady, 1952; Gasson, 1973; Perkin and Rehman, 1994) that family farms are very resilient in the face of adverse trading conditions because they do not operate simply as businesses. One way of investigating this complex situation is to consider explicitly the varying decisions facing farmers. They face conflicting goals and have to decide how to allocate the income generated by the farm between family consumption and reinvestment in the productive unit. From a 1995 survey of farms, six farm clusters were identified, each representing groups of farms which differed not only in type and size, but also in terms of technical efficiency and household dependence on farm income. Using numerical scaling techniques, farmers' goals were investigated and, in a separate clustering analysis, three distinct goal preference ratings were identified and classified as follows: growth/investment, consumption/ profit and cash flow/consumption.

The growth/investment goal structure placed greatest importance on the goal of growth in net farm worth. The second and third goal structures differed primarily in terms of the priority given to a cash flow goal of avoiding borrowing. Consequently, the cash flow/consumption goal structure examined a situation where the farmer was opposed to borrowing capital beyond a very modest level. In contrast, the consumption/profit structure prioritised annual family consumption and farm profit necessary to finance consumption. Under this goal structure, the cash flow goal was given a lower priority, implying a greater likelihood of borrowing in order to finance consumption.

Four scenarios were examined using the farm models. Firstly, a baseline solution was generated applying a conventional profit-maximising model formulation. Secondly, the three separate goal structures were examined using a weighted goal programming formulation (WGP). The aspiration or target levels attached to the individual goals under the WGP scenarios are presented in Table 2.1.

In the event of all other goals being satisfied in the WGP models, profit maximisation became the determining goal and prevented the possibility of an inferior solution. The planning horizon in the analysis covered the period 1991/92 to 1997/98.

Neither the consumption nor investment aspiration levels in the models could be considered over-generous. The consumption targets were average family expenditure levels of households in Northern Ireland where the head of household was in manual employment. They were adjusted to take account of existing off-farm income of the farmer and spouse and assumed there were no mortgage costs associated with the family dwelling. The very low level of consumption required for the small beef and sheep farm households reflected the high incidence of off-farm income in these households. The investment target provided only for the maintenance of the fixed asset base at the initial level and did not imply any desire to increase the value of fixed capital on the farm. Consequently, the target represented only the cost of replacing fixed assets over time.

TABLE 2.1: ASPIRATION LEVELS FOR EACH OF THE GOALS INCLUDED IN THE WGP MODELS

Goal	Target/Aspiration Level
Farm profit	maximum feasible
Family consumption	£15,600 per annum — large and medium dairy and large beef models
	£11,700 per annum — small dairy model
	£10,400 per annum — medium beef model
	£ 5,200 per annum — small beef model
Growth in net worth	2 per cent per annum — all beef models
	5 per cent per annum — all dairy models
Fixed investment	Maintain fixed capital base at or above initial level, i.e. maintain sufficient investment to offset rate of depreciation of fixed capital
Short run borrowings (Cash flow)	Maintain borrowings at under 2 per cent of the value of assets

The results of the models highlighted wide differences in profitability among the representative farms, which was confirmed by the farm incomes published by the annual Farm Business Survey for Northern Ireland. The model results also identified wide differences among groups of farms in terms of their ability to satisfy key goals concerning farm profitability, family consumption, farm investment, farm growth and cash flow. There were clear conflicts between the achievement of separate goals, most notably between family consumption, farm investment/growth and avoidance of borrowings. In particular, model solutions indicated that only the larger farms could simultaneously attain, out of farm returns, both their family consumption goal and the maintainance of the value of fixed assets. This is of particular concern in the context of the Northern Ireland farming population, as these 'larger' holdings represent just under 14 per cent of dairy and beef/sheep farms (Department of Agriculture for Northern Ireland, 1997).

The most important constraint faced by the smaller farms was shortage of capital due to poor returns from farming. This capital problem restricted the choice of enterprises, inhibited growth potential, gave rise to overdraft problems and resulted in a trade-off between family consumption and farm investment. By contrast, over the period covered by the models, the larger dairy farms exhibited considerable potential for capital accumulation, thereby avoiding the need to borrow, provided for the satisfaction of basic family consumption aspirations and generated the liquidity for farm investment and expansion.

For the smaller farms, the low level of expected farming returns resulted in a decline in living standards over time to levels well below those in wider society. Furthermore, lack of capital restricted the possibility of alleviating low income through farm expansion and led to the running down of farm assets over a prolonged period of time, in an attempt to maintain consumption levels. It was anticipated that such farmers would come under increasing economic pressure, which is likely to accelerate their need to seek alternative sources of income or face the prospect of ceasing farming altogether.

It was recognised that many small farm holdings, however, have the important fallback of non-farm income generated by family members maintaining off-farm employment or receiving social transfers. The presence of such income can remove the pressure of having to meet all family consumption needs from farming income. To this extent, non-farm earnings can subsidise the farming activities of such households, and may enable them to make farm investments or sustain farming activity that would not be justified by the potential economic returns.

There is also the possibility, put forward by Hannan and Commins (1992), that the continued existence of apparently 'uneconomic' farm businesses may reflect the enjoyment of status in rural society conferred by land ownership, a status diminished if the land is let rather than actively farmed, and lost if land is sold. Nonetheless, the farm incomes generated over the last three years have been very poor and any appraisal of the future of Northern Ireland family farms must consider whether the current exceptionally low farm incomes are likely to persist into the future.

The representative farm models covered the period from 1991 to 1997. From a peak in 1995, farming incomes have plummeted; indeed negative incomes have been recorded for the beef and sheep farm types. The main reasons cited for the pattern of farming income throughout the 1990s were as follows: the MacSharry CAP reforms which resulted in farmers receiving compensatory payments for price reductions which did not materialise; sterling dropping out of the Exchange Rate Mechanism in 1993 and the subsequent devaluation of sterling against the major European currencies, which continued until 1995; and finally there began a period of gradual revaluation of sterling, which became more acute with the inception of the euro at the beginning of 1999.

Projections of sectoral income

Schuh (1974) and Güzel and Kulshreshtha (1995) have shown the importance of exchange rate fluctuations on agricultural prices and farm incomes in export-dependent sectors. The strength of sterling relative to the main European currencies,

48

and the euro since the beginning of 1999, is very important for Northern Ireland's agriculture because:

(1) The region is heavily dependent on exports to the EU and the rest of the world. The Northern Ireland agricultural sector is very small and is, in effect, a price taker in export markets. When the exchange rate is weak, exports are more competitive and vice versa;

(2) A strong sterling, relative to the euro, encourages imports from other EU countries into the UK markets, exerting a downward pressure on local market prices and thereby on producer prices;

(3) Northern Ireland farmers receive direct payments from the EU under the CAP. These payments are denominated in euros. Consequently, the £/euro exchange rate impacts directly on farm receipts. The weaker the euro is relative to sterling, then the lower are the direct payments.

The potential impact of differing exchange rate scenarios on the Northern Ireland farm sector has been analysed using the Northern Ireland FAPRI agricultural model system (Moss et al, 2000). The NI agricultural model and the FAPRI Global and EU Gold models, to which the NI model is linked, were solved for three different exchange rate scenarios:

(1) A baseline (ESRI) scenario projection using exchange rate forecasts provided by the Economic and Social Research Institute in Dublin where the £/euro exchange rate holds constant in 2000 and then recovers to 1 euro equal to 69 pence by the end of the projection period;

(2) A second (WEFA) scenario using more optimistic exchange rate forecasts provided by Wharton Econometric Forecasting Associates in Philadelphia, USA, where the euro appreciates against the pound sterling to 1 euro equals 75 pence by the end of the projection period;

(3) A parity scenario where the £/euro exchange rate is maintained at 1 euro equal to 62 pence over the projection period and, as the name suggests, the US dollar is at parity with the euro under this scenario. This was considered a worst-case scenario (see Figure 2.2).

FIGURE 2.2 HISTORIC EXCHANGE RATES AND PROJECTION (£/EURO)

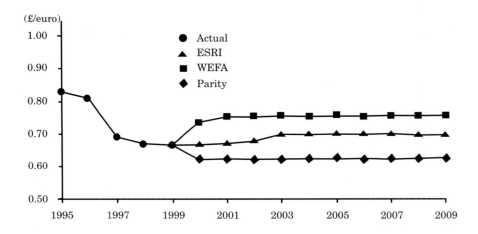

The results of the investigation of different exchange rate scenarios indicated that under the Baseline and WEFA scenarios, the net receipts (total gross receipts minus variable costs) for the aggregate dairy, beef and sheep sectors increased immediately and then became fairly stable after 2003, after the impact of the premium changes from the Berlin Agreement had worked through the system (see Figure 2.3). This was at a level commensurate with 1996/1997 levels of net receipts for the three livestock sectors. Under the Parity scenario, which reflected the most pessimistic exchange projections, however, the net receipts did not recover to 1997 levels.

50

FIGURE 2.3 TOTAL NET RECEIPTS FOR DAIRY, BEEF, SHEEP AND INPUT
SECTORS (£M)

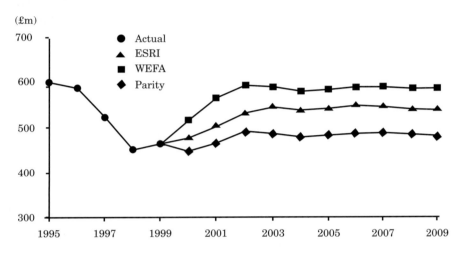

It can be concluded from Figure 2.3 that, even under the most
optimistic sterling/euro exchange rate forecast, with the euro
strengthening steadily to 75 pence by the end of the projection
period, the net receipts for the dairy, beef and sheep sectors
would not exceed the peak levels of 1995/6. Consequently, if it
is accepted that the sterling/euro exchange rate is a major
determining factor in the magnitude of farming incomes, the
medium to longer term dairy, beef and sheep farm incomes are
unlikely to return to levels that would lessen the need for the
majority of farm families to augment their farming incomes.

OFF-FARM EMPLOYMENT

At the time of writing, a study is being undertaken to investigate further the nature and extent of off-farm employment,
which appears to be making possible the continuation of the
small farm businesses. A survey was conducted in rural areas of
Northern Ireland in November 1999 focusing upon rural household structure, educational attainment and labour market
participation. Sample selection concentrated on those 'target'

areas which have been classified for policy purposes as disadvantaged rural areas of Northern Ireland (Robson et al, 1994; Rural Development Council, 1999). A criterion of housing density of between one and ten households per square kilometre was also applied. The survey area was defined, identified and mapped using geographical information systems (GIS), and a sample of seventy grid squares (excluding replacements), each being one kilometre square, was selected randomly. The questionnaire was structured to enable information to be obtained on two levels; firstly, at household level and secondly, at the level of each household member (over the age of sixteen) considered to be living permanently within the household.

Household structure

In total, 259 rural households were surveyed, 39 per cent of which, hereafter referred to as farm households, were associated with farmland, i.e. either by owning, letting or renting. The remainder of households, defined as non-farm households, had no association with farmland. Information was obtained on 661 individuals, 44 per cent of whom were members of farm households. The distribution within the final sample between farm and non-farm households and among the individuals comprising the households allowed for comparisons to be made between the sub-populations.

At an individual household level, farm households had a higher percentage of adults under the age of twenty-five and over the age of fifty-five compared to non-farm households. Furthermore, there were significantly more farm households with three or more adults permanently resident, compared to non-farm households. These findings reflect the intergenerational nature of many farming households, with household income shared with elderly relatives and pension income making an important contribution to overall household income (Gasson and Errington, 1993). Furthermore, the higher percentage of adults under the age of twenty-five may be indicative of young people from farming households remaining at home with their parents to an older age because they have not attended higher education (Pavis et al, 2000).

Respondents were asked to identify the proportion of income derived from various sources for each individual within the household, but not their actual income levels. For those households associated with farming (101 in total) the sources of income for the main adults in the household, i.e. the main respondent and/or spouse, were examined in order to assess the household's level of dependency on farming income (see Table 2.2). For 11 per cent of farm households the income of the main respondent and spouse (if relevant) was not from farming. In addition, 58 per cent of farm households were only partially dependent on farming-related income. Consequently, less than one third of farm households in the survey indicated that their income derived solely from farming. This confirmed a trend identified by Moss (1992) and Davis et al (1997). A possible source of additional income was a diversified enterprise. Investigating the incidence of farm diversification in the Republic of Ireland, Cawley et al (1995) identified a variety of reasons why producers in disadvantaged areas had a limited interest in farm diversification. The reasons included farmers' preferences for traditional farm enterprises, insufficient capital, lack of knowledge, the age of the farm operator and risk aversion. The Northern Ireland survey also demonstrated a very low incidence of on-farm diversification with only five farm households (5 per cent) engaging in some form of on-farm diversification.

TABLE 2.2 FARM HOUSEHOLD DEPENDENCE ON INCOME FROM FARMING

Dependence on farm income	Percentage of households
totally independent	11
partially dependent	58
fully dependent	31

Of the individuals under the age of fifty-five and associated with farming, 43 per cent claimed that they earned income from off-farm employment. The incidence of off-farm employment declined significantly, the older the farm male. This indicates the extent to which the income of farm households is reliant, to a greater or lesser extent, on off-farm employment. This involvement with the wider economy is considered in the following section.

Labour market participation

The employment status of the 548 individuals in the sample, who did not define themselves as retired, categorised by household type and gender, is summarised in Table 2.3. There is no significant difference between the activity rates of farm and non-farm males. The slightly higher percentage of farm males working part-time can be attributed to the relatively common phenomenon of older farmers remaining in farming to beyond the 'normal' age of retirement (Gasson and Errington, 1993).

TABLE 2.3. EMPLOYMENT STATUS BY HOUSEHOLD TYPE AND GENDER

	Male*		Female*	
Employment status	**Non-farm** (%)	**Farm** (%)	**Non-farm** (%)	**Farm** (%)
working full-time	74	75	40	34
working part-time	2	6	17	9
registered unemployed	11	6	2	4
sick or disabled	3	5	3	Nil
full-time housewife	Nil	Nil	26	35
student	10	8	12	18
Total % (count)	100(145)	100(137)	100(157)	100(109)

*Excludes those who classify themselves as retired.

In relation to the activity levels of females from farm households, 35 per cent were classified as full-time housewives. In total, 43 per cent of farm females were engaged in the labour market, compared to 81 per cent of farm males. Like the farm males, the older the farm females, the less likely they were to have off-farm employment. Of the non-farm females, 57 per cent were engaged in the labour market. A significantly higher percentage of the non-farm females were engaged in both part-time and full-time employment than their female counter-parts in farm households.

Type of off-farm employment

The study examined the type of employment for all those engaged in the labour market, to investigate whether or not distinctive employment patterns for the various categories of individuals could be ascertained. The results, outlining the nature of off-farm employment, excluding full-time farmers but including the off-farm employment of part-time farmers, are given in Table 2.4. Of the 261 individuals in paid employment, 36 per cent were from farm households and 64 per cent were from non-farm households.

TABLE 2.4 TYPE OF OFF-FARM EMPLOYMENT

	Male*		Female*	
Industrial classification	**Non-farm** (%)	**Farm** (%)	**Non-farm** (%)	**Farm** (%)
Agriculture and related occupations*	8	9	2	Nil
Construction and related occupations	35	59	5	Nil
Transport, travel and related occupations	17	15	2	3
Education, training and related occupations	7	6	31	15
Health, social services and related occupations	2	9	28	45
Manufacturing	12	2	7	12
Other (i.e. wholesale, retail, banking, finance, legal and protective services)	19	Nil	25	25
Total (Count)	100(86)	100(53)	100(82)	100(40)

* Excludes those who farm full-time and have no off-farm employment.

For non-farm males, the main sectors providing employment were construction, 'other', transport, and manufacturing. For farm-associated males, construction, transport and agriculturally related work accounted for 83 per cent of their off-farm employment. There were relatively few farm males working in the tertiary sector, which has experienced the most growth in recent years. It has been observed that male employment, in general, in Northern Ireland is concentrated in the more traditional industries, and indications are that these industries will show the most marked decline over the next ten years (NIERC, 1999; DANI, 2000). Moreover, the current skills which farm males acquire from their farm work are most likely to be matched with these declining industries. For females, both farm and non-farm, however, employment is concentrated in the areas of education, health and the service sector, reflecting a higher level of public sector dependency amongst female employment in the rural areas.

TABLE 2.5 NATURE OF EMPLOYMENT

Employment	Male*		Female*	
	Non-farm (%)	Farm (%)	Non-farm (%)	Farm (%)
Manual/unskilled*	22	34	11	15
Skilled/semi-skilled	55	49	26	25
Clerical/secretarial	1	4	18	35
Sales	3	N/A	4	N/A
Professional/managerial	19	13	41	25
Total (Count)	100(86)	100(53)	100(82)	100(40)

* Excludes those who farm full-time and have no off-farm employment.

Having identified the main sectors of employment, the nature of employment was also examined and the main categories are outlined in Table 2.5. For those males in employment, whether farm-based or otherwise, employment was concentrated in manual/unskilled and skilled/semi-skilled jobs. In farm households there was a significantly higher proportion of females engaged in professional or managerial activities, compared to their male counterparts. In addition, females from non-farm households were more likely to be engaged in professional or managerial work than females from farm households.

Education and training

In terms of access to employment and the gaining of suitable employment, lack of skills and/or training are often cited as barriers to labour market participation (Monk et al, 1999). The rural household survey indicated that for those in employment, there was a significant difference between the type of employment farm males engaged in, compared to their non-farming male counterparts. They were much less likely to be employed in professional and managerial positions. Consequently, it is important to consider educational attainment and training levels.

An examination of the educational attainment of males below the age of sixty-five years indicated a significant difference between non-farm and farm males in relation to university and/or college education. Sixteen per cent of non-farm males had obtained a university and/or college qualification, whilst only 8 per cent of farming males had achieved a similar qualification. Moreover, when all post-secondary level training was considered, i.e. agricultural, vocational, trade and further education, males from non-farming households were more likely to have obtained some form of post-secondary level qualification than their counterparts in farm households. There was no significant difference between the overall incidence of post-secondary training of males and females in farm households. However, when the existence of university and/or college attainment was examined, a significantly higher percentage of farm females had completed further education, compared to farm males.

Although there was no significant difference in the proportions of farm and non-farm males working, farm males were disadvantaged by the type of off-farm employment that they could undertake, due to their lack of training and overall level of educational attainment. The survey indicated that the level of educational attainment, specifically higher education, of farm females was higher than that of their male counterparts, but this was not reflected in their uptake of professional employment. When comparing farm females with non-farm females, there was no significant difference in the level of all post-secondary training undertaken and university and/or college attainment. Although farm females were educated to similar levels as their non-farm counterparts, when they entered employment they were less likely to be engaged in professional and managerial posts. This supports the findings of Shucksmith and Chapman (1998), who suggested that women's aspirations took second place to their male partners or male peer group and this disparity is reinforced in rural areas through inadequate childcare provision and transport services.

Distances travelled to work

Farm households had a higher percentage of females at home than non-farm households. It is possible that the longer working hours and commuting time of farm males may have placed greater restrictions on opportunities for farm female off-farm employment. The observed high level of dependency on personal transport in rural areas placed considerable financial constraints on households. If the male member of the household was travelling long distances to employment and using the sole household vehicle, then the female member of the household may not have been able to engage in employment.

In terms of distance travelled to work (see Table 2.6), two-thirds of non-farm males and over three-quarters of farm males were travelling more than ten miles, single journey. Furthermore, 40 per cent of non-farm males travelled more than twenty-five miles, whereas over 65 per cent of farm males travelled similar distances.

A high percentage of males, both farm and non-farm, travelled lengthy distances to work. Moreover, 30 per cent of males worked more than forty hours per week. In light of the earlier findings, regarding the sectors in which these males were employed, the recorded commuting distances reflected the nature of their occupations, i.e. construction, agriculture-related and transport, which are associated with long commuting distances and also long working hours. The farming enterprises were not restricting the location of off-farm employment nor the long hours worked by farm males.

TABLE 2.6 SINGLE JOURNEY DISTANCES FROM HOME TO WORK

Distance travelled	Male*		Female*	
	Non-farm (%)	Farm (%)	Non-farm (%)	Farm (%)
Up to ten miles	33	24	64	54
Greater than ten miles	67	76	36	46

Just over 60 per cent of employed females, both farm and non-farm, travelled ten miles or less to their place of employment, significantly shorter distances than the males. This may reflect the desire/need for working women to be close to their children's schools or childcare facilities. The vast majority (90 per cent) of the people in employment, both male and female, farm and non-farm, declared a high reliance on private transport, as the main means of transport to work was by car, van or lift. Public transport was considered too infrequent or unreliable to be used for travel-to-work purposes. This created difficulty for those females who either worked part-time or engaged in manual or semi-skilled work. Their earning potential was insufficient to finance their own private vehicles and, furthermore, public transport was inadequate outside standard commuting times. Over four-fifths of respondents considered the road network to be poor or only adequate.

CONCLUSIONS

The representative farm models presented have identified that although farmers may have a range of objectives and goals for their farming enterprises, in terms of profitability only the larger farm operators can achieve an adequate level of return which will provide for household consumption and maintain the capital base of the enterprise. Even when farming incomes were at historically high levels, in the mid-1990s, the limited earning potential of the majority of Northern Ireland farm businesses resulted in difficulty in financing basic farm household consumption levels, despite the presence of off-farm earnings and, at the same time, maintaining the value of the fixed assets associated with the farm business. There is little prospect of farming incomes returning to or exceeding those relatively high levels.

Consequently, off-farm employment or diversification, which has recently been recommended by policy makers as a possible solution to low farm incomes, can be expected to play an ever more important role in generating adequate income for farm families. In the situation where the farms' fixed assets are not being maintained, it is difficult to envisage farmers being in a financial position to consider new diversification start ups, especially when the risk associated with new small business ventures is known to be high. There is also evidence that small farmers have not engaged in such ventures in the past and are not trained for such ventures.

Smaller farmers are under continued pressure to identify and access other sources of income, and for those of working age, the indications are that off-farm employment is of increasing importance. Farming enterprises such as beef and sheep production are sufficiently flexible, in terms of labour requirements, that members of the household can engage in off-farm employment in the wider economy. Small dairy farmers, however, have difficulty accessing off-farm employment due to the labour demands of a dairy enterprise.

Evidence suggests that males below retirement age in farm households are as economically active as their non-farming counterparts, are equally mobile and are prepared to work long hours off-farm. However, farm males have a lower level of training and educational attainment, and a skills base which is mainly trade or agriculture related. Consequently, their off-farm employment is concentrated in sectors such as construction, transport and agriculture, which do not require advanced training/education. Jobs in these sectors are characteristically lower paid, involve long working hours and have limited growth potential. Given the willingness of farm and non-farm males to commute, rural development policies targeted towards highly localised job creation may be more appropriately concentrated in growth centres. There is also a need to address the training and skills deficit amongst males in farming households, targeting the training requirements of the 'new technology' industries and other emerging sectors.

In contrast, females from farm households are not so constrained by training or educational attainment, as they are better qualified than their male counterparts, but they are more restricted in where and when they can work due to family responsibilities. Consequently they constitute a less mobile workforce. Female employment is concentrated in the public sector activities of health and education. Clearly the existence of public sector jobs in locations easily accessed by rural dwellers is particularly important. The recent trends in rationalising the provision of public services in rural areas will diminish the employment opportunities for rural females, both farm and non-farm. Since many educational and health jobs are professional in nature, the loss of this higher paid employment from the commuting range of rural, and especially farm-based females is a concern.

A higher number of farm females than non-farm females of working age remained at home. The main constraints cited were transport availability, childcare and feeling responsible for the farm business. They were very often the only people at home due to their partners being employed off-farm. In relation to caring for children and other dependent relatives, there may be a need for greater emphasis on grant provision for community-based initiatives which would allow women to engage in the wider economy.

For many rural households, ownership of a second car is essential in order to gain access to employment. There is no viable alternative to private transport and over half of the households surveyed had two or more vehicles. This pattern of private transport usage conflicts with current environmental policies aimed at reducing private car use, i.e. through increased road tax and higher fuel prices. For some individuals in rural households, particularly women seeking part-time, semi-skilled employment, ownership of a second car may not be an economically viable option.

Past experience shows that the small farm families that dominate the Northern Ireland farm sector are capable of withstanding severe financial pressure. Their tenacity, however, has been won at the cost of long working hours both on and off-farm. The desire to retain their farmland and engage in farming, albeit on a modest scale, is very strong. If these farming families are to have a more financially secure future, their skills and training base will have to be enhanced. Better paid employment in the growth sectors of the wider Northern Ireland economy is their best route to sustaining their small farm businesses.

ENDNOTES

The FAPRI global modelling system, described in Brandt et al (1991a; 1991b), is a system of partial equilibrium models for different regions of the world, which are solved simultaneously. The FAPRI EU model is one of the regional models, which, when solved as part of the FAPRI global modelling system, produces price projections for EU agricultural goods. These prices are transmitted to the Northern Ireland model via price linkage equations, reflecting the price-taking nature of Northern Ireland's small, highly export-dependent agriculture sector. The Northern Ireland Agricultural model comprises sub-models of the Northern Ireland dairy, beef, sheep and input sectors. The four Northern Ireland sub-sector models are inter-linked, as illustrated in Figure 2.3. In the analysis of the Northern Ireland agricultural model for the period 2000 to 2009, it was assumed that the Berlin Agreement of Agenda 2000 policies had been fully implemented, as described in McErlean et al (1999), and the growth rate of the Northern Ireland economy followed Northern Ireland Economic Research Centre forecasts.

The research project investigating rural household decision making has received the financial support of the Rural Innovation and Research partnership (NI) Ltd through the EU LEADER 2 programme.

The analysis of the impact of policy scenarios is associated with the Northern Ireland FAPRI Project.

REFERENCES

Brandt, J.A., R.E. Young II and A.W. Womack (1991a), 'Modelling the Impacts of Two Agricultural Policies on the US Livestock Sector: A Systems Approach', *Agricultural Systems* 35: 129–155.

Brandt, J.A., K.W. Bailey and P. Westhoff (1991b), 'Food Costs and 1988 US Drought: An Assessment of Stock Policies', *Food Policy,* October: 362–370.

Cawley, M., D.A. Gillmor, A. Leavy and P. McDonagh (1995), *Farm Diversification Studies Relating to the West of Ireland,* Dublin: Teagasc.

Davis, J., N. Mack and A. Kirke (1997), New Perspectives on Farm Household Incomes, *Journal of Rural Studies,* vol. 13, no. 1: 57–64.

Commisssion of the European Communities (1992), Directorate General for Agriculture, *The Reform of the Common Agricultural Policy,* Brussels: CAP Working Notes.

Department of Agriculture for Northern Ireland (1997), *Farm Incomes in Northern Ireland,* Belfast: HMSO.

Department of Agriculture for Northern Ireland (2000), *Scoping Study: Supplementation of Family Farm Income.* Belfast: HMSO.

Department of Agriculture and Rural Development for Northern Ireland (2000a), Economic and Statistics Division, personal communication.

Department of Agriculture and Rural Development for Northern Ireland (2000b), Rural Development Division, personal communication.

Department of Agriculture and Rural Development for Northern Ireland (2000c), *Farm Incomes in Northern Ireland,* Belfast: HMSO.

European Commission (1997), *Agenda 2000: For a Stronger and Wider Europe,* Strasbourg/Brussels: DOC/97/9.

European Commission (1999), 'Berlin European Council: Agenda 2000, Conclusions of the Presidency', *DG Agriculture Newsletter,* Brussels: April 1999.

Gasson, R. (1973), 'Goals and Values of Farmers', *Journal of Agricultural Economics,* 24: 521–537.

Gasson, R. and A. Errington (1993), *The Farm Family Business,* Wallingford, Oxon: CAB International.

Güzel, H.A. and S.N. Kulshreshtha (1995), 'Effects of Real Exchange Rate Changes on Canadian Agriculture: A General Equilibrium Evaluation', *Journal of Policy Modelling,* vol. 17, no. 6: 639–657.

Hannan, D.F. and P. Commins (1992), 'The Significance of Small-scale Landholders in Ireland's Socio-economic Transformation', in J.H. Goldthorpe and C.T. Whelan (eds), *The Development of Industrial Society in Ireland: Proceedings of the British Academy,* vol. 79, Oxford: Oxford University Press.

Heady, E.O. (1952), *Economics of Agricultural Production and Resource Use,* Englewood Cliffs, New Jersey: Prentice Hall.

McWhinney, G. (2000), *Information Technologies and E-commerce in Rural Areas and Adding Value to Local Primary Produce,* Report of Proceedings of the UK LEADER 2 Network Workshop held in Limavady, Northern Ireland, 23–24 March, Northern Ireland LEADER Network.

Monk, S., J. Dunn, M. Fitzgerald and I. Hodge (1999), *Finding Work in Rural Areas: Barriers and Bridges,* Work and Opportunity Series 13, Joseph Rowntree Foundation, York Publishing Services.

Moss, J.E. (1992), 'The Role of Pluri-active Family Farms in the Development of a Marginal Area of the European Community, in *Spatial Dynamics of Highland and High Latitude Environments,* Occasional Papers in Geography and Planning 4, Boone, North Carolina: Appalachian State University.

Moss, J.E., S.A. McErlean, Z. Wu, J. IJpelaar and A. Doherty (2000), *Impact of Exchange Rates on Northern Ireland Agriculture,* AFED Occasional Paper, Queen's University Belfast.

McErlean, S.A., J.E. Moss, Z. Wu, A. Doherty and J. IJpelaar (1999), *Analysis of the Impact of CAP Reform Measures (Berlin Agreement) on the NI Beef and Dairy Sectors*, Northern Ireland FAPRI Project Research Report commissioned by DANI Policy Divisions (published as AFED Occasional Paper).

Northern Ireland Economic Research Centre (1999), *Regional Economic Outlook, Autumn 1999*, Belfast.

Pavis, S., S. Platt and G. Hubbard (2000), *Young People in Rural Scotland: Pathways to Social Exclusion*, Joseph Rowntree Foundation, York Publishing Services.

Perkin, P. and T. Rehman (1994), 'Farmers' Objectives and their Interaction with Business and Life Styles: Evidence from Berkshire, England', in J.B. Dent and M.J. McGregor (eds), *Rural and Farming Systems Analysis: European Perspectives*, Wallingford, Oxon: CAB International.

Robson, B., M. Bradford and I. Deas (1994), *Relative Deprivation in Northern Ireland*, Policy Planning and Research Unit Occasional Paper **28**, Belfast: HMSO.

Rural Development Council for Northern Ireland (1999), *GIS Mapping of Disadvantaged Wards in Northern Ireland*, Cookstown.

Schuh, G.E. (1974), 'The Exchange Rate and U.S Agriculture', *American Journal of Agricultural Economics* 67: 1–13.

Shucksmith, M. and P. Chapman (1998), Rural Development and Social Exclusion, *Sociologia Ruralis*, vol. 38, no. 2: 225–242.

CHAPTER 3

SUSTAINING RURAL ECONOMIES: ENTERPRISE FORMATION IN RURAL NORTHERN IRELAND 1994–1999

Mark Hart, Maureen O'Reilly
and Michael Anyadike-Danes

INTRODUCTION

The ability to generate a large flow of good quality new businesses is a prerequisite of a dynamic growing economy. These new businesses serve to renew the existing stock of businesses as well as contributing to innovation, the development of new industries and employment creation. In general, a link can be developed between entrepreneurship and economic prosperity. Enterprising individuals, or entrepreneurs, are vital in this process as they respond to market opportunities by combining the necessary people and resources (Best, 2000; Anyadike-Danes et al, 2001; Global Entrepreneurship Monitor, 2002).

A number of previous research studies have demonstrated that small firms located in rural areas generally outperform comparable firms in urban areas (Curran and Storey, 1993; Keeble et al, 1992). More recent evidence is not as clear-cut, with SMEs in rural areas of Great Britain containing a significantly higher proportion of stable or declining enterprises compared to comparable firms in other areas in the period 1994–1999 (Cosh and Hughes, 2000). However, from the same study, there do not appear to be any significant differences in employment or turnover growth rates between SMEs across urban/rural groups.

The primary aim of this chapter is to analyse trends in new business formation at the sub-regional level in Northern Ireland for the period 1994 to 1999 and to set them within the context of wider employment growth. This analysis will be based on VAT registrations and de-registrations for the 26 District Council Areas (DCAs) in Northern Ireland. From the outset it should be acknowledged that it is not being assumed that the VAT data provides the only or best measure of enterprise formation and closure in the business sector.[1] The analysis presented here does not attempt to 'explain' any differences in formation rates between rural and urban areas, as collection of the vast array of data required for that exercise has not yet been completed by the authors. The paper concludes with an assessment of the extent to which the rural economy can be seen as 'enterprising' and capable of providing sustainable economic development opportunities for its residents and communities.

For the purposes of the analysis presented here the definition of 'rural' will be defined as all those DCAs outside the Belfast Metropolitan Area (which is defined as Belfast, Castlereagh, Carrickfergus, Newtownabbey, North Down and Lisburn DCAs) and Derry (Figure 3.1). A further grouping of DCAs will be used, which corresponds to the NUTS III level of disaggregation, and will provide a useful sub-division of this broad 'rural' category by distinguishing between rural areas in the east of Northern Ireland, and those in the west and south and the north (Figure 3.2; Annex 1).

---

1. The VAT data does not include information on the self-employed and is only a partial dataset for business as a result of the VAT threshold (currently £54,000), which excludes many small business start-ups. For a fuller discussion of the issues and problems surrounding the use of VAT data as a proxy for business formation, the reader is referred to Storey (1994) and Johnson and Conway (1997).

FIGURE 3.1 DISTRICT COUNCIL AREAS IN NORTHERN IRELAND

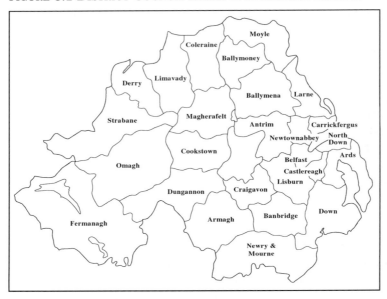

FIGURE 3.2 NUTS III SUB-REGIONS IN NORTHERN IRELAND

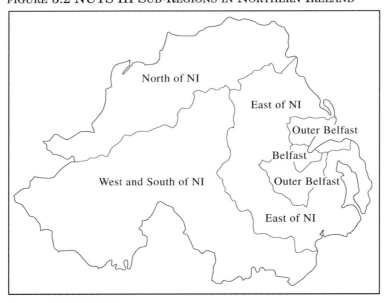

Source: DETI (2001).

EMPLOYMENT CHANGE IN RURAL AREAS, 1995–1999

In the 1970s and 1980s there was clear evidence that total employment in rural areas in Northern Ireland was growing faster than in urban areas (Hart, 1993). These trends have continued into the 1990s. Using data from the Northern Ireland Census of Employment (CoE), the number of employees in employment (all sectors) increased by 11 per cent (58,523 *net* jobs) in the period September 1995 to September 1999 (Table 3.1). At the sub-regional level it is clear that rural areas in Northern Ireland are continuing to grow faster in terms of total employment than the Belfast Region and Derry. In absolute terms rural areas contributed 56 per cent of total net jobs in the period.

TABLE 3.1: TOTAL EMPLOYMENT CHANGE IN RURAL AREAS, 1995–1999

Sub-Region	Net Change in Jobs (Number)	Net Change in Jobs (%)
Rural	32706	13
Urban		
(Belfast Region and Derry)	25817	9
NUTS III		
• Belfast Region	22782	9
• East of NI	12539	12
• North of NI (exc. Derry)	5105	12
• West and South of NI	15062	16
Northern Ireland	**58,523**	**11**

Source: *Labour Market Bulletin* (November 2001), no. 15, DEL, constructed from Table 2, p. 33.

Furthermore, within the rural areas, there is a clear difference in employment growth rates between the rural areas in the east and north of the region compared to those in the west and south of Northern Ireland. As in the previous period 1971–1990, net employment growth is much higher in the western and southern rural regions compared to other rural areas in Northern Ireland. This would tend to suggest that it is the more 'remote' rural regions in Northern Ireland that are experiencing faster growth in employment compared to the more 'accessible' rural areas around the Belfast Region and Derry.

Figure 3.3 presents the total employment growth rates between 1995 and 1999 for all 26 DCAs in Northern Ireland. Clearly, not all rural DCAs are experiencing above-average growth rates (e.g., Strabane, Ards and Banbridge), but three DCAs, all within the broad 'rural' category, experienced the highest growth rates in the period, of around twice the Northern Ireland average: Limavady (26%), Cookstown (23%) and Dungannon (21%). This pattern is also in evidence when one looks only at service sector employment over the same period (Figure 3.4). However, it is important to remember the small base upon which these changes are taking place in some of the rural DCAs.

FIGURE 3.3 TOTAL DISTRICT EMPLOYMENT GROWTH RATES, 1995–1999

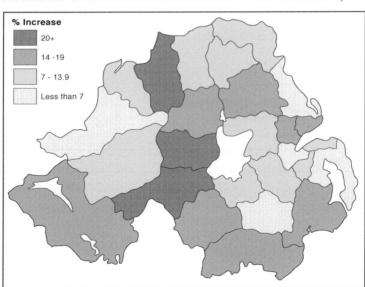

Source: DETI (2001).

FIGURE 3.4 TOTAL DISTRICT SERVICE SECTOR EMPLOYMENT GROWTH
RATES, 1995–1999

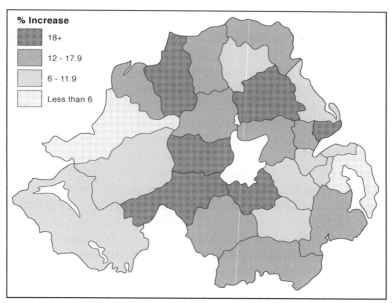

Source: DETI (2001).

While it is possible to document that faster employment growth
is taking place in the rural areas of Northern Ireland, it is perhaps more difficult to 'explain' these dynamics and to present
an argument for the sustainable nature of that employment
growth. One possible connection to these trends in employment
growth is the process of new business formation, and the following section presents the available evidence for each of the
DCAs. In the absence of alternative measures[2] of enterprising
activity, data on VAT registrations and de-registrations are
used as a proxy for new business formation over the period
1994–1999.

---

2 Although the Labour Force Survey (LFS) for Northern Ireland collects
data on the self-employed by DCA, the sample size in 1999 (n=79) is too
small to enable meaningful analysis at the sub-regional level.

71

NEW BUSINESS FORMATION IN RURAL AREAS: VAT TRENDS
1994–1999

Stock of Businesses

At the start of 1999 the total stock of businesses registered for
VAT[3] in Northern Ireland was 54,615, which represented an
increase of 3.7 per cent since 1994. Rural areas contained
almost three-quarters (73.6%) of this stock of VAT registered
businesses, a proportion that has remained stable since 1994.
Standardising the data by the adult resident population facili-
tates a proper comparison between rural and urban areas in
Northern Ireland (Table 3.2). Using this method it emerges that
there are almost twice the number of businesses registered for
VAT in rural areas compared to urban areas. However, as the
VAT data contains businesses registered in the agriculture
sector it is further necessary to exclude this sector when
making the urban/rural comparison. For all industries (excluding agriculture) the number of business registered for VAT in
rural areas per 10,000 adult resident population (ARP) was 298
at the start of 1999 compared to 254 for urban areas. While the
number of businesses per 10,000 ARP in rural areas has
remained static over the period, urban areas have experienced
a decrease of 6 businesses per 10,000 ARP over the period 1994
to 1999. An examination of the data using the NUTS III regions
highlights more clearly the differences between the rural and
urban areas in Northern Ireland. In particular, the stock of
businesses in the west and south is 23 per cent higher than the
Northern Ireland average and 40 per cent higher than the
Belfast Region. In addition, the west and south is the only
sub-region that has experienced any noticeable increase in the
number of businesses per 10,000 ARP.

At the level of the individual DCA there is a great deal of variation in the stock of VAT registered businesses in 1999 (Figure
3.5). In the light of the analysis presented in Table 3.2 it is
not surprising that the DCAs with the highest stock of VAT

---

3   The annual turnover threshold for VAT registration is currently £54,000.

businesses per 10,000 ARP are located in the western and southern locations of Northern Ireland and, in particular, in Magherafelt, Dungannon and Cookstown. In contrast, the four DCAs with the lowest number of VAT registered businesses per 10,000 ARP are all located in the Belfast Region: Castlereagh, Carrickfergus, Newtownabbey and North Down.

TABLE 3.2: STOCK OF VAT REGISTERED BUSINESSES IN NORTHERN IRELAND, 1994–1999

Sub-Region	Stock of Businesses in 1999 (Number)	Stock of Businesses in 1999 (%)	Per 10,000 ARP 1994	Per 10,000 ARP 1999
All Industries				
• Rural	40,185	73.6	532	530
• Urban*	14,430	26.4	282	276
Northern Ireland	**54,615**	**100**	**429**	**427**
All Industries (exc. Agriculture)				
• Rural	22,585	63.6	298	298
• Urban*	12,950	36.4	254	248
Northern Ireland	**35,535**	**100**	**280**	**278**
NUTS III				
• Belfast Region	12,515	37.1	258	247
• East of NI	8,515	25.3	289	282
• North of NI (exc. Derry)	3,435	10.2	270	272
• West and South of NI	9,245	27.4	334	344
Northern Ireland	**33,710**	**100**	**284**	**280**

* Includes the Belfast Region and Derry DCA.
Source: DTI.

FIGURE 3.5: STOCK OF VAT REGISTERED BUSINESSES PER 10,000 ARP BY DISTRICT, 1999

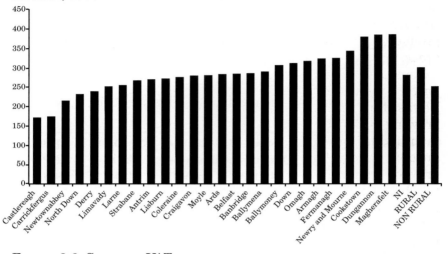

FIGURE 3.6: STOCK OF VAT REGISTERED PRODUCTION BUSINESSES PER 10,000 ARP BY DISTRICT, 1999

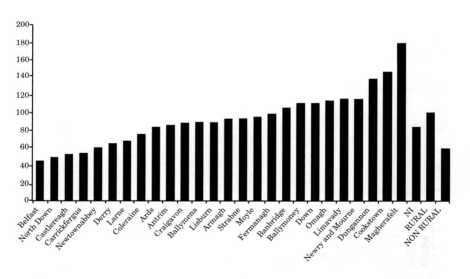

An important dimension of the debate on the sustainability of the rural economy is the nature of the businesses that are operating from these locations. Figure 3.6 shows that there is a clear spatial pattern to the distribution of businesses in the production sector (manufacturing and construction) in Northern Ireland in that the rural areas have on average twice as many production businesses per head of population than do urban areas.

Obviously, a large part of the explanation of this divergent pattern relates to the decline of the manufacturing sector in the Belfast Region (Hart, 1990), but nevertheless, the presence of a growing production sector (in terms of actual businesses in manufacturing activities) in rural areas does at least provide an opportunity for future trading activity beyond the boundaries of the local rural economy. The critical issue is the extent to which these production businesses are in sectors which are growing at regional and national level and further, so that they can draw upon the requisite skills in the local labour market to facilitate their expansion. The pattern is rather different in respect of business services, with the Belfast Region and Derry, not surprisingly, having higher concentrations of businesses in this sector compared to rural areas (Figure 3.7).

FIGURE 3.7: STOCK OF VAT REGISTERED BUSINESS SERVICE BUSINESSES PER 10,000 ARP BY DISTRICT, 1999

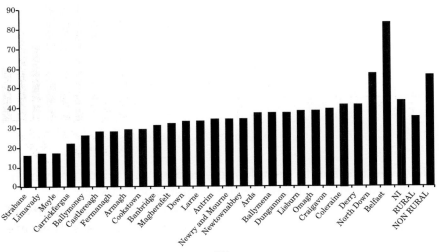

Business births and deaths

The number of businesses registering for VAT can be used to create a data series which can act as a proxy for new business formation at the sub-regional level in Northern Ireland. Once again it is important to standardise the number of registrations per 10,000 ARP in order to make comparisons between rural and urban areas as well as across the individual DCAs.

From Figure 3.8 it is clear that, although the number of VAT registrations in Northern Ireland has remained constant (28 per 10,000 ARP) in the period 1994–99, the difference between rural and non-rural areas has converged a little. In 1994 there were 32 new VAT registrations per 10,000 ARP in rural areas compared to 22 in urban areas. By 1999 the advantage of rural areas over urban areas had fallen slightly as the number of new VAT registrations per 10,000 ARP were 31 and 23 respectively.

FIGURE 3.8: VAT REGISTRATIONS PER 10,000 ARP, 1994–1999

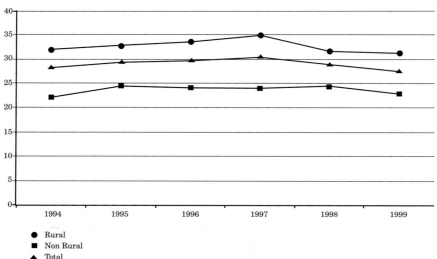

● Rural
■ Non Rural
▲ Total

However, these data include registrations in agriculture which, as argued above, complicate the comparison between rural and urban areas. If these registrations are removed, a more useful comparison between these two broad sub-regions is arrived at.

The differences between rural and urban areas over the 1994–99 period remain, but they are much reduced. For example, in 1999 the number of non-agricultural registrations was 26 per 10,000 ARP compared to 22 registrations in the Belfast Region and Derry, which was a marginal widening of the differential observed in 1994.

Apart from the obvious difference in agricultural registrations it is important to consider the main types of businesses registering for VAT in the rural areas of Northern Ireland and how they compare with registrations in urban areas. Figure 3.9 illustrates that at a broad sectoral level rural areas in 1999 had a higher number of registrations in construction, manufacturing, hotels and restaurants, transport and communications and wholesale and retailing, whereas urban areas have an advantage in business services and finance. It might, therefore, be concluded from this aggregate level analysis that whilst rural areas have experienced higher levels of business births, compared to urban areas, they were perhaps in sectors which suffer from low value-added and may have difficulty trading beyond their local area. However, in the absence of more detailed data from the VAT dataset it is impossible to be more precise on this issue.

FIGURE 3.9: VAT REGISTRATIONS PER 10,000 ARP BY SECTOR, 1999

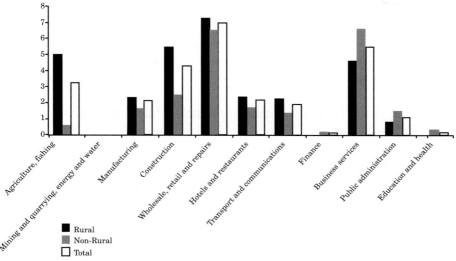

A closer look at the pattern of average annual non-agricultural VAT registrations by DCA over the period 1994–1999 reveals that the four highest rates were found in DCAs within the NUTS III region 'West and South of Northern Ireland', namely, Dungannon, Magherafelt, Cookstown, and Newry and Mourne (Figure 3.10). These four DCAs achieved business formation rates well above the Northern Ireland average in the six years since 1994. Overall, the rate of registrations is higher in rural areas (26 per 10,000 ARP) compared to urban areas (23 per 10,000 ARP).

FIGURE 3.10: AVERAGE ANNUAL NON-AGRICULTURAL VAT REGISTRATIONS PER 10,000 ARP BY DISTRICT, 1994–1999

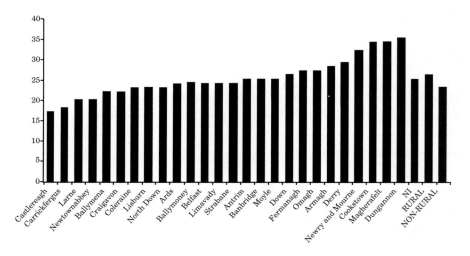

Turning to VAT de-registrations, which is used here as a proxy for business failure, Figure 3.11 illustrates that in 1994 the number of de-registrations in rural areas (35 per 10,000 ARP) was higher than in urban areas (23 per 10,000 ARP). Over the six-year period, however, these two figures converged so that by 1999 they were almost identical at around 28 and 29 de-registrations per 10,000 ARP respectively. Once again the agricultural de-registrations were removed from the analysis to enable a more appropriate comparison between rural and urban areas. The overall trend remains broadly unchanged with de-registrations remaining static in rural areas, after an initial fall, and rising in urban areas over the period. By 1999, the level of de-registrations in rural areas was 24 per 10,000 ARP compared to 27 per 10,000 ARP in urban areas.

FIGURE 3.11: VAT DE-REGISTRATIONS PER 10,000 ARP, 1994–1999

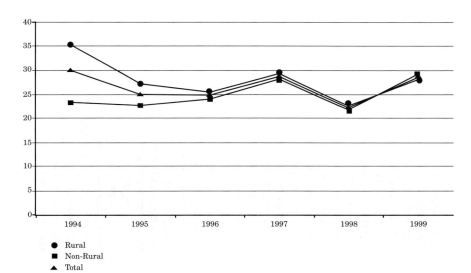

● Rural
■ Non-Rural
▲ Total

Putting the registration and de-registration aggregate data together demonstrates that, whereas in 1994 rural areas exhibited a net fall in the number of businesses registered for VAT (de-registrations were greater than registrations), by 1999 this had been reversed with an overall net increase in the stock of businesses in rural areas registered for VAT. This has been due to a rising number of registrations combined with a static level of de-registrations. This would tend to support the view that businesses in rural areas in Northern Ireland are surviving longer than their counterparts in urban areas

Figure 3.12 examines the pattern of non-agricultural VAT de-registrations at the level of the individual DCA for the period

1994–1999. The results reveal a much less straightforward pattern than that for VAT registrations for the same period, with the highest rates found in the Belfast region (Belfast, North Down and Ards DCAs) as well as DCAs in the 'West and South' NUTS III region (Dungannon, Cookstown, and Newry and Mourne). Overall, the rate of de-registrations in rural areas in Northern Ireland over the period is only marginally lower than that for urban areas: 23 and 24 de-registrations per 10,000 ARP respectively.

FIGURE 3.12: AVERAGE ANNUAL NON-AGRICULTURAL VAT DE-REGISTRATIONS PER 10,000 ARP, 1994–1999

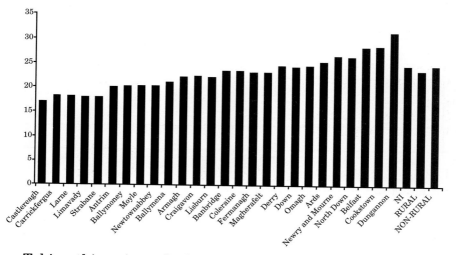

Taking this point a little further it is helpful to examine the relationship between business births and deaths as represented by the VAT registrations and de-registrations data at the level of the individual DCA for 1999 (Figure 3.13). Overall, there is a positive and significant relationship between births and deaths across the 26 DCAs in Northern Ireland as represented by the solid trend line on the graph. For example, Dungannon, Cookstown and Newry and Mourne DCAs, all located in the NUTS III 'West and South' region, display above-average business birth rates as well as above-average business death rates. By way of contrast, Castlereagh, Larne and Carrickfergus DCAs have the lowest rates of business birth and death.

In other words, the higher the rate of business births the higher the rate of business deaths, lending support to the notion of 'churning'. What this means is that DCAs with above-average rates of business birth in the period 1994–99 are also those DCAs with above-average rates of business death. In business start-up policy terms the implication here is that 'success' and 'failure' are intrinsically linked. However, the precise direction of causality in the data is difficult to interpret at this level of analysis and requires more detailed analysis. Two simple interpretations will illustrate the problem. First, it could be the case that high levels of business birth lead to higher levels of business death, as less competitive firms are forced out of the market place. Second, high levels of business death may lead to start-up opportunities as other businesses seek to fill gaps in the market place and take advantage of the resources released by failing businesses. Clearly, both processes can be in operation simultaneously and the analysis presented here sheds no real light on the dynamic processes of start-up and closure, and their inter-relationships, which are at work in the local economy.

FIGURE 3.13: VAT NON-AGRICULTURAL REGISTRATIONS AND DE-REGISTRATIONS BY DISTRICT, 1994–1999

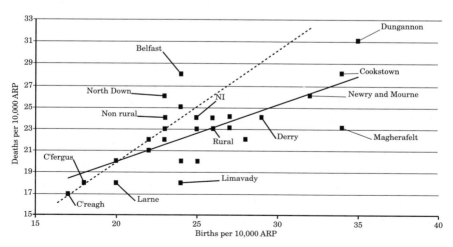

However, the strength of the relationship between registrations and de-registrations is not completely linear, a finding which is supported by a closer examination of the rank order of DCAs in Figures 3.10 and 3.12. This indicates that there are important exceptions to this general rule. The relationship is weakened, for example, by the presence of Belfast and North Down in the top five DCAs in terms of business death rate. These two DCAs have business birth rates at or below the Northern Ireland average, which has led to a declining stock of business registered for VAT in these areas. At the other extreme, Limavady DCA has experienced above average birth rates and below average death rates in the six years since 1994, which has led to an increase in the business stock in the area.

Nevertheless, as noted above, within the context of this broadly positive relationship between business births and deaths, the net outcome for rural areas is an increasing stock of businesses over the period 1994–99. This is illustrated in Figure 3.13 by the 'rural' data point lying below the dotted line which connects points where birth and death rates are equal and the "non-rural" point lying above it. A further point to note is that a growing business stock (excess of births over deaths) can be achieved through both high and low registrations rates as illustrated by the case of Limavady and Larne, which have below average birth rates combined with even lower death rates.

The implication here for rural enterprise policy is clear. If the objective is to develop a growing business community in rural economies, as measured by an increase in the stock of businesses, then this can equally be achieved at high and low levels of business birth rate. This is important because the relationship between business birth and death rates might suggest that a volume start-up strategy, without too much regard for the quality of the start-up business, may well lead to higher closure rates through the process of displacement in local markets. This is of particular concern for the Business Start-up Programme in Northern Ireland, which was operated in partnership between LEDU, formerly the Northern Ireland small business agency, and the District Councils in an attempt to increase the level of business start-up activity across the region (Hart and Scott,

1994; Hart and O'Reilly, 2000). The broader lessons from Figure 3.13 might be to encourage policy makers, not least those associated with the Northern Ireland Rural Development Programme, to think in terms of reducing the number of business failures by developing a 'business death rate strategy'!

EMPLOYMENT GROWTH AND BUSINESS BIRTHS

It has been shown earlier in this chapter that rural areas in Northern Ireland have been experiencing faster employment growth in the late 1990s compared to urban areas, and thus it is useful to consider the extent to which the higher levels of business birth rate in rural areas over the same period are related to that broader growth trend. This section will address the nature of any relationship between employment growth and birth and death rates at the DCA level for the period 1994–99.

The relationship between employment growth and business birth rates over the period 1994–99, although positive, is a weak one (Figure 3.14). There is some evidence to suggest that those DCAs with the highest employment growth rates between 1995–99 are also those that have achieved the highest rates of VAT registrations: for example, Dungannon and Cookstown. However, Ballymena and Newtownabbey have experienced above-average employment growth rates and below-average business birth rates in the period, illustrating the weakness of the relationship. The analysis also points to a weak association between business start-up and employment growth and says nothing about the direction of causality. It is not clear, for example, whether employment growth drives higher business births or whether a greater number of new businesses generates employment growth.

What this suggests is that there are 'missing' variables in the analysis which are necessary to insert before it is possible to construct an explanation of the spatial variations in business birth in Northern Ireland. Future research, following the broad conceptual frameworks developed in earlier modelling work into the spatial variations in new business formation (see Reynolds et al, 1994; Hart and Gudgin, 1994), will be an important next step in the research agenda for understanding the dynamics of business birth and death in rural areas. Such an analysis would incorporate a range of socio-economic variables that can, a priori, be related to the process of setting up a new business activity. These would include information on demand (population growth and GDP), urbanisation (population density), unemployment, personal or household wealth, proportions of small firms, industrial structure, occupational structure and government spending policies either through direct programmes designed to promote increased levels of business start-up in an area or economic development/regeneration policies in general.

FIGURE 3.14: AVERAGE ANNUAL NON-AGRICULTURAL VAT REGISTRATIONS PER 10,000 ARP BY EMPLOYMENT GROWTH, 1994–1999

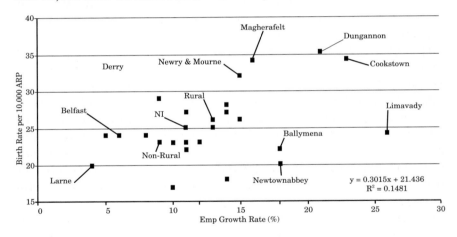

CONCLUSION

Rural areas in Northern Ireland have exhibited faster rates of growth in total employment between 1995 and 1999 than urban areas. Moreover, net employment growth is much higher in the west and southern rural regions of Northern Ireland compared to other rural areas in Northern Ireland.

The analysis of the VAT dataset, despite its weaknesses, has provided an important narrative about the enterprising nature of rural Northern Ireland in the late 1990s. At the level of the individual DCA there is a great deal of variation in the stock of VAT registered businesses. The DCAs with the highest stock of VAT registered businesses per 10,000 ARP are located in the western and southern regions of Northern Ireland, while in contrast, the four DCAs with the lowest number of VAT registered businesses per head of population are all located in the Belfast Region.

With respect to business start-up activity it is clear that rural areas, and particularly those in the west and south of Northern Ireland, have managed to achieve and maintain above-average business birth rates. What can be concluded from this is that there is an important positive dynamic in the rural economies of Northern Ireland which requires further monitoring and research in order to arrive at some meaningful explanation of these spatial variations in enterprise activity at the DCA and NUTS III level.

However, what has been reported here is only a small part of the analysis that is needed on the rural economies of Northern Ireland. The VAT data provide only a partial view of the scale of start-up activity across Northern Ireland, and it is important to develop datasets which will provide a more accurate measure of the scale of entrepreneurial or enterprise capacity. With more comprehensive datasets on business start-up and the performance of surviving cohorts of small firms, it may be possible to understand more clearly the development trajectories of the *variety* of rural economies in Northern Ireland.

Finally, this analysis has revealed once again the dangers of treating the rural economy in Northern Ireland as a homogeneous entity. Clearly, it is not, and the challenge for policymakers in government, whether they be in the Department of Agriculture and Rural Development, the new industrial development agency, Invest NI, or the Department for Regional Development, is to develop coherent and integrated policies which respond to this emerging diversity. Too often, spatial stereotypes, as evidenced by the content of the Northern Ireland Regional Development Strategy with its emphasis on the Belfast Region as *the* economic engine, have served to constrain the formulation of innovative and imaginative sub-regional development strategies.

REFERENCES

Anyadike-Danes, M., M. Hart and M. O'Reilly (2001), 'Watch That Space! The County Hierarchy in Firm Births and Deaths in the UK, 1980–1999', paper presented at the 24th ISBA National Small Firms Policy and Research Conference, De Montfort University, 14–16 November 2001.

Best, M.H. (2000), *The Capabilities and Innovation Perspective: The Way Ahead for Northern Ireland,* Belfast: Northern Ireland Economic Council.

Cosh, A., and A. Hughes (2000*), British Enterprise in Transition: Growth, Innovation and Public Policy in the Small and Medium-Sized Sector 1994–99,* Cambridge: Centre for Business Research (CBR), University of Cambridge.

Curran, J. and D.J. Storey (1993*), Small Firms in Urban and Rural Locations*, London: Routledge.

Global Entrepreneurship Monitor (2002), *Global Entrepreneurship Monitor 2001: UK Executive Report,* London: London Business School.

Hart, M. (1990), 'Belfast's Economic Millstone? The Role of the Manufacturing Sector since 1973', in P. Doherty (ed.), *Geographical Perspectives on the Belfast Region,* Dublin: Geographical Society of Ireland, Special Publication No. 5.

Hart, M. (1993), 'Enterprise in Rural Areas', in M. Murray and J. Greer (eds), *Rural Development in Ireland*, Aldershot: Avebury.

Hart, M. and G. Gudgin (1994), 'Spatial Variations in New Firm Formation in the Republic of Ireland, 1980–1990', *Regional Studies,* vol. 28, no. 4: 367–380.

Hart, M. and R. Scott (1994), 'Measuring the Effectiveness of Small Firm Policy: Some Lessons from Northern Ireland', *Regional Studies*, vol. 28, no. 8: 849–858.

Hart, M. and M. O'Reilly (2000), 'Enterprise Start-up Policy in Northern Ireland: An Agenda for Social Inclusion?', paper presented at the 23rd ISBA National Small Firms Policy and

Research Conference, Aberdeen University, 15–17 November 2000.

Johnson, P. and Conway, C. (1997), 'How Good are the UK VAT Registration Data at Measuring Firm Births?', *Small Business Economics*, vol. 9, no. 5: 403–409.

Keeble, D., P. Tyler, G. Broom and J. Lewis (1992), *Business Success in the Countryside: The Performance of Rural Enterprise*, London: HMSO.

Reynolds, P., D.J. Storey and P. Westhead (1994), 'Cross-national Comparisons of the Variations in New Firm Formation Rates: An Editorial Overview', *Regional Studies,* vol. 28, no. 4: 343–346.

Storey, D.J. (1994), *Understanding the Small Business Sector*, London: Routledge.

ANNEX 1

NUTS III regions in Northern Ireland and their constituent District Councils

Belfast	Belfast
Outer Belfast	Carrickfergus
	Castlereagh
	Lisburn
	Newtownabbey
	North Down
East of Northern Ireland	Antrim
	Ards
	Ballymena
	Banbridge
	Craigavon
	Down
	Larne
North of Northern Ireland	Ballymoney
	Coleraine
	Derry
	Limavady
	Moyle
	Strabane
West and South of Northern Ireland	Armagh
	Cookstown
	Dungannon
	Fermanagh
	Magherafelt
	Newry and Mourne
	Omagh

CHAPTER 4

THE ROLE OF COMMUNITY TOURISM DEVELOPMENT: INSIGHTS FROM SOUTH ARMAGH

Maureen O'Reilly and Mark Hart

INTRODUCTION

In many ways tourism is unusual due to its ability to affect the lives of the majority of people within a community irrespective of their direct involvement as providers of a tourism-related service. Tourism has the potential to positively contribute to the development of a community's socio-economic well-being through the creation of employment opportunities, reducing the flow of outward migration and alleviating problems associated with unemployment. The Commission of European Communities recognises the widespread impact of tourism and the fact that it is linked with all sectors of socio-economic and cultural activity: *'Tourism influences, and is directly influenced by, many of these sectors* [cultural and socio-economic] *and is a source of revitalisation for many others'* (Commission of European Communities, 1992). Clearly therefore, tourism and the community are regarded as being of central interest, with considerable potential for local community-led development.

At the beginning of its boom, tourism was viewed as being a 'natural' renewable resource industry, with visitors portrayed as coming only to admire — not consume — the landscape, customs, and monuments of a destination area. However, as tourism grew in size and scope, it became apparent that this

89

industry, like others, competed for scarce resources and capital, and that its non-consumptive attributes did not necessarily prevent the erosion or alteration of attractions. With this came recognition that to become a renewable resource, tourism requires careful planning and management. Specifically, the industry possesses great potential for social and economic benefits if planning can be redirected from a purely business and development approach to a more open and community-oriented approach which views tourism as a local resource (Murphy, 1993). Such an approach recognises the uniqueness of tourism as an industry in its reliance on the goodwill and cooperation of local people as part of its product.

Further evidence of the need for a changed approach to public involvement in tourism planning has come from the numerous tourism impact and resident attitude studies conducted over the past two decades. These studies have shown that while tourism's economic impacts are generally welcomed (Keogh, 1990; Kendall and Var, 1984; Liu and Var, 1986), many of the social and ecological consequences of tourism development are perceived in a more negative light (Cooke, 1982; Pizam, 1978; Liu, Sheldon and Var, 1987) and, if allowed to build, may ultimately be reflected in deteriorating and even hostile attitudes towards tourism and tourists. When this happens everybody loses: residents, visitors and the tourist industry. The outcome of such studies has been a call for increased public participation and, in particular, a more community-oriented approach to tourism planning (Cooke, 1982; Getz, 1983; Haywood, 1988; Loukissas, 1983; Murphy, 1988, 1993). The central objective is to maximise the potential and sustainability of tourism development by optimally combining the commercial priorities of the tourist provider with the needs and objectives of the community.

Community involvement in tourism planning can serve several purposes. First, it can provide residents with information. A basic aim of any public participation programme should be to provide concerned citizens with adequate information. As Lucas (1978) observes, 'if full information is not available on issues under consideration, opportunities or even rights to participate become meaningless'. It is, therefore, important in any programme to determine what data are needed and by whom, and to do so throughout the planning process. This requires identifying the issues at stake in the community and the potential public or interest groups involved.

Second, it can help to identify the existing and potential tourism product. In community-based tourism management, residents themselves are seen as an essential part of an area's 'hospitality atmosphere' (Simmons, 1994). Securing their support is thus essential. The same public has considerable tourism experience both as hosts and visitors, providing a reservoir of information and enthusiasm if properly tapped. Public participation in tourism planning can enable the community to identify the existing 'tourism product' of the area, to provide suggestions regarding possible future potential and to indicate the range of constraints. Also at this stage, residents can attempt to reach consensus regarding the goals they wish to achieve. These might include reducing unemployment, promoting economic development, revitalising deprived areas or conserving landscape or wildlife.

Third, it can highlight and resolve possible conflicts. The reason for this is that the impacts of tourism, both positive and negative, are felt most keenly at the destination area. For example, negative spill-over effects will arise, such as congestion, particularly with respect to traffic and parking, but also in terms of longer shopping lines and overcrowding at local pubs or restaurants. Furthermore, there is a concern that as tourism grows in importance local authorities may begin to give it preferential treatment with the result that the personality of their communities can be changed (e.g. 'from a rural way of life') for the convenience of visitors rather than for local people. Other concerns might be the growth of litter and vandalism. Indeed, where development and planning do not fit in with local aspirations and capabilities, resistance and hostility can raise the cost of business or destroy the industry's potential altogether. Public participation, however, can enable residents to address such fears.

Fourth, the community-based approach to tourism can encourage and assist residents to develop specific tourism strategies by offering support, training and advice. Such advice should draw on research to provide conceptual and predictive support for planners, and also on the evaluation of planning efforts to maximise the use of existing knowledge. *Ex post* evaluations are necessary, especially where public funding is involved, for in-built accountability and as a measure of impacts and performance. These findings can then be used to increase the effectiveness of future projects.

The arguments in favour of community tourism are persuasive. A community-based approach to tourism recognises the fact that tourism has many complex inter-relationships with those communities which host it and that the success of any tourist development is heavily dependent on the goodwill of the community. The central objective of community tourism is to maximise the potential and sustainability of tourism development by optimally combining the commercial priorities of the tourist provider with local needs and objectives. Clearly, strong community benefits accrue as a result of such 'bonding' as a viable social unit through interactive, locally based economic activity, not to mention the increased sense of responsibility and pride fostered amongst residents as they work together for the common good.

In summary, within a community-based tourism framework the goals of the tourist provider should be integrated into overall community objectives in order to maximise the potential impact and sustainability of tourism activity within the local economy. The integration process that effectively weds the objectives of tourism development with community needs should ideally be:

- *goal orientated* — with a clear recognition of the role to be played by tourism in achieving broad societal goals;
- *democratic* — with full and meaningful input from community level up;
- *integrative* — placing tourism planning issues into the mainstream of planning for parks, heritage, conservation, land use and the economy;
- *systematic* — drawing on research to provide conceptual and predictive support for planners, and drawing on the

evaluation of planning efforts to maximise the use of existing knowledge.

It is within this conceptual context that this chapter critically examines the ability of a community-based initiative to establish and sustain tourism in, perhaps, one of the most socially and economically deprived rural areas in Northern Ireland — South Armagh. For more than thirty years the name 'South Armagh' has been perceived externally as the frontline of military and paramilitary contestation in Ireland. From that stark poverty of tourist resources, image and capacity, what follows in this chapter is a narrative of the attempts by community groups, in partnership with a variety of organisations and agencies ranging from the EU to the local District Councils, to develop a viable tourist venture titled the South Armagh Tourism Initiative (SATI). The discussion of the origins and evolution of SATI, together with an assessment of its impact, are drawn from the results of a more detailed evaluation carried out by the Northern Ireland Economic Research Centre (NIERC) throughout 1999.

SOUTH ARMAGH TOURISM INITIATIVE (SATI)

Background

The International Fund for Ireland (IFI), in conjunction with the Northern Ireland Tourist Board (NITB), has operated a Tourism Programme since 1989 with the aim of stimulating the private, public and community sectors to invest in novel and innovative tourism initiatives. In the early 1990s the IFI and NITB became concerned about the development unevenness of this Programme. Counties such as Down, Antrim and Fermanagh had developed a significant number of tourism projects, but only a limited number had come forward in Armagh and Tyrone. Given a commitment to tackling disadvantage across all areas of Northern Ireland, the IFI and NITB believed that an individual approach to tourism in these latter areas was required.

Accordingly, the IFI launched the Rural Community Tourism Initiative (RCTI) in South Armagh and the Sperrins in 1993. At that time each territory comprised a designated Area of Outstanding Natural Beauty (AONB) and was recognised as an IFI designated disadvantaged area. Both Initiatives were established as demonstration projects to encourage tourism development in deprived rural areas of Northern Ireland and to provide valuable lessons for any future community tourism projects which may emerge. They were to be imaginative, innovative and targeted at areas with untapped tourism potential. Central to the RCTI was the understanding that it should be:

- a regional approach targeted at those areas which had not performed to date;
- focused on the central role of the host community;
- not only an action-oriented initiative but also a research initiative which would record and facilitate valuable lessons at all levels for planning, developing, resourcing, delivering and marketing rural tourism, with the added capability of replication elsewhere.

The RCTI had a number of specific operational aims: first, to harness and channel community energy by making tourism expertise available at an early stage of community group development; second, to encourage the community to make optimum use of what already exists by way of tourism infrastructure; third, to support both community and private sector projects provided they were within the context of an agreed viable approach; fourth, to operate as a partnership between the local community and a variety of agencies; fifth, to broaden knowledge and horizons beyond the 'heritage centre mentality'; and sixth, to offer genuine opportunities for communities to shape and control their futures.

The geographical remit of the South Armagh Tourism Initiative (SATI) straddles the two District Councils of Newry and Mourne and Armagh. It covers 17 wards in total, 10 in Newry and Mourne and 7 in Armagh. The total population of the area in 1991 was just over 40,000 residents, representing around 30 per cent of the population in each District Council area. Overall, SATI extends across almost half the territory of each District Council area (Figure 4.1).

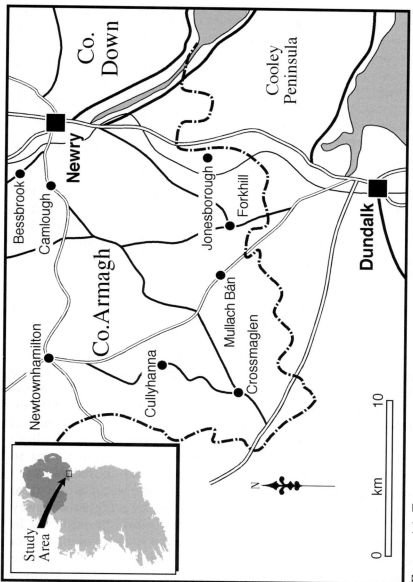

FIGURE 4.1: THE LOCATION OF THE SOUTH ARMAGH TOURISM INITIATIVE

Evolution of the South Armagh Tourism Initiative

In South Armagh, community groups had already been brought together under the umbrella of ROSA (Regeneration of South Armagh) in its capacity as the sub-regional rural support network. Tourism was a direct action of a number of these groups and had resulted in the opening of the Slieve Gullion Courtyard, Ti Chulainn Cultural Centre, the Cardinal O'Fiaich Centre and the Bessbrook Development Centre, most of which had received direct assistance from the IFI. Communities in South Armagh were intent on broadening this tourism base. The total amount of assistance approved under the Initiative was £350,000, split equally between South Armagh and the Sperrins. The Initiative was to run on a pilot basis encompassing three key components: the appointment of a tourism officer and administrator as well as a fully constituted management committee; the facilitation of business plan preparation for individual projects; and acting as a funding top-up to community groups or the private sector or alternatively as a single funding source.

A preliminary meeting of local people to discuss the Rural Community Tourism Initiative took place in March 1994. In March 1995 ROSA met with the IFI and other parties to identify next steps. The Sperrins component of the Initiative got underway in October 1994 with the appointment of a tourism officer. The managing agent for that Initiative was the Rural Community Network (RCN). The South Armagh Tourism Initiative (SATI) was established in 1995 as a result of the mutual recognition by a range of interests of the potential for tourism development to contribute to rural regeneration and economic development in the South Armagh area. ROSA, under a contractual arrangement with NITB, became responsible for holding the funds of the project and ensuring proper expenditure of the budget. It was selected because of its close links with communities in the area, acting as a network, which, it was hoped, would bring other actors into the Initiative. At the outset, these interests included the community sector, manifested through ROSA, the IFI and the NITB. However, as the

Initiative evolved, other core funders and interested parties came on board. These included Newry and Mourne District Council, Armagh City and District Council, the Area-Based Strategy Partnership for South Armagh (ABSAG), the Department of Agriculture for Northern Ireland (DANI), the South Down/South Armagh LEADER local action group, and a number of private sector tourism providers. A partnership-based approach was regarded as being central to their interaction.

The operation of SATI

From the outset it was determined that SATI would put in place a sustainable tourism strategy which would help create local jobs for local people, take account of the physical environment and improve the image of South Armagh. A three-year pilot period was originally planned for, around a suite of priority development themes which included tourist accommodation, signage and visitor information, tourism attractions and activities, the coordination of activity holidays, marketing, tourism training on a North–South basis and action research.

During the 1990s the nature of SATI's role changed quite substantially. This has been documented by the preparation of three successive Operational Plans in 1996, 1997 and 1998. This reflects to a large degree the scaling down of SATI's planned activities from a spending programme of £1.2m over a three-year period outlined in the 1996 Operational Plan to £0.55m in 1997 and finally £0.26m in 1998. The main changes to the Operational Plan were:

- *Accommodation*
  The 1996 study indicated the need to upgrade thirty existing B&Bs and register a further fifty. This was totally at odds with the 'Baseline Study' undertaken by SATI, which highlighted the existence of just fifteen B&Bs in the area at that time. No attempt was made to quantify the actual demand for increased accommodation in the area. In 1997 the B&B plans were downsized to twenty, but further accommodation developments were set out, which included eleven self-

97

catering units under LEADER 2, a feasibility study for a rural hotel and one fully serviced camping site.

- *Product development*
  SATI's product development plans evolved into a more narrowly focused set of proposals over the life-span of the three operational documents. The 1996 plan focused on the general tidiness and appearance of towns, villages and the local environment but to a large extent lacked detail on areas of specific product development. The 1997 Operational Plan was much more definite on the issue of product development, concentrating on the upgrading of monuments, the development of themed trails and organised events such as the package holiday. Finally, the 1998 Plan was essentially a slightly downscaled version of the 1997 Plan. Most notably proposals relating to the monument upgrading appeared to have been dropped. In addition the 1998 Plan did not specify any actions relating to the development and upgrading of equestrian and golfing activities. However, LEADER II took these on board.

- *Marketing*
  In the 1996 Plan, marketing was split into two key functions: a) the production of marketing material and implementing marketing activities, and b) marketing and promotion of a coordinated events programme. In 1997 the marketing element was much more detailed and included the development of a marketing strategy, a cross-border tourism initiative, the provision of small levels of grant aid to individual operators and the development of an arts and crafts marketing group. By 1998, the Plan had focused on the marketing and promotion of SATI along with the marketing of South Armagh, including marketing literature, trade exhibitions and hosting visiting groups.

- *Signage and visitor information*
  Signage and visitor information was the one area where a strategy had developed and expanded over the three

Operational Plans. The 1996 Operational Plan did not contain any proposals for signage or visitor information facilities, whereas the 1997 document outlined the need for a signage audit and tourism information programmes. SATI's approach to this issue was further refined in the 1998 Operational Plan, which included an Ordinance Survey map of the area and the development of a funding programme aimed at ensuring adequate signage provision in the future.

OPERATIONAL PLAN FUNDING

TABLE 4.1 OPERATIONAL PLAN FUNDING FOR SOUTH ARMAGH TOURISM INITIATIVE

	Community Tourism Initiative/ IFI	ABSAG	Newry and Mourne DC	Armagh City and DC	NITB	All Funders
	£'000	£'000	£'000	£'000	£'000	£'000
Tourist accommodation		47.5			2	49.5
Signage and visitor information	49	8.7	10		2.5	70.2
Tourism attractions and activities	42.8	25	9.5	5	10	92.3
Activity holiday coordination	5					5
Marketing	2	5			12	19
Action research	8				15	23
Total	**106.8**	**86.2**	**19.5**	**5**	**41.5**	**259**
Tourism training and promotion*		30	30	30		90

* Administered by the Regional Tourism Training Network (RTTN).
Source: South Armagh Tourism Initiative.

Following the preparation of the 1998 Operational Plan, a detailed programme of work was launched which incorporated resources from the five principal funding partners. As illustrated in Table 4.1, just over £350,000 was allocated to implementation over the period March 1998 to March 2000. SATI identified tourism training as an important component of its operational strategy. It allocated £90,000 of its budget, secured from Newry and Mourne District Council, Armagh City and District Council and the ABSAG, towards the Regional Tourism Training Network (RTTN). This was developed through Newry College of Further Education to coordinate tourism training in the border areas of Counties Armagh, Down, Louth, Monaghan and Cavan. INTERREG and LEADER also funded this programme. However, as this element of the Plan was undertaken by the RTTN, and SATI did not have any operational role in it, this amount has been excluded from the analysis.

Thus the actual funding available for developments under the Operational Plan was £259,000. The most significant elements of the Plan were Accommodation, Signage and Attractions/ Activities. More than one-third of funding was for projects developed under Tourism Attractions and Activities, largely concentrated on walking. Signage/Visitor Information and Accommodation developments accounted for 27 per cent and 20 per cent of funding respectively. The principal funders of the Initiative were the IFI and the South Armagh ABSAG, each contributing 41 per cent and 33 per cent of funding respectively. Newry and Mourne District Council, and particularly Armagh City and District Council, made relatively small contributions to the operational elements of the Initiative. However, the former had offered £20,000 on an annual basis to the Initiative should projects become available in that timescale and in addition made a significant contribution to administration funding. Each partner's contribution to the individual elements of the Operational Plan can be separately identified. Thus, for example, while the majority of ABSAG funding focused on the Accommodation component, the Community Tourism Initiative, funded through the IFI, focused largely on Signage and Visitor Information along with Tourism Attractions and Activities.

CRITICAL REFLECTIONS ON THE PROCESSES OF CREATING A
COMMUNITY TOURISM INITIATIVE

In this section, a critical commentary is provided on the
processes which have helped shape the Initiative. Based on an
understanding of the origins and evolution of the Initiative, as
outlined above, the following issues can be identified:

(1) *At the outset, there was poor communication between SATI,
key players and funders, and between the funders themselves.*
There was a lack of adequate consultation with key players
operating in the area during the establishment of the Initiative
and thus it proved difficult to get everyone on board. This was
exacerbated by the lack of any clear understanding of the role
of certain current stakeholders, most notably the District
Council Tourism Officers. As a result, a significant amount of
time was spent finding a role for the Initiative which 'fitted in'
with existing provision. There was also some confusion between
the IFI and the NITB, which acted as the IFI's agent for the
Initiative. The issue concerned the absence of a shared view of
the process and outcomes required from the Initiative. The
emphasis of the IFI on flagship projects was the principal
reason for this slight tension.

(2) *Time was required to build trust relationships.* It took two
years to settle the remit of the Initiative. This in part reflected
the complex set of actors involved, complicated even further by
the need to develop relationships between the funders. These
relationships straddled Northern Ireland-wide public bodies
(operating regionally and locally), local authorities, community
and private sectors. In addition, community-led initiatives by
their very nature can take a long time to establish and are
dependent on the building of capacity and confidence.

(3) *lack of strategic direction.* Because the Initiative was established as a pilot project, there was no explicit model to provide
guidelines on its development and, in fact, flexibility was viewed
as essential. However, the remit of the Initiative kept changing
as it evolved and although this might have been expected from
a pilot scheme, it actually led to disenchantment, particularly
among the private sector participants. The Initiative was constantly trying to find its place in the broader picture.

(4) *Unrealistic expectations over funding.* The precise parameters for the Community Tourism Initiative were unclear. The Initiative developed ambitious plans for the provision of grants totalling £1.2m over the three-year period which were difficult to connect back to the notion of a community-based venture.

(5) *Over-ambitious development plans.* There appeared to be no attempt to link the strategic components of the Operational Plans with the 'Baseline Study' or the 'Record of Interest Forms' compiled by the Initiative. In addition, there was no evaluation of tourism performance within the area in order to set proposed developments in context.

(6) *Duplication of effort.* Despite best efforts, there was duplication in the two tourism officer roles: the Community Tourism Officer and the South Armagh Tourism Officer for Newry and Mourne District Council. As the functional boundaries of the two jobs had not been sufficiently defined, it proved difficult for the officers to work effectively together.

(7) *Disillusionment by the private sector.* Confusion over the remit of the Initiative and subsequent delays led to the disillusionment of the private sector. In 1999 there was just one private sector representative on the management committee. A further two private sector individuals had previously been involved but resigned as operational issues continued to remain unresolved. This had clear implications for the ability of the Initiative to claim to have an effective public/private/community partnership.

Notwithstanding these difficulties, it has to be recognised that SATI formed only a relatively small part of the tourism base in the area and that, in line with its scale of operation, did manage to secure a wide range of process- and product-related accomplishments. These can be summarised as follows:

- providing an 'almost one-stop shop' for tourism development in South Armagh;
- offering a *local* support mechanism for tourism providers in the area;
- facilitating partnership, particularly by encouraging the two District Councils to work together;

- making available a significantly larger pool of resources for small-scale tourism development;
- maintaining two Tourism Offices and a Tourism Information Point at what can be considered a 'cross-border gateway' into Northern Ireland;
- providing for the erection of the first tourism 'brown signs' in South Armagh;
- encouraging accommodation providers to put signs on properties;
- initiating through the ABSAG an Accommodation Programme which is now being replicated in other parts of Newry and Mourne District;
- improving the quality of accommodation in the area;
- publishing professional literature on the area;
- giving South Armagh a positive public profile through advertisements and press coverage.

In summary, the achievements of SATI have been small, incremental and in many ways hard to measure. Actual impacts have related more to improving the image of the area as a tourist destination.

THE FUTURE OF SATI?

It was originally anticipated that the Rural Community Tourism Initiative (RCTI) would be three years in timescale following its launch in 1993. SATI was established under its auspices in 1995 but is currently still active in 2002. The Initiative was due to complete its Operational Plan in March 2000 and thus, in anticipation of that dateline, questions were posed in late 1999 regarding its future direction, if any. In this section of the chapter the views of tourism providers and community groups in the local area are reported regarding who should take responsibility for the future development of tourism in South Armagh. It should also be appreciated that at the stage of the NIERC evaluation in late 1999, all of the funders were reviewing their programme activities and how SATI could fit into those plans. Other relevant views on the way forward for the South Armagh Tourism Initiative are included in the narrative.

A total of sixty-two tourism providers and community groups were surveyed by NIERC. The responses highlighted a variety of views about the way forward in South Armagh, which can be summarised as follows: SATI is the preferred initial point of contact on tourism issues for the area; there is a broad range of views on how South Armagh should be marketed/developed, with a marginal majority wishing to retain South Armagh as a separate entity; and SATI should have responsibility for marketing/developing South Armagh as a tourist destination.

The more detailed responses to the survey are as follows:

(1) Preferred initial point of contact?
- almost 1 in every 2 respondents stated that SATI would be their preferred initial point of contact on tourism issues;
- SATI was the preferred point of contact for accommodation providers and community groups;
- one-third of tourism amenity respondents highlighted that NITB would be their preferred initial point of contact and a further 27 per cent highlighted that they would initially contact SATI;
- 30 per cent of community groups said that they would contact ROSA initially.

(2) How should South Armagh be marketed / developed?
- 1 in every 3 respondents felt that South Armagh should be marketed /developed as a separate entity;
- 22 per cent felt it should be marketed/developed on a cross-border basis, and a further 18 per cent as part of Northern Ireland as a whole;
- 13 per cent felt it should be marketed/developed as part of the Island of Ireland and 12 per cent as part of the South-East Region (mostly amenity respondents);
- accommodation providers were most split on this issue with 25 per cent opting for a separate entity, 25 per cent for a cross-border dimension, and 25 per cent suggesting an Island of Ireland perspective.

(3) Who should have responsibility for marketing / developing South Armagh?

- almost 60 per cent of respondents felt that SATI should have responsibility for marketing/developing South Armagh;
- a further 17 per cent felt it should be the responsibility of NITB;
- 25 per cent of amenity respondents felt it should be the responsibility of a cross-border body and 23 per cent of accommodation providers felt it should be within NITB's remit;
- community groups were overwhelmingly in favour of the responsibility being with SATI.

The research also sought feedback from the funding partners of the Initiative. First, in relation to NITB, it was pointed out that the organisation remains committed to the concept of *local* rural community tourism development. In fact, this may play a more significant role in future tourism development plans, particularly if linked to 'natural resource tourism'. The NITB, together with the Department of Agriculture and Rural Development (DARD) and the Department for Regional Development (DRD), put forward an integrated bid to the Structural Funds, which develops a framework for assistance in natural resource areas including the Ring of Gullion. Each area has a different set of priorities focused on the natural environment, disadvantage and tourism. As well as the strategic and regional focus, there is a strong role for local input into developments in these areas. However, the other funding partners raised a number of concerns. These can be summarised as follows:

- that any future Initiative should be first and foremost about delivery mechanisms and not about the organisation in itself;
- that as a Community Tourism Initiative, the community representation in SATI should be re-examined and enlarged;
- that the funding contributions of each partner be combined to create a pooled resource. This would differ significantly

from the then current arrangement whereby funders required direct association with individual projects. This would free up significant administration time;

- SATI should move towards natural resource tourism and involve the farming community more fully;
- a review of a greater role for the LEADER programme in SATI is needed;
- the Environment and Heritage Service of the Department of the Environment (DOE) should be represented on any future management committee;
- there was a preference for 'flagship' projects to be developed in the area, which would fit more easily with the IFI 'project by project' approach under its Tourism Programme.
- the tensions between the two District Councils, within whose territories SATI operates, need to be resolved. The Armagh City and District Council questioned the benefits of the Initiative focusing on South Armagh as a separate enti-ty; its preference would be to see the development of an 'Armagh rural tourism product'. By contrast, South Armagh remains a distinct and integral component of the Newry and Mourne District Council area tourism product. In addition, this Council remains supportive of the developmental role of the Initiative in rural South Armagh;
- the balance between funders and community/private sector representation in the Initiative needs to be addressed, with the latter two groups still under-represented;
- it was clear from many sources that in the future SATI should have a focus which is not marketing-orientated but rather should be about product development and packaging. Marketing, from either a domestic or an international per-spective, should not be within its remit;
- finally, one observation on SATI concerned the degree of involvement of the South Armagh ABSAG. The ABSAG accounted for one-third of SATI's Operational Plan budget. However, it is widely accepted that the ABSAG's intervention at a critical point for the Initiative was pivotal in developing the current approach of partnership and an almost 'one-stop shop' for tourism development in the area. In addition, it is

the funders' view that one of the successes of the Initiative over the two years leading up to late 1999 was the effective degree of collaboration between the ABSAG and the Initiative. This is, perhaps, reflected in the high degree of spending on the ABSAG elements of SATI's Operational Plan.

THE WAY FORWARD — SOME ISSUES

In assessing the way forward for the Initiative there are a number of interconnected issues which need to be discussed and resolved in order to build on the foundations of this community-based approach to rural tourism. These range from the strategic development of tourism policy in Northern Ireland, to the involvement of local communities and indeed to the original spatial remit of the Initiative.

(1) The change in strategic direction for marketing Northern Ireland
New and evolving structures concerning the way in which the tourism marketing of Northern Ireland is to be undertaken will provide a greater degree of definition over the content of local tourism initiatives such as SATI. Figure 4.2 provides a summary outline of the arrangements in place. The implication here is that any future local community tourism initiative would have no explicit marketing function. However, product development and packaging could remain within its remit.

(2) The market failure argument for some form of intervention
NIERC estimates that there has been approximately £4.5 million of tourism investment in South Armagh over the period 1994–1999. This has ranged from some very large-scale projects, such as Ti Chulainn, to some very small projects, such as those developed by SATI. The IFI has been responsible for funding the majority of this investment. One of the critical issues to arise out of both the NIERC tourism provider survey and the consultation process is that, whilst the supply of tourism amenities has improved immensely over recent years, tourism demand is still mainly absent. The B&B occupancy

FIGURE 4.2: STRUCTURES FOR MARKETING NORTHERN IRELAND AS A TOURIST DESTINATION

Responsibility   *Spatial Remit*

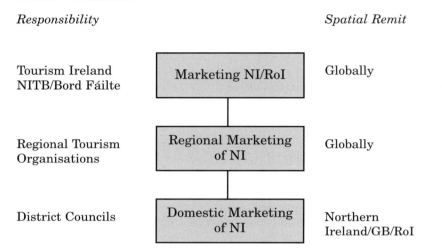

Tourism Ireland NITB/Bord Fáilte — Marketing NI/RoI — Globally

Regional Tourism Organisations — Regional Marketing of NI — Globally

District Councils — Domestic Marketing of NI — Northern Ireland/GB/RoI

rate for 1998, for example, was estimated at 2.5 per cent. Visitor numbers to amenities in the area were only 28,000 in that year.

Potentially the strongest justification for public sector intervention in the past in South Armagh has been on the basis of 'missing markets', that is, the market potential existed but the private sector did not have the capacity to develop it. The argument in favour of retaining some form of intervention is equally as strong in terms of the private sector's inability to coordinate and deliver on the product which has been developed. Some B&Bs have already indicated that they cannot sustain their businesses with the low level of visitor numbers to the area. This may also be the case for tourist amenities, many of which rely on the highly competitive schools' market to survive. There is an urgent need to begin to draw together the current tourism product and to package it in a way which can benefit the maximum number of stakeholders in the area. It is clear that if this does not happen much of the investment highlighted above may be lost.

The demand for a local approach

There is a very strong sense that the tourism and broader community is supportive of a local initiative. For the majority, SATI would be the first point of contact for tourism development plans and would be responsible for the marketing/development role of the area. The fact that the local District Councils featured so far down the list of who should take responsibility for future developments perhaps most strongly reflects the trust of the local community in the primacy of local contact. And yet, as pointed out above on several occasions, South Armagh straddles both the Newry and Mourne District Council area and the Armagh City and District Council area. The current tourism product is thus important to both areas.

A number of issues have been raised on this issue of the relationship between a local approach and the spatial remit of the Initiative. First, there is a belief that the spatial remit of the Initiative is too small, that is, South Armagh does not offer sufficient scope for development. Second, South Armagh is a politically contentious area. This causes difficulties in terms of selling the area as a tourism destination and in getting tourism providers, the community sector and funders to work together. Third, the core product, the Ring of Gullion, is 'off centre', whereas in areas such as the Sperrins, Mournes and Fermanagh Lakelands the core product is at the centre of developments. This can cause difficulties with identification, for example, the Ring of Gullion Marketing Initiative against marketing South Armagh as a whole. In fact, the tourism providers and local communities do not appear to be wholly convinced that South Armagh should be marketed/developed as a separate entity. Although 1 in 3 thought that the separate identity of the area should be retained, equally it could be said that 2 in 3 had varying opinions of how this should be taken forward.

CONCLUSIONS: COMMUNITY BASED TOURISM —
THE WAY FORWARD

The South Armagh Tourism Initiative was launched in a vacuum of amenity development in South Armagh. The accommodation base was relatively low and, more importantly, of low standard. With the exception of Slieve Gullion, there were no major tourism amenities in the area. Since then, it is estimated that around £4.5m has been invested through to late 1999 in tourism development in the South Armagh area, largely as a result of substantial funding from the International Fund for Ireland. South Armagh is now an important tourism product for both Newry and Mourne District Council and Armagh City and District Council.

The concept behind the Initiative was to develop tourism in deprived rural areas of Northern Ireland where tourism potential existed but had not yet been exploited. The Initiative had a number of key features. It was to be run on a pilot basis, it was to be innovative in nature and it was to recognise the central role of the host community. As highlighted above, the achievements of the Initiative have been small, incremental and in many ways hard to measure as actual impacts have been more concerned with improving the image of the area as a tourist destination.

It is very clear from the feedback of the tourism providers/ community sector and wider consultation that the market failure argument for this type of intervention still exists in South Armagh. At the outset, the argument was centred more on 'missing markets', that is, that the potential existed but the supply did not. There is no doubt that this gap in provision has been filled over the last several years and a tourism market now exists. However, there is an insufficient flow of visitors into South Armagh. Occupancy rates amongst B&B providers are extremely low and some have highlighted that they will be unable to sustain their businesses in the medium/long term if this does not improve. Although many of the amenities are relatively new, visitor numbers are low and would be cause for concern.

Tourism providers and the community sector overwhelmingly endorse the role of the Initiative in taking responsibility for future tourism developments in the area. In addition, the funders have been largely supportive of the operation of the Initiative since its relaunch in 1998. Under the framework of the Northern Ireland Rural Development Programme 2006,

SATI has been selected as one of five recipients of funding for the development of natural resource-based tourism. The allocation is competitive and will depend on the quality of the strategy submitted by SATI in 2002 to the Department of Agriculture and Rural Development. However, evidence from the NIERC evaluation indicates that 'South Armagh' may not present the most appropriate geographical focus for the Initiative. NIERC has, therefore, advanced two strategic possibilities as the way forward for SATI.

The first option is built around a 'Ring of Gullion Tourism Initiative' which would focus directly on the AONB as its core product. As highlighted earlier, one of the difficulties with the spatial remit of SATI is that it does not have a central focus. The core product is the Ring of Gullion, which is a designated AONB and naturally lends itself to tourism development. For example, during the 1995 ceasefire year, visitor numbers to Slieve Gullion Forest Park doubled to 20,000. There may, therefore, be potential in focusing the Initiative on the Ring of Gullion as the core product and undertaking marketing/development around the core and its periphery, however far that might extend. This would be similar in concept to arrangements for the Sperrins and the Mournes. In addition, there is significant potential for cross-border development because of the close proximity to the Cooley Mountains.

The second option calls for a broader rural community tourism initiative. One of the strongest comments made about the concept of a rural community tourism initiative was that it should be about *'delivery mechanisms'* and not *'the organisation'*. In many ways the Initiative has come a long way in establishing a delivery mechanism for the rural tourism product in South Armagh, but this has been largely overshadowed by the need to establish the Initiative as an organisation. What is important now is to develop a mechanism that can begin to deliver sustainability to the existing tourism providers in the local area and help rural communities to bring forward tourism developments where the potential exists.

However, it is the authors' view that the second of these two options presents the most appropriate option for sustainable

111

tourism development in the area. The underlying rationale behind this is that:

- the Ring of Gullion is potentially too small, tourism is not the top development priority and the AONB Countryside Officer has responsibility for some tourism functions in the area;
- the Ring of Gullion is located in Newry and Mourne District and would not command the support of Armagh City and District Council. The Initiative to date has achieved much in terms of the two District Councils working together. It would be unfortunate if this were lost;
- tourism in the Ring of Gullion can be accommodated through a broader rural community tourism initiative;
- by avoiding the label 'Ring of Gullion', the identity of the Initiative becomes less of an issue in the sense that it serves more of a developmental than marketing role;
- a more broadly based Initiative can encompass a range of programmes including the Ring of Gullion, Cross-Border, South Armagh, and North Armagh. In this way the different cultural identities of distinct areas within the remit of a new Initiative could be maintained. It therefore presents the potential to establish wider networks, but the corollary is the need for more broadly based community participation. This approach could draw on the support of both Newry and Mourne District Council and Armagh City and District Council;
- South Armagh ranks high in terms of disadvantage and thus funding would be skewed towards this area. The adoption of a Ring of Gullion label runs the risk of diluting that focus and consequent public sector intervention.

In conclusion, the attempts to develop a community-based tourism initiative in South Armagh illustrate the scale of the problem to be overcome in this part of rural Northern Ireland. While the rhetoric of the role and value of community-based tourism initiatives is widely rehearsed, the practice as evidenced in this chapter has been somewhat different and the challenges ahead are daunting. Furthermore, the public sector has an important role to play in continuing to support such initiatives. However, the success of community-based tourism initiatives needs to be judged in the medium to longer term and therein lies the potential tension with public policy. The major funders of initiatives, such as SATI, are perhaps more concerned with the creation of 'flagship' tourism products in an area without necessarily establishing the foundations for the community sector to engage with the opportunities such projects can bring to an area. At a time when a fresh round of rural development related expenditure is about to commence in Northern Ireland, there are indeed insights with wider applicability to be drawn from the South Armagh experience.

REFERENCES

Commission of European Communities (1992), EEC SEC/92/702 Final, 27 May 1992.

Cooke, K. (1982), 'Guidelines for Socially Appropriate Tourism Development in British Columbia', *Journal of Travel Research*, vol. 21, no. 1: 22–28.

Getz, D. (1983), 'Capacity to Absorb Tourism: Concepts and Implications for Strategic Planning', *Annals of Tourism Research*, vol. 10, no. 2: 239–263.

Haywood, K.M. (1988), 'Responsible and Responsive Tourism Planning in the Community', *Tourism Management*, vol. 9, no. 2: 105–118.

Kendall, K. and T. Var (1984), *The Perceived Impact of Tourism: The State of the Art*, Vancouver: Simon Fraser University.

Keogh, B. (1990), 'Public Participation in Community Tourism Planning', *Annals of Tourism Research*, vol. 17, no. 3: 449–465.

Liu, J.C. and T. Var (1986), 'Resident Attitudes Towards Tourism Impacts in Hawaii', *Annals of Tourism Research*, vol. 13, no. 2: 193–214.

Liu, J.C., P.J. Sheldon and T. Var (1987), 'Resident Perception of the Environmental Impacts of Tourism', *Annals of Tourism Research*, vol. 14, no. 1: 17–37.

Loukissas, P.J. (1983), 'Public Participation in Community Tourism Planning: A Gaming Simulation Approach', *Journal of Travel Research*, vol. 22, no.1: 18–23.

Lucas, A.R. (1978), 'Fundamental Prerequisites for Citizen Participation', *Involvement and Environment: Proceedings of the Canadian Conference on Public Participation*.

Murphy, P. (1988), 'Community-driven Tourism Planning', *Tourism Management*, vol. 9, no. 2: 96–104.

Murphy, P. (1993), *Tourism: A Community Approach*, London: Routledge.

O'Reilly, M. and M. Hart (1999), *Evaluation of the South Armagh Tourism Initiative*, Belfast: Northern Ireland Economic Research Centre.

Pizam, A. (1978), 'Tourism's Impact: The Social Cost to the Destination Community as Perceived by its Residents', *Journal of Travel Research*, vol. 17, no. 1: 8–12.

Simmons, D.G. (1994), 'Community Participation in Tourism Planning', *Tourism Management*, vol. 15, no. 2: 98–108.

SECTION THREE:
MEETING THE CHALLENGES
IN RURAL COMMUNITIES

CHAPTER 5

THE COUNTRYSIDE AESTHETIC AND HOUSE DESIGN IN NORTHERN IRELAND

Ken Sterrett

INTRODUCTION

An estimated 2000 single houses are built each year in the open countryside of Northern Ireland. This represents approximately 27 per cent of all the private sector houses completed in the region. Outside the Belfast City Region this figure increases to 40 per cent. In the south and west of the region the share of build-out during much of the 1990s was even higher. Government planners and major amenity groups argue that the external design and appearance of many of these houses are inappropriate for a countryside setting. Rural dwellers, on the other hand, often employ a different aesthetic rationale, and want to live in what they consider to be bright, modern homes located in areas where they have strong family and community connections. Consequently, aesthetics and design are highly charged socio-political issues in rural areas, particularly in the more peripheral districts of Northern Ireland. Indeed, housing in the countryside is regarded by many people as possibly the most controversial rural planning issue in Northern Ireland.

This chapter deals with the conflict between the state and the supporters of countryside dwellings and attempts to understand the origin and nature of their respective aesthetic preferences.

The chapter chronicles the emergence and adjustment over time of policy and practice in this sphere and offers an analysis of the contrasting characteristics of housing design associated with these contested perspectives.

THE COUNTRYSIDE AS LANDSCAPE

In Great Britain, Urry (1992) notes how the concept of 'landscape' was initially a technical term for natural inland scenery but came to refer to an area of land which should be viewed as though it were a picture. The redefinition of nature and the countryside as scenic landscape, as something to be visually consumed, occurred during the nineteenth century and may, therefore, be considered as a historically specific social and cultural construction. Urry argues that the process of a changing perception of the countryside was already underway in the eighteenth century among the aristocracy and gentry. This was evident in the development of gentry commissioned landscape painting, which either romanticised the rural poor or else excluded them from the scenery. The upper classes were becoming mobile during this period, and 'this helped them develop the cultural capital necessary for judging and discriminating between such different environments' (4).

Interestingly, Kennedy (1993) notes that picturesque theory of the late eighteenth and early nineteenth centuries provided artists with definitions of what the 'gentleman connoisseur' might expect in landscape painting. He records how Uvedale Price, in his *Essay on the Picturesque* (1794), explained the picturesque as a category of aesthetic values that supplemented those expounded thirty-eight years earlier by Edmund Burke in his essay *A Philosophical Inquiry into the Origin of our Ideas of the Sublime and the Beautiful*. Irish landscapes painted by English artists around this time were faithful to these theoretical maxims. They took care, as Kennedy suggests, to distinguish 'between the moral view, in which the industrious mechanic was a pleasing subject, and the picturesque, which rejects industry and in which idleness adds dignity' (166). Consequently the thatched houses of the rural poor are presented as 'neat and well maintained, symbols of rural contentment, nestling into the landscape' (166).

While the romanticisation of the Irish landscape was a developing phenomenon amongst the leisured classes during the nineteenth century, the peasantry continued to struggle for economic existence. Evans (1981) has commented 'that it would be difficult to find a more rigid example of a simple caste system than that of nineteenth century rural Ireland with its landlords and peasants, reflected in the landscape of the big house with its high walled wooded demesne and the naked countryside with its teeming tenantry' (57). The attachment to the land, traditionally almost the sole means of support in rural Ireland, comes from this long history of struggle. For the 'rural peasantry', therefore, the countryside was not a contemplative landscape, but rather a terrain of exploitation, a social and cultural place and a means for economic livelihood.

The translation into state policy of an emerging dominant view of the countryside as landscape did not occur in Northern Ireland until the 1940s. Arguably, this was imported in large part from Great Britain, where a sometimes uneasy mix of land use and aesthetic ideologies were driving planning and environmental policy. Punter (1987) records how the influence of organisations such as the Society for the Preservation of Rural England (later to become the Council for the Protection of Rural England), and the articulation of the interests of the architectural profession helped to shape the post-war modernist planning rationale. This was a rationale that offered to bring order to sprawling cities and to promote an almost spiritual respect for the countryside. Reade (1987) makes a number of similar points about this period. He argues that the main source of planning ideas 'centred on the one hand, on the propagandist bodies such as Howard's Garden Cities and Town Planning Association, and on the other hand on the design and land use professions' (42). The main body of ideas underpinning this ideology were largely aesthetic and technical. The contemporary city was seen as 'unhealthy and undesirable', while the 'countryside and small towns [were] the source of much that [was] good and wholesome in our national life' (43).

The same set of aesthetic concerns, educated attitudes and ideological visions began to permeate the language of planning in Northern Ireland. This was reflected in a report by the Planning Advisory Board's Amenity Committee in 1947. In the Foreword to the report, the Board's chairman, Sir David Lindsay Keir, praises the unique quality of the Ulster country-side with its 'restfulness and unspoiled charm'. However, he notes some instances of 'irreparable damage by thoughtless and careless development. Scenes once typical of the beauty of Ulster have ceased to be so, not so much from any deliberate intention to despoil, as from lack of taste and a sense of responsibility'.

However, very few of the recommendations made by the Planning Advisory Board were implemented (Caldwell, 1992). A continued distrust of planning by the Unionist oligarchy, together with problems arising from compensation rights, meant that the region's second planning statute, the Planning (Interim Development) Act, 1944, lacked the sort of authority needed to produce an effective development plan and control system. Indeed, it was not until the early 1960s that planning in the strategic sense, as well as in the local development control sense, was introduced. In 1960 the Northern Ireland government appointed Sir Robert Matthew to prepare an advisory plan for the Belfast Region and 'to relate the survey and plan in the broadest terms to the geographical, economic and cultural patterns of Northern Ireland as a whole'.

The Matthew Plan (Matthew, 1964) was essentially about giving physical shape to a modernisation process that had started in the 1940s but had quickened its pace by the 1960s. In overall terms the plan and its underpinning rationale were imbued with a fusion of ideologies that brought together the per-ceived requirements of multinational capital for green field sites, a ready supply of labour and fast, efficient infrastructure with a body of conservative planning ideas that were given legal form in the British Town and Country Planning Act 1947. The latter stressed the separation of town and country, an aesthetic of order and clarity and an ethos of countryside preservation (Matless, 1990). Although the focus of the Matthew Plan was on the Belfast region, it became, as Caldwell notes, 'the strategic blueprint for the Province as a whole and provided the *raison d'être* for rural settlement policy and the control of housing in the open countryside' (46). The growth centres in the Belfast City Region were to be complemented by six key centres located in a 'rural remainder' which would form a passive backdrop for modernised urban concentrations. It is significant to note that while Matthew did not make any specific recommendations for the planning and development of rural areas, his comments about the character of the Ulster countryside reflect the broad economic rationale underpinning the overall initiative:

> The character of the Ulster countryside is one of the most precious assets, both for the well-being, enjoyment and stimulation of her people and for those who visit the Province. There are all too many signs throughout the region of neglect and indifference. There is little sign of appreciation of the value of the natural environment and in particular the special endowment with which many parts of the region are blessed ... The maintenance and enhancement of amenities ... is not a matter of sentiment, it is a matter of making the best use of available resources. Northern Ireland in this highly competitive, modern world cannot afford to neglect, or even unwittingly destroy this resource. (Matthew, 1964: 25–26)

The countryside was presented here as an economic asset for a modern urban region. It was to be preserved as a scenic context and as a distinctive attraction for foreign investors looking for branch plant opportunities on the edge of Europe. There was no scope here for any perceived sentimental Irish attachment to the land and no space for a rural culture which stays in place and seeks to develop its own future. Caldwell and Greer (1984) make a similar point about the Matthew approach:

> there prevailed little perception of the personality of the countryside and its people, save a somewhat inconsistent, negative and regulatory attitude to amenity and preservation of the landscape; a seeming unawareness of the unique and complex inheritance of history and culture and, above all, a

lack of understanding of the consequences of the persistent drift from the land, particularly in peripheral rural areas where the agricultural base was in severe decline. (4)

RURAL POLICY 1974–1978

The increasing influence of the local amenity lobby in the late 1960s and early 1970s contributed to the publication in 1974 of a consultation paper on the control of residential development in rural areas. In the introduction, the Department of Housing, Local Government and Planning quite explicitly states that:

gradually over the years there has been ... a growing expectation that planning authorities should exercise their powers of control to limit scattered housing development in the countryside. In recent years, various voluntary organisations whose aim is to preserve the amenity of the countryside have become much more influential and questions of the effect of development on the rural scene now evoke widespread interest and comment.

Two years after the publication of this consultation paper, a policy note on rural residential development was issued as part of the Regional Physical Development Strategy (RPDS) 1975–95. The RPDS was effectively the region's first comprehensive planning strategy. While the concept of concentration was sustained, the distribution of growth centres was widened. A District Towns Strategy resulted in the designation of one town in each of the 26 District Council areas for economic and residential growth. In addition, a number of other towns and villages were identified for further expansion. The rural content of the strategy continued to pursue the re-organisation and rationalisation of the traditional dispersed settlement pattern. This was largely presented as the only viable means of ensuring the efficient provision of services and the facilitation of new employment. The implementation of this policy was to be achieved through settlement planning in Area Plans, and through the operation of the policy note on rural residential development, where the critical criterion remained the demonstration of need to live in the countryside.

Milton (1993) has commented that under the RPDS, residential development was to be discouraged for two reasons: to prevent the countryside being disfigured by unsympathetic development, and secondly, to avoid the cost of providing services such as electricity, telephone and mains water to isolated houses. It is interesting to note, however, that while the aesthetic aspiration was to be achieved largely by controlling the number of houses being built in the countryside, reference is also made for the first time in rural policy to the application of siting and design criteria. Significantly too, the criteria referred to were contained in the Ulster Countryside Committee's booklet entitled *Building in the Countryside*.

THE COCKCROFT REPORT

Opposition to the operation of what was widely regarded as a restrictive rural policy, particularly by District Councils in the south and west of Northern Ireland, led to the Labour Government appointing a Review Body in 1977, under the chairmanship of Dr W.H. Cockcroft. The published report represented a turning point in rural planning policy, not only in terms of its recommendations, but also in terms of its recognition of the distinctive rural settlement tradition in the region. This is captured in the Foreword:

the planning policy at present applicable to Northern Ireland is derived from policies devised for the densely populated and highly urbanised areas of lowland Britain where the major criterion is based on the historical need to prevent suburban sprawl and ribbon development. We do not regard that to be the major criterion of a rural planning policy for Northern Ireland. We consider that a set of criteria applicable to and consonant with the particular urban characteristics of one area of the United Kingdom cannot be assumed to be applicable to another area in which different rural characteristics and traditions apply. (Cockcroft, 1978)

The Committee made a total of thirty-one recommendations, but perhaps the most crucial, in relation to the theme of this chapter, were those to relax the existing rural policy, widen the categories of people permitted to live in the countryside, and introduce new methods of improving aesthetic control. In relation to the latter, the Committee noted that out of 121 planners in the Department of the Environment, only six had an architectural qualification. Consequently it favoured a stipulation that all housing and some other categories of building in rural areas should be designed by architects. The Committee made two other recommendations: the provision of design guides and the setting up of advisory or consultative panels, especially in Areas of Outstanding Natural Beauty. Arguably the Committee's faith in architectural design as a solution to the aesthetic problem was encouraged by the architect on the Committee, but the recommendation also offered the amenity lobby some crumbs of comfort in a report that, in its terms, would be seen as regressive. Moreover, the Committee had accepted the argument of the rural lobby that new houses do not necessarily detract from the countryside, and suggested that the building of well-sited houses of good design in some of the more sparsely populated areas could enhance the natural beauty of the landscape.

The Department's response to the report of the Cockcroft Committee was made in a statement published in November 1978. While not accepting all the recommendations, the new policy did relax the conditions on single house development. Outside of a number of designated Areas of Special Control, planning applications would not be judged on the basis of the need criterion. In terms of the issue of aesthetic control, the Department accepted that more could be done to ensure better siting and design decisions. The follow-on Practice Notes published two months later (DOE, 1979) provided more detail on the aesthetic criteria to be applied to all applications for the erection of buildings in rural areas. These offered advice to planners and applicants on choosing an appropriate location for a new dwelling, as well as suggesting some siting and design standards that would help protect or even enhance the visual quality of the existing scene. Although the guidance on aesthetic considerations represented the Department's first attempt to engage directly with the issue, it nevertheless fell short of the more comprehensive approach recommended by Cockcroft.

A 'NEW RIGHT' ADMINISTRATION FOR NORTHERN IRELAND

The collapse of the Labour Government in 1979 and the installation of the Thatcher administration brought a radically new agenda to state policy. Gaffikin and Morrisey (1990) note that in general terms, the New Right rhetoric was one of less government, less welfare, lower taxation, and curbed trade union power. Government would get off people's backs and out of their pockets. But, in return, individuals would have to rediscover the virtue of self-reliance. In Great Britain this brought immediate effects across a range of policy sectors. However, the initial rhetoric of Michael Heseltine, the Secretary of State for the Environment, about the unnecessary imposition of design standards in planning practice was tempered in his circular 22/80 *Development Control: Policy and Practice* (DOE, 1980). Nevertheless, as Punter (1987) argues:

the broad message was the same — aesthetics were subjective, taste or fashions should not be imposed on developers, and there had to be fully justified reasons for the control of external appearance. (50)

This first flush of dogma could not be sustained, particularly given the ideological project which combined an aggressive modernisation of the economy with reference to pre-modern values.

In Northern Ireland the direct-rule administration did not have to mediate the shaping or implementation of its policies through local government, and new ministers were keen, where possible, to show their radical Thatcherite credentials. Consequently in August 1981, Mr David Mitchell, Parliamentary Under Secretary of State with responsibility for the Department of the Environment, issued a development control policy statement (DOE, 1981) which echoed, and perhaps even went beyond, the sentiments of Circular 22/80 in Great Britain. The main thrust of the statement was about removing state constraints on economic development, particularly on small business development. It was suggested that planning must not unnecessarily impede developments such as new industry, commerce and housing, which are of fundamental importance to the well-being of the community. The statement endorsed the existing rural policy, but in what was to become normal Thatcherite language, it cautioned against development that might require additional public spending on services. Only one paragraph in the statement was devoted to aesthetic control. This was strongly worded and, although it had a general application for town and countryside, it would effectively prevent any attempt to implement the location, siting and design criteria set out in the Practice Notes:

> It is recognised that aesthetics are a subjective matter and the Department will not seek to impose its tastes on developers at the expense of individuality, originality or traditional styles. Nor will developers be asked to adopt designs which are unpopular with their customers or clients. However, in areas of scenic importance and in conservation areas more strict standards have to apply in order to prevent the incongruous, unsightly and dominant from spoiling the landscape or townscape. At the same time the Department wishes to encourage high standards of design, particularly for buildings occupying prominent positions. (DOE, 1981: 19)

Considered in a historical political context, the statement is particularly interesting. The uneasy alliance of a modernisation rhetoric with a preservation of the countryside ethos had at that time given way to a market dogma which eschewed collectivist thinking and stressed individual self-determination. The notion that aesthetics are a subjective matter broke with the conservative cultural tradition. As Rustin (1985) has argued, the traditional conservatives within the Thatcher administration

126

did not agree in philosophical fundamentals with the possessive individualists of Thatcher, but they decided, particularly in the early years, 'to give them unstinting support against the common progressive enemy' (21).

LOCATION, SITING AND DESIGN

The Mitchell statement had clearly articulated the main thrust of Thatcherite ideology and had the effect of undermining any potential to impose siting and design restrictions on the more liberal post-Cockcroft approach to single house developments. Consequently, during the early 1980s not only did the number of houses being built in the countryside increase, but their some-times prominent location and elaborate design became a major irritant for the environmental lobby. The rather functionalist rectangular suburban bungalows which had replaced the often 'damp and dark' traditional cottages were now being superseded by more expressive designs which drew upon a wide range of inspirations, including 'Spanish haciendas'.

Continuous pressure from the environmental lobby eventually met with some amount of sympathy from Richard Needham, the Minister of State responsible for the Environment. His own aristocratic heritage in Ireland, together with a re-emerging interest in environmental aesthetics in Great Britain, persuaded him to endorse a new initiative. Nevertheless, in shaping a new initiative, the semi-autonomous planning administration had to weave a path through a political minefield. It could not offend Conservative ideology on the one hand, and yet had to offer some sort of compromise between rural political interests and environmental conservation groups on the other. The focus was back on design.

A major initiative was launched to address the problem of the quality of rural houses, not their quantity. Design was to be used as a political tool in an attempt to deal with conflicting definitions of the countryside. The initiative had a number of elements, including design competitions, but its primary com-ponent was a statement published in 1987, on standards to be applied to new development in the countryside, titled *Location,*

Siting and Design in Rural Areas (DOE, 1987). In composing the standards, the planners had to be sensitive to a number of concerns. Firstly, in order to maintain some policy consistency, the key points from the largely ignored 1979 Practice Notes were identified. The rural lobby had regarded the Cockcroft Report and the subsequent policy as a political victory. Any amendment or revision which might undermine that victory would be perceived as regressive. Secondly, the language had to be broadly conceptual and not overly specific in terms of pre-ferred designs. The Conservative intolerance of bureaucratic prescription still prevailed, as did a continued reverence for the imaginative and interpretative skill of the architect. And thirdly, the standards had to be seen as a marker of change in aesthetic control by the environmental lobby.

Although the key terms in the document *Location, Siting and Design* had been employed before, a more methodology-driven approach to aesthetic appreciation was now evident. This is captured in the first paragraph where it is stated:

> the aspects of siting and design which are important depend on whether a house is seen from a distance or close up — its critical viewpoint. (DOE, 1987)

In other words, new development must be considered within a wider composition, and the frame of that composition will be determined by the location of the contemplative viewer. Where 'the critical viewpoint is a long-distance one, colour, scale, form and relationship with existing buildings are the important aspects of design'. The document goes on to define how these con-cepts can be employed in this context. The scale and form of a new house, for example, 'must be measured against local topography, natural features and existing buildings', all of which combine to create the aesthetic composition. Of course when the critical view-point is close to the development, the composition is not the land-scape context but rather the building and siting elements.

The introduction of these standards in November 1987 was preceded by a series of meetings with all 26 District Councils and with the main environmental lobby groups. In relation to the Councils, particularly the rural Councils in the south and west of the region, the purpose was to promote the idea that better quality development in the countryside could be achieved without affecting the number of houses being built. The issue was quality, not quantity. Reaction to the initiative was largely predictable. The southern and western District Councils voiced some concerns but reserved judgement until the impact on development control decisions could be assessed. Within the Greater Belfast Area councillors mostly welcomed the initiative, with some seeking tighter controls. In view of the Cockcroft remarks about the lack of architectural expertise in the Planning Service of the Department of the Environment, in-house training of planning officers on how to employ the standards and on aesthetic appreciation was undertaken.

A number of points can be made about this initiative. Firstly, the design advice was not so much based on replicating or re-interpreting tradition, but rather focused on aesthetic appreciation. It might even be argued that a didactic approach to aesthetic appreciation was employed. *Location, Siting and Design* sought, on the one hand, to inform the design decision makers about how to make an aesthetic judgement based on pictorial composition and on key aesthetic concepts such as form, scale, relationship and proportion. On the other hand, it explained how inappropriate and intrusive elements could disrupt a composition. Secondly, a complementary design competition for qualified architects sought to promote aesthetic skills that neither the plan-drawers nor rural residents might have. Arguably, the overall initiative was rather high-minded and showed little appreciation of rural culture or, even more particularly, of how rural dwellers make their individual location, siting and design decisions.

Almost inevitably, the implementation of the standards triggered problems in the District Council chambers. Interestingly, a siting standard based on the aesthetic merits of the late nineteenth-century practice of seeking privacy was translated into a setback rule. The policy document states that

where the Department considers that from the critical viewpoint, the nature of the site would not permit a new

129

dwelling to be satisfactorily integrated with the landscape other than by setting it well back on its site, it will require a building line of not less than 50 metres from the road edge. (DOE, 1987: paragraph 2)

The application of this standard led to planning refusals and to renegotiated siting, all of which caused considerable political tension between Department of the Environment planners and District Councils. To meet the standard, developers had to incur the additional costs of either enlarging the site or of creating a longer access to a hidden site. Councillors also reminded the planners that rural people 'did not want to hide in the hills', but rather they wanted to live on the road network that connected them to their family and community. A new house, moreover, had symbolic importance, as it represented a living country-side, and for its occupants it communicated improved status to their community.

But even within its own terms, the initiative did not have the desired effects. Where dwellings were set back 50 metres from the roadside, formal elaborate gardens filled the space. The realisation of the theory that a building should be set into the landscape, so that the natural landscape is the dominant fea-ture of the composition was being undermined by additional, distracting elements.

While the operation of the new standards was causing tension with many District Councils, the amenity lobby was equally unhappy with the outcomes. Milton (1993) relates that in this post-Cockcroft period, and particularly after the perceived fail-ure of the *Location, Siting and Design* initiative, the amenity lobby stepped up its opposition to then current policy in all of its dimensions. Indeed, Milton claims that the arguments and supporting evidence presented to the House of Commons Select Committee on the Environment led to the recommendation '... that the Department of the Environment carry out a review of the effects of current policies on residential development in the countryside and reconsider the changes introduced follow-ing the Cockcroft Report' (Milton, 1993: 142).

The evidence presented to the Select Committee from a

number of environmental lobby groups included comments on siting and design as well as on the number of houses being built. One referred to 'the peppering of Spanish style and other inappropriate new buildings throughout the countryside, and a disastrous ribbon type development pattern along roadways' (House of Commons Environment Committee, 1990: 157). Another spoke of the minimal effect of the standards and suggested that the initiative did 'nothing to address the real problem which is quantity' (177). However, while the environmental lobby's evidence showed some appreciation of the fierce attachment to land in rural areas, it arguably failed to comprehend the deep rural cultural heritage. Commenting on the replacement dwelling category in rural policy, for example, the Ulster Society for the Preservation of the Countryside queried the insistence 'in keeping an old settlement pattern' (185). In a similar vein, the Historic Buildings Council decried the loss of thatched cottages in the countryside and commented that 'at the moment, negative social attitudes seem to prevail in Northern Ireland towards old vernacular buildings' (157).

Almost certainly the recommendations of the Select Committee contributed to the initiation of a fresh review of rural planning policy. The political strength of the two main contesting lobbies and a well-developed and demanding civil society led the Department of the Environment in 1991 to launch a consultation exercise premised on the question: *What kind of countryside do we want?* Design issues featured quite prominently in many submissions and again the two principal and competing rationales were evident. For example, a report (Rural Development Council et al, 1992) from a series of rural meetings argued that the emphasis on aesthetics and visual amenity was overly dominant in policy practice. On the other hand the amenity lobby suggested that design guidelines should not only be improved but that there should be a greater commitment from government to their implementation and enforcement. Some rural community groups also suggested that a range of acceptable designs for local areas should be published to allow people to select a solution which would reflect their social and personal aspirations.

In September 1993, following this exercise as well as direct consultations with District Councils, the Department of the Environment published a more comprehensive set of policies for rural areas titled *A Planning Strategy for Rural Northern Ireland*. Rural Northern Ireland was defined as all of the towns, villages and countryside of the region outside Belfast and its adjoining built-up areas and Derry/Londonderry. Two of the key issues raised in the strategy document have particular relevance for this chapter. One refers to the amount of housing development which has already taken place in the countryside as well as continuing development pressures, and asserts the need to establish 'the extent to which future development can be accommodated ... without detriment to the environment'. The second reflects the amenity lobby's concern about 'the quality and impact of much recent development in the open countryside and about the standards which should be applied to ensure that new development is satisfactorily integrated into its rural setting' (17). In rather crude terms, perhaps, the first is about density and capacity, while the second refers to siting and design standards. Arguably though, both are essentially concerned with the visual impact of development. Indeed, this becomes clearer in the policy response to these issues.

The issue of capacity was destined to be the central concept in a new Countryside Assessment approach to rural planning which would be carried out as part of the development plan-making process. Allen (1995) notes that Countryside Assessment as defined in the Strategy appears to have two main objectives: to assess the capacity of the landscape to absorb further development and to environmentally appraise lands being considered for development within towns and villages. Other ancillary purposes could be subsumed under these headings. In relation to the former, the assessment would identify the environmental and topographical aspects of the landscape as well as its settlement heritage, in order to allow the subdivision of the countryside into areas of broadly similar character. In turn, the development capacity of each sub-landscape area would be assessed.

This new approach represented a response to a number of political pressures. On the one hand it appeared to offer the environmental lobby a methodology-grounded and comprehensive approach to rural planning and protection of the countryside. Planning was frequently criticised as a reactive process, directed by broad, non-place-sensitive policies. Countryside Assessment thus seemed to offer a finer-grained approach for development control purposes and even potentially for countryside management, based on an evaluation of the particular and distinctive quality of local areas. For the rural development lobby, on the other hand, assessment could offer clearer direction on where to build and, perhaps, also on acceptable siting and design. Significantly though, while the text of the policy was replete with the language of amenity and environment, the essential focus was on capacity and placed special emphasis on the visual capacity of the countryside to accommodate more dwellings. It might be argued, therefore, that yet again the state was pursuing a conservation agenda, and was not simply arbitrating between two contesting ideologies. The countryside was defined as landscape, a visual resource and an environmental amenity. Countryside Assessment would be largely single-dimensional and would not include consideration of the social, cultural or economic dimensions of rural areas.

The policy response to the more specific issue of siting and design standards is set out under the heading 'Buildings in the countryside'. The language is stronger and more assertive than before and combines an almost romantic adoration for the vernacular tradition, or at least for its external visual form, with an imperative to preserve the scenery of the countryside. In relation to the former, there is some recognition that vernacular style has been influenced by formal architecture. Indeed the policy now promotes this:

> some (traditional) buildings were altered over time and they may show the influence of a more formal architecture. Indeed there are many rural houses of a formal design which could act as appropriate models for modern houses in the countryside. (DOE, 1993: 128)

More forceful direction is provided on how to blend a new house into the countryside:

A new building in the countryside will be acceptable if, when viewed from these surrounding vantage points, it meets all of the following criteria:

- it blends sympathetically with landform;
- it uses existing trees, buildings, slopes or other natural features to provide a backdrop;
- it uses an identifiable site with long established boundaries, which separate the site naturally from the surrounding ground; and
- it does not spoil any scenic aspect or detract from the visual appearance of the countryside. (126)

The imperatives underpinning this approach aim to sustain the notion of the countryside as aesthetic composition. To put it rather bluntly perhaps, a new house and its site from the vantage point should either look as if it is naturally part of a romanticised version of nineteenth-century countryside scenery, or else it should be camouflaged by existing natural features. The key concept is 'natural'. Any new development in the landscape should not disturb its natural quality. Traditional houses, outbuildings, trees, vegetation and field patterns are considered to be natural and to be either part of nature or to be an integral part of an unaffected rural idyll.

The follow-on publication by the Department of the Environment in 1994 of *A Design Guide for Rural Northern Ireland* is the first region-wide illustrated guide for rural house development. The initiative was guided by a steering group comprised of representatives from what could be regarded as the key institutions of professional influence: the Royal Society of Ulster Architects, the Institute of Landscape Architects, the Northern Ireland Housing Executive and the Ulster Folk and Transport Museum. The product of this collaboration reflects an approach which fuses architectural methodology with references to vernacular tradition. Interestingly too, there is explicit recognition of the actual design practices in rural areas. The guide is targeted at house designers who are not architects and who would normally use a standard set of suburban house plans for rural sites. Moreover, the approach is educative and steers the designer/applicant through a process of analysis from site selection to site and building design. The rationale underpinning this is much more dependent on the aesthetic merits of traditional design. It is almost implied, for example, that traditional builders/designers selected sites and building forms for aesthetic reasons, or that at the very least their functional concerns coincided with appropriate aesthetic outcomes: buildings tucked into the folds of the hillside to avoid the wind, finding a sheltered site among the trees, and selecting building materials and forms that are plain, simple, even austere.

During the preparation of the guide, the opinions of amenity groups and some District Councils were invited. The rural development lobby echoed previously articulated views about the need to facilitate the desire by rural people for modern contemporary design. In response to this, the guide specifically outlaws the styles perceived as more appropriate to suburban locations, but suggests that a sensitive interpretation of vernacular design can produce a modern house:

> In recent years ... there has been a marked tendency for new dwellings in the countryside to adopt the style and appearance of typical suburban development of the period e.g. mock Georgian and Tudor with the addition of the Spanish hacienda. While some of these styles may not look out of place in a housing estate in a town, they are generally incongruous in a rural setting. They have the effect of debasing the distinctive regional character and blurring the contrast between town and country. ... This guide does not suggest that modern rural dwellings should look like reproductions of traditional houses or cottages. On the contrary, there is no reason why a modern house, designed in accordance with this guide, should not look like a modern house and at the same time be entirely appropriate to its rural setting. (DOE, 1994: 21)

THE STATE'S AESTHETIC AND THE POPULAR RURAL AESTHETIC

This narrative of the evolution of rural house design policy has identified an ongoing contestation between the state and what might be termed the rural development lobby. It has been argued that during the course of the post-war years the state steadily embraced an ideological position that, in one sense, was simply a reflection of the preservation ethos prevalent in lowland Britain. The tradition in Northern Ireland of communities living in the open countryside required, however, an approach that was sensitive to the development needs of an increasingly politicised constituency. Policy development, therefore, moved beyond the initial, rather blunt attempts to prevent development, to focus more on the aesthetics of development conjoined with a nostalgic reverence for traditional siting and design practices.

On the basis of existing policy and guidelines it is possible to construct an ideal type of the state's preferred aesthetic (Fig. 5.1) to allow comparison with actual rural development practices. This may be summarised as follows:

- The new house should be grouped with existing traditional buildings in the landscape or should be set back into the countryside scenery and separated from the public road by agricultural land.
- The site should be bounded by indigenous trees and shrubs, preferably making use of existing field boundaries.
- The site should be accessed by an existing laneway bordered by existing mature hedgerows.
- The dwelling should be moderately sized, but, more importantly, should have a linear plan form with annexes to the rear. The traditional building unit could also be used to create an interesting composition of forms.
- Windows should be vertically proportioned and should be arranged on the elevation to allow a strong solid to void relationship. Window arrangement should also contribute to a satisfactory visual balance between the overall horizontal and vertical forces.
- The roof should be gable pitched at between 30° to 40° with natural slate and chimneys situated on the ridge.
- The building should be rendered and painted white or a pale neutral colour.

- The garage should be either attached to the main building under a dropped roof, or should be a separate structure situated at the rear or as part of a visually satisfactory grouping.
- Detailing or ornamentation should be minimal, using if necessary traditional plaster banding or colour on the door.
- The overall siting and design should be the outcome of an evaluation and design process undertaken by a qualified architect.

FIGURE 5.1 AN ILLUSTRATION OF THE STATE AESTHETIC

Source: Department of the Environment for Northern Ireland (1994), *A Design Guide for Rural Northern Ireland,* p. 23.

The popular rural aesthetic is to some extent moderated directly and indirectly by planning practices and by local trends. However, research (Sterrett, 1999) suggests that there is a high degree of consistency in design and siting preferences, particularly in the south and west of the region, where living in the open countryside is the ideal for many people. The main characteristics of the popular rural aesthetic (Figure 5.2) can be summarised as follows:

- A site with an approximate area of 0.32 hectare (¾ acre), situated between 10–30 metres from the public road.
- The dwelling to be separated from the road by a formal garden, and bounded by some form of landscaping including coniferous trees.
- The dwelling to be accessed directly off the public road by a formal entrance or driveway.
- The dwelling to be a single-storey building with a living area of approximately 185 square metres (2,000 sq. feet).
- The building to be a rectangular plan form with a gable pitched roof and finished in painted render.
- The front elevation to feature horizontal picture windows sometimes with feature archways or bay/bow windows or an external chimney.
- The building to include an integral garage under the same roof.
- The house plans to be prepared by a plan drawer, normally chosen from an already completed set of drawings.

FIGURE 5.2 AN ILLUSTRATION OF THE POPULAR AESTHETIC

CONCLUSION

The state's aesthetic is essentially a hybrid, cleaned-up vernacular concept fused with a reverence for form and composition. This is regarded as the superior aesthetic. It has a superior tone and quality and evokes the taste of the middle class conservation and amenity groups. The popular rural aesthetic, on the other hand, is perceived to be vulgar and tasteless. But the popular rural aesthetic is driven by a number of imperatives. Family ownership of land, for example, largely determines the choice of location and site. This practice can extend beyond immediate family members to sometimes include distant relations, and in rural culture the offering of a site to a newly married couple has long been regarded as almost an obligation. Increased affluence, among at least some in rural communities, can facilitate this move to a new house in the first place.

The final built form, its location and siting is the outcome of what Bourdieu (1984) calls 'functional considerations'. These embrace utility and sign values. Thus the sheer size of the new dwelling is designed to facilitate all the conveniences of modern life: the bathroom or bathrooms, the *large* kitchen, separate bedrooms for children, dining room and formal lounge, and indeed other spaces which may be in fashion at any given time. The size and layout of internal space can be perceived as the manifestation of the aspiration to move on from the past and to purposefully enjoy the material comforts that this past denied. But the new house has other functions and important sign values. It communicates to others a sign of progress, a sign of having achieved a degree of material wealth, of having left poverty behind. There is a certain sense of defiance here as well. Many rural communities are mindful of an exploited past and of rural relations which Evans has described as the equivalent of a caste system: 'The big house with its high walled wooded demesne and the naked countryside with its teeming tenantry, [are] ingrained in rural memories' (Evans, 1981). So to get out of 'the bog' and on to 'the hill', and to build a big house of one's own is to defy a history of subordination.

Of course the building of a new house is also about a feeling of self-worth that comes from community assent, and what

Bourdieu calls 'the norms of morality and agreeableness'. The ethos underpinning rural culture is certainly about collective and supportive community, but it also encourages self-advancement. Indeed to some extent, evident self-improvement reflects on the wider community. A broader culture of enterprise and individuality has prevailed since the late 1970s and has created, therefore, a moral sanction for increased wealth. The political difficulty has come with its conspicuous expression. For the amenity lobby, the vulgar expression of wealth is distasteful; it is a reminder of the social reality of capitalist economics and of aspiring classes; it celebrates a crude pretentiousness and it distracts from the real object of aesthetic merit and of harmony in nature — the landscape.

But from the rural community's point of view new wealth is demonstrably good. It is an expression of rural regeneration and of come-back after decades of depopulation and economic decline. A new house is a social aspiration for many in rural society and should be proudly proclaimed. There are virtually no design objections to new houses in the countryside from within the rural community, particularly in localities away from the two main urban areas of Northern Ireland. And for many in the rural community a well-designed house is located on top of the hill, with arches and columns and large picture windows. There is agreement in this arena about design, but it is about a design that communicates, not a design to contemplate.

What then is the source of design choice? What are the social and design references for rural people? The ideal type, as outlined above, suggests a straightforward reference to suburbia. Suburban estates are replete with bungalows of the type described, or with variations of it. One rural planner commented during the research underpinning this chapter that 'rural people are obsessed with things urban'. What this means is that 'urban' is regarded as more sophisticated than 'rural' and that the 'rustic' and 'backward' labels imposed on declining rural areas during the progressive 1950s and 1960s are still retained in the rural psyche. The suburban bungalow is a symbol of new wealth and a social aspiration in urban areas and, therefore, is something to imitate in rural areas. But if a new house is to communicate, what other readable references are possible? The imagery of the popular aesthetic is that a new house must visibly contrast with the old. A new house should have large windows instead of small windows, colour and ornamentation instead of utilitarian blandness, curved and rounded forms instead of lines and angles, garden instead of field, garage instead of workspace and should be big instead of small.

Essentially, therefore, the preferences of the popular rural aesthetic are derived from cultural heritage and from contemporary social aspiration. The language of the designs speaks to the rural community and is about communication within that community. The popular rural aesthetic is, in Bourdieu's terms, 'pluralistic and conditional'; pluralistic in the sense that there are no aesthetic pretensions beyond the community and no claims for universal validity. When presented with an alternative architectural solution, rural people have not disparaged it but rather suggested that it is not for them: 'Others may like it, perhaps architects themselves or urban people moving to the countryside, but it is unlikely to be the sort of house a rural person would want to build'.

On the other hand, the superior aesthetic rejects the popular inclination to humanise subject matter and to connect it to the concepts of everyday life: 'a bracketing of form in favour of 'human' content, ... is barbarism par excellence from the standpoint of the pure aesthetic' (Bourdieu, 1984). Countryside as landscape form, as subject matter to be contemplated, is a key part of the state's design rationale, as it is for amenity groups. In the language of the amenity lobby there is also a sense in which the popular rural aesthetic can be regarded as almost immoral: "Here is nature, here is God's natural world being destroyed by a tawdry materialism. Look back at how your ancestors looked after the countryside, how they respected nature and didn't challenge its divine power!'

But rural people do not make choices on this basis. A very different rationale is employed. It is one based on a different set of meanings and on a very different understanding of what the countryside is. In conclusion, this is similar to the distinction that Williams makes in his novels between the 'tourist gaze' and 'lived lives in place'. In *Border Country*, for example, Will returns home to Wales after a long absence:

It was one thing to carry its image in his mind, as he did, everywhere, never a day passing but he closed his eyes and saw it again, his only landscape. But it was different to stand and look at the reality. It was not less beautiful; every detail of the land came up with its old excitement. But it was not still, as the image had been. It was no longer a landscape or a view, but a valley that people were using. He realised as he watched, what had happened in going away. The valley as landscape had been taken, but its work forgotten. The visitor sees beauty: the inhabitant a place where he works and has friends. Far away, closing his eyes, he had been seeing this valley, but as a visitor sees it, as the guidebook sees it: this valley, in which he had lived more than half his life. (Williams, 1960: 75)

REFERENCES

Allen, N. (1995), *Countryside Assessment: A New Initiative for Rural Planning in Northern Ireland,* Unpublished MSc. dissertation, School of Environmental Planning, Queen's University, Belfast.

Bourdieu, P. (1984) *Distinction: A Social Critique of the Judgement of Taste*, London: Routledge and Kegan Paul.

Caldwell, J.H. (1992), 'Policies for the Control of Rural Housing', unpublished PhD thesis, Queen's University, Belfast.

Caldwell, J.H. and J.V. Greer (1984), *Physical Planning in Rural Areas of Northern Ireland,* Occasional Paper No. 5, Department of Town and Country Planning, Queen's University, Belfast.

Cockcroft, W.H. (1978), *Review of Rural Planning Policy: Report of the Committee under the Chairmanship of Dr W.H. Cockcroft*. Belfast: Department of the Environment for Northern Ireland.

Department of the Environment for Northern Ireland (1978), *Review of Rural Planning Policy*, Belfast: HMSO.

Department of the Environment for Northern Ireland (1979), *Policy for the Control of Development in Rural Areas: Practice Notes,* Belfast: HMSO.

Department of the Environment (1980), *Circular 22/80: Development Control — Policy and Practice,* London: HMSO.

Department of the Environment for Northern Ireland (1981), *Planning: Development Control,* Statement by Mr David Mitchell, Parliamentary Under Secretary of State with responsibility for the Department of the Environment.

Department of the Environment for Northern Ireland (1987), *Location, Siting and Design in Rural Areas,* Belfast: HMSO.

Department of the Environment for Northern Ireland (1993), *A Planning Strategy for Rural Northern Ireland*, Belfast: HMSO.

Department of the Environment for Northern Ireland (1994), *A Design Guide for Rural Northern Ireland*, Belfast: HMSO.

Evans, E. (1981), *The Personality of Ireland: Habitat, Heritage and History*, Belfast: Blackstaff Press.

Gaffikin F. and M. Morrisey (1990), *Northern Ireland: The Thatcher Years,* London: Zed Books Ltd.

Harvey, D. (1996), *Justice, Nature and the Geography of Difference*, Oxford: Blackwell.

House of Commons Environment Committee (1990), *Environmental Issues in Northern Ireland*, London: HMSO.

Kennedy, B.P. (1993), 'The Traditional Irish Thatched House: Image and Reality 1793–1993', in A. Dalsimer (ed.), *Visualising Ireland: National Identity and the Pictorial Tradition,* London: Faber and Faber.

Matless, D. (1990), 'Definitions of England 1928–89: Preservation, Modernism and the Nature of the Nation', *Built Environment*, vol. 16, no. 1: 179–191.

Matthew, R. (1964), *Belfast Regional Survey and Plan*, Belfast: HMSO.

Milton, K. (1993), 'Land or Landscape: Rural Planning Policy and the Symbolic Construction of the Countryside', in M. Murray and J. Greer (eds), *Rural Development in Ireland,* Aldershot: Avebury.

Punter, J. (1987), A History of Aesthetic Control: Part 2, 1953–1985', *Town Planning Review,* vol. 58, no. 1: 29–62.

Reade, E. (1987), *British Town and Country Planning*, Milton Keynes: Open University Press.

Rural Development Council, Rural Community Network and Community Technical Aid (1992), *Rural Planning Strategy Review: A Community Consultation Response,* Belfast: Community Technical Aid.

Rustin, M. (1985), 'English Conservatism and the Aesthetics of Architecture', *Radical Philosophy*, no. 40, Summer: 21–28.

Sterrett, K.W. (1999), 'The Sociology of Design and Aesthetics: The Case of Housing in Rural Northern Ireland', unpublished PhD thesis, Queen's University, Belfast.

Urry, J. (1992), 'The Tourist Gaze and the Environment,' *Theory, Culture and Society*, vol. 9, no. 1: 1–26.

Williams, R. (1960), *Border Country*, London: Hogarth Press.

CHAPTER 6

BUILDING AT THE CROSSROADS: RURAL HOUSING POLICY IN NORTHERN IRELAND

Michael Conway

INTRODUCTION

One of the landmarks in the evolution of rural development policies in the past two decades is the European Commission's 1988 publication *The Future of Rural Society* (Commission of European Communities, 1988). In the debate which followed this, it was reported that there existed 'a weight of evidence suggesting that the largest and in some ways the most intractable problem affecting rural areas in the United Kingdom is the provision of affordable housing for local communities' (HMSO, 1990: 52). A variety of studies (Phillips and Williams, 1982; Shucksmith et al., 1987; Shucksmith 1990; Scottish Homes, 1993) have highlighted the key role that housing can play in the regeneration of rural areas. Policies formulated and implemented by government departments and housing agencies can be pivotal in deciding the future of rural communities in a variety of ways. From an economic perspective, statutory authorities can help provide employment through house building initiatives, thus having a direct economic benefit in rural localities. As well as assisting rural shops and schools, new housing provision can also act as a confidence-building measure and catalyst for further development.

Statutory housing policies can bring social benefits through community development. Young and Lemos (1997) have argued that a strong attachment to place, together with multi-generation family ties, can help create close-knit communities. Thus housing policies can encourage such community development by retaining and building networks in rural areas. And finally, housing policies can address environmental issues by tackling dereliction and promoting retention of the built heritage.

As outlined, therefore, housing affects the future of both individuals and communities in rural areas, with statutory policies having a particularly significant impact. This chapter examines some aspects of rural housing in Northern Ireland by looking first at the policy framework within which housing issues are determined. It discusses the particular role of the Northern Ireland Housing Executive (NIHE) as a comprehensive housing authority and considers how the NIHE rural housing policy has developed. Attention then turns to the Crossroads initiative as a specific example of policy in action. Finally, the chapter looks at contemporary rural housing issues and concludes with the identification of some of the future housing challenges with relevance to rural places.

RURAL HOUSING: THE PUBLIC POLICY FRAMEWORK

In Northern Ireland, public policy on rural housing has evolved primarily from a complex inter-relationship between the responsible government department (currently the Department for Social Development) and the responsible statutory agency (the NIHE). The policy environment also includes the housing association movement, District Councils (primarily by way of the consultative Northern Ireland Housing Council), and tenant/ community representatives through the NIHE's community involvement framework. While such bodies can influence policy, the main players in policy evolution have traditionally been the NIHE and the Department. Connolly (1990) comments on the relationship between the Department (at that time the Department of the Environment for Northern Ireland) and the NIHE as follows:

The simplistic but erroneous view is that the Department is responsible for policy formulation and the NIHE for service delivery. This view ignores two complementary factors. First on questions of housing, the Department and the Minister operate in a sensitive political manner and matters of detail can become highly contentious. Second within the NIHE there is the strongly held view that as a considerable amount of housing expertise lies within the organisation, it should contribute to the development of policies in housing. Staff in the NIHE constantly argue that they are in a 'comprehensive housing agency' with a responsibility for housing throughout Northern Ireland. The result is that a clear role definition is difficult with much negotiation and interplay taking place between the two organisations. (129)

The relationship described above has operated in a stable and coherent fashion for many years. In recent times this relationship and the general policy framework has been adapting to changing circumstances arising from two specific developments. The first of these was the Department of the Environment's 1996 housing policy review. This review was predicated on the continuation of the NIHE as the single comprehensive regional housing authority, together with an expanding voluntary housing sector and a growing private sector. The most notable aspect of the review was the enhancement of NIHE's strategic and enabling role, with the housing association movement taking over the role of provider of new social housing. It was proposed that apart from exceptional circumstances the NIHE would no longer build public housing, but would take over some of the Department's former operational roles, such as the regulation of housing associations and the private rented sector. Some of the review proposals have still to be implemented and the transfer of the Department's operational roles to the NIHE has still to occur. However, the transfer of the Department's regulatory role in relation to housing associations seems increasingly unlikely. Such developments combined with the enhanced provider role for housing associations will undoubtedly affect the longstanding inter-relationship between the

NIHE and the Department, and increase the housing associations' influence on policy.

The second recent development within the public policy environment has been the establishment of devolved government structures. As a result of this, departmental structures changed considerably, with the redistribution of many of the housing policy overseeing responsibilities of the Department of the Environment. The NIHE now comes under the remit of the Department for Social Development (DSD), although other housing-related matters, which inevitably have an effect on rural policy, rest with other departments. For example, spatial planning control has remained with the Department of the Environment, while strategic regional planning has become the responsibility of the Department for Regional Development. Rural development rests primarily within the Department of Agriculture and Rural Development. Again the impact of such structures is still evolving at present, but the splitting of departmental responsibilities will inevitably increase the need for the meritorious but obstacle-ridden concept of 'joined up government'. Increased rural demands, a complex administrative structure, and a changing balance in the relationship between the NIHE, housing associations and the Department for Social Development could potentially produce a tension-filled policy arena. These changing circumstances will require a high degree of flexibility on behalf of statutory bodies to respond to the variety of issues within their remit, both to prevent public policy disarray and to maximise benefits for rural Northern Ireland across government departments.

THE NIHE AND THE RURAL HOUSING PROBLEM

The NIHE was founded by the Housing Executive (NI) Act 1971 following a government decision that all public housing should be removed from political control and all housing powers should be located within a single housing authority. The NIHE currently has three main roles:

1   assessment of housing need, housing market research and production of local housing plans;

2   landlord responsibilities for some 130,000 dwellings; and
3   a facilitating role to enable other bodies to meet special and general housing needs.

The evolving circumstances mentioned in the previous section might well affect the NIHE role in future, but in its relatively short existence the organisation has shown an aptitude to adapt successfully. This can be seen in the crisis era of the 1970s when, as a new agency, the NIHE assumed the housing functions of sixty-five separate housing authorities and set about tackling high levels of housing unfitness through stock clearance and new building. The NIHE subsequently adapted to the Thatcherism of the 1980s by developing closer links with the private sector, while in the 1990s the organisational focus switched to a more strategic and enabling direction. Since its formation, the NIHE 'has been credited with achieving fairness and impartiality, particularly in its programmes, openness in its administrative procedures and high quality standards in the homes it provides' (DOE, 1996).

The NIHE's successes are certainly wide ranging, but it is fair to say that for at least half of its existence, the NIHE has been an organisation with a strong urban focus. McPeake and Murtagh (1993) have charted the NIHE's involvement in rural housing until 1990–91 when its first rural housing policy review was undertaken. As McPeake and Murtagh note, 'although the NIHE billed its exercise as a review of rural housing policy, in reality there was no rural housing policy as such. Rather, there was a broad set of housing policies, the objectives of which were set out each year in the government's expenditure plans' (167). Effectively, therefore, the first attempt to develop a rural housing approach only came about in 1991 when a major public consultation and research exercise led to the formation of a policy framework underpinned by seven key principles (NIHE, 1990):

1   Rural housing policy should contribute towards rural development objectives.
2   Partnership with others in developing and implementing a rural housing policy is critical for success.

3   A new rural approach is necessary not a revised urban approach.
4   Tailoring to local circumstances is a critical success factor.
5   Working with rural communities is essential for effective rural development.
6   Affordability lies at the core of potential housing solutions.
7   Investment and resources should be directed to where they are needed and to those who need them most.

A variety of follow-on policy instruments were developed from these principles. For example, latent demand testing emerged to identify hidden rural housing need; replacement grants were introduced to tackle the worst private housing; crossroads schemes were proposed to provide housing in communities beyond villages; and a Rural Housing Association was created in 1992 to complement public sector housing activity. However, during the subsequent period of implementation the profile of the rural housing initiative diminished somewhat within the NIHE. The Rural Co-ordinator, who had devised and driven much of the policy effort, returned to his former post and a replacement was not appointed. Policy implementation was left to the NIHE network of five Regional Offices and thirty-eight District Offices. However, in February 1995 a progress assessment noted that there was a need to move from a reactive to a more proactive stance in contributing to rural development.

In 1997, the NIHE again appointed a Rural Co-ordinator and shortly after decided to undertake a second formal policy review. The reasons for this were varied. The 1996 House Condition Survey and the work of the new Rural Co-ordinator created fresh interest in rural issues within the NIHE. Externally, the NIHE was aware of the changing rural dynamic. In the UK context, the 1995 Rural White Paper for England (DOE /MAFF, 1995) had emphasised the need for integrated rural policy. In Scotland, Scottish Homes (1998) had produced a rural position statement emphasising empowerment, inclusion and partnership as key issues. In the Republic of Ireland, a White Paper on Rural Development was also pending. From a European perspective, continuing changes in agricultural policy and the preparation of the 2000–2006 Structural Funds bids all had a bearing on the NIHE decision to re-examine its stance. The eventual outcome was the publication of a consultation document, *Places for People* (NIHE, 1999).

PHOTOGRAPH 6.1 ADDRESSING RURAL UNFITNESS THROUGH REPLACEMENT GRANT AID

PHOTOGRAPH COURTESY OF NIHE

This document included an examination of the progress made by the NIHE in rural areas since the 1991 review. It highlighted the following achievements:

- a decrease in rural housing unfitness from 17.2 per cent in 1991 to 12.1 per cent in 1996 (although the corresponding 1996 urban figure was around 5 per cent);
- substantial improvements to over 50 per cent of the 2,000 NIHE-owned rural cottages;
- the acknowledgement of a hidden demand for rural housing which led to 73 latent demand tests resulting in 136 housing units being programmed;
- the ring-fencing of around 10 per cent of the social new build programme for rural housing and the provision of almost 1400 new units from 1991–96;
- the identification of some key policy failings. For example, efforts to target grant aid and to reduce the number of empty rural dwellings had not been wholly successful.

Overall then, as a performance report the *Places for People* assessment of the NIHE since 1991 was of the 'well done but can do better' variety. But given that the period under review had been the NIHE's first attempt to proactively address rural housing issues, it is only fair to suggest that these endeavours should be regarded as both exploratory and tentative. One such endeavour is the Crossroads initiative, which is examined next as an illustration of policy in action.

POLICY IN ACTION: THE CROSSROADS INITIATIVE

The Crossroads initiative was an integral part of the NIHE's 1991 rural policy and was defined as follows:

Crossroads refers to those small settlements beyond existing villages which have over time, evolved around a church, hall, school, or shops or some combination of these facilities, and which are considered by residents to be primary focal points for their communities. In such key locations, the NIHE will consider small-scale developments based on an assessment of current and latent demand to include the need for low-cost shared ownership dwellings. (NIHE, 1991: 36)

PHOTOGRAPH 6.2 CROSSROADS SCHEME, COUNTY DOWN

PHOTOGRAPH COURTESY OF NIHE

The NIHE was to act as land assembler and was to take account of the need for mainstream renting, special needs renting and shared ownership. It was intended that each scheme would be on a small scale of around six dwellings and be provided by a combination of the NIHE, the Rural Housing Association and private developers. The main objectives of the Crossroads initiative were:

- to provide satisfactory housing for those in most housing need, who wish to live in rural areas outside villages;
- to maintain existing rural communities;
- to assist in wider rural regeneration.

An examination of NIHE records for all new build housing from 1991 to 1996 shows that fifty-two schemes were provided in rural areas. No specific records of Crossroads schemes are held but by excluding projects of less than three properties, replacement schemes (where no housing gain resulted) and village schemes (within villages defined by statutory Area Plans), eleven new build schemes remain. These can, therefore, be properly classified as crossroads developments. The schemes in question are geographically spread (Table 6.1), with four of the schemes (twenty-one properties) being provided by the Rural Housing Association and the remainder by the NIHE.

TABLE 6.1 LOCATION OF CROSSROADS SCHEMES, 1991–1996

County location	No. of schemes	No. of properties
Armagh	3	22
Down	2	19
Fermanagh	2	14
Tyrone	2	12
Londonderry	2	7
Total	**11**	**74**

In order to evaluate the impact of the Crossroads initiative, research was undertaken in 1998–1999 primarily by means of a questionnaire survey targeted at residents of these eleven schemes. Fifty residents in total were interviewed to establish views on a range of issues. Some 66 per cent of those interviewed were females and 34 per cent were males. Eight per cent of heads of household were in full-time employment and 8 per cent in part-time employment, while 80 per cent were reliant on state benefits. The household types residing in the 50 properties are outlined in Table 6.2. Analysis of age profile showed a high proportion (54 per cent) in the 20–39 age group. This age group (significant in rural development terms) has previously been shown to be under-represented in rural Northern Ireland (NIHE, 1999).

TABLE 6.2 HOUSEHOLD COMPOSITION OF CROSSROADS SCHEMES

Household type	No. of households	%
Single adult with 0 children[*]	13	26
Single adult with 1–2 children	8	16
Single adult with 3+ children	4	8
2 adults with 0 children	5	10
2 adults with 1–2 children	7	14
2 adults with 3+ children	9	19
Other	4	8
Total	**50**	**100**

* Children = under 16 years of age.

The research results and conclusions are set out below against the defined objectives of the Crossroads initiative.

Objective One: to provide satisfactory housing for those in most housing need, who wish to live in rural areas outside villages

The first element of this objective is the provision of satisfactory housing. From a variety of perspectives, Crossroads schemes were found to have achieved this. The eleven Crossroads schemes demonstrated a high proportion of detached housing (20 per cent), which contrasts with a low proportion (approximately 1 per cent) throughout all NIHE stock. The use of Parker-Morris standards also points to a satisfactory design in crossroads provision. The perceptions of the occupants showed that 86 per cent were satisfied with their properties and a similar proportion (88 per cent) felt the houses had a beneficial impact on the locality. The only notable aspect of dissatisfaction was in relation to rent levels among those 25 per cent of residents who were not in receipt of support through housing benefit.

The second component of this objective is to target those in most housing need and who wish to live in rural areas outside villages. An analysis of the housing status of Crossroads dwellers prior to being housed showed that (excluding transfers from other NIHE stock), 86 per cent were in the NIHE's priority categories. This compared with a Northern Ireland average of 55 per cent and effectively, therefore, illustrates that those housed in Crossroads schemes were indeed those in most housing need, as measured under the NIHE's assessment system. The main attraction of the Crossroads areas for over 70 per cent of residents related to peace and quiet and similar aspects of the rural environment which is consistent with the wish of such residents to live outside larger settlements. The additional factor that almost 40 per cent of Crossroads residents had never lived in a village or town also illustrates a strong attachment to the countryside.

Objective Two: to maintain existing rural communities

The maintenance of rural communities and stemming outward migration are clearly central to all rural development policies. While the NIHE's allocation policies allow little 'protection' for local applicants, the Crossroads initiative has been successful in this regard mainly because it is usually local people who have sought local housing. Eighty per cent of those housed had previously lived within a 5-mile radius of their scheme. Furthermore, 70 per cent indicated they had existing family connections in the area, with more than half of these going back over two generations. The success of Crossroads schemes in retaining local populations was illustrated by the finding that around half the residents stated that they would have to live outside the Crossroads localities had the schemes not been provided. Residents also indicated their intention to remain (i.e. 94 per cent hoped to still be there in five years time), which would certainly suggest the maintenance of rural communities, through an emphasis on locational stability, attachment to place and family ties.

Objective Three: to assist in wider rural regeneration

Interviewees were asked questions about their attitude to their local area, their usage of local facilities and their involvement in local community activity. The guiding assumptions were that a positive attitude to the locality might indicate confidence in its future well-being, use of local facilities could highlight whether housing provision could assist the local school, shop, etc., and the extent of involvement might point to a degree of cohesiveness within the local community.

In relation to attitudes to the local area, the research clearly shows high satisfaction levels. Of particular note is the finding that those who lived within a two-mile radius before moving to their current home were three times more likely to think the locality was improving than did those from further afield. This does suggest that the provision of new housing can lift an area and contribute as a confidence-building measure to those resident in a particular locality. The knock-on effect of housing provision in assisting local services was also considered. In the schemes surveyed, only church, school, and social facilities (often a public house) were within close proximity. It was evident that such facilities were being used by Crossroads dwellers. Some 78 per cent of residents attended a church within a two-mile radius, while 36 per cent availed of similarly local social facilities. In relation to the local primary school, 56 per cent of residents had children aged under eleven and 71 per cent of these indicated that their children attended or would definitely be enrolling at the local rural primary school. Evidence on the involvement of residents in community organisations demonstrated not only low levels of participation, but also a limited number of organisations with which to become associated. Just over half the residents had a local community centre, but 87 per cent of residents never or very rarely attended this centre.

The research also sought to identify in what ways the NIHE and Rural Housing Association had taken proactive steps to encourage broader rural regeneration. For example, it has been suggested that housing providers can assist rural employment through the use of local contractors. Of the eleven schemes, 64 per cent were built by contractors based within a fifteen-mile radius of the relevant scheme. However, the policies of the NIHE and housing associations do not advocate specific use of local contractors, due to tendering and anti-discrimination rules, and thus this economic contribution cannot be treated as a deliberate employment effort by housing providers. Moreover, neither the housing providers, nor the Department of Agriculture (DANI) with responsibility for a number of integrated area-based strategies, had consciously sought to link housing with other forms of rural regeneration. It would seem to have been the case, therefore, that social housing providers in the 1991–1996 period adopted a 'hit and hope' policy, whereby houses were built and wider development spill-overs may have resulted. The research shows that local facilities did benefit and that local confidence was enhanced. However, a more proactive approach involving collaboration with other agencies and encouraging greater community participation could have created a better environment for deeper rural development outcomes.

Finally, a number of more general matters also emerged from the research which are not specific to any of the three guiding objectives. Firstly, given that the initiative was a response to past investigations, which highlighted that many rural dwellers were not happy to live in towns and villages, it was notable that the NIHE did not record or monitor Crossroads schemes separately from other rural new build projects. Secondly, the original policy intention was to provide mixed tenure schemes for general and special needs. However, the Crossroads housing has instead consisted of single landlord, general needs schemes. Thirdly, to determine where to build, the NIHE and Rural Housing Association usually tested latent housing demand. But there was no consistent approach in deciding where such tests should take place, and test locations often relied on requests from local councillors or community groups. It is significant that many of these criticisms have since been addressed through the NIHE's recent policy review (NIHE, 1999). Nevertheless, as illustrated below, there remain a number of current issues to be addressed in the years ahead.

CURRENT RURAL HOUSING ISSUES

The need for integration

A comparison of the 1991 NIHE policy document with its 1999 equivalent reveals a notable shift in emphasis towards the role of housing in rural regeneration. This reflects the government's 'joined-up' philosophy where housing should not be treated as a stand-alone response to rural problems. But as Hood (2000) notes in regard to England, attempts by social housing providers to gain resources for wider rural regeneration have often met with little success. She observes that there is often a lack of co-ordination between departments and agencies responsible for housing provision and those responsible for social and economic regeneration. The 1999 policy document by the NIHE seeks to counter this by proposing enhanced links with District Councils and other statutory agencies responsible for physical planning, health and social services.

The building of bridges with rural communities is a further important issue and is especially significant for the NIHE, which has reasonably strong links with estate-based groups but much less connectedness to rural people beyond its estates. For housing to contribute to wider regeneration, the need for the NIHE to be involved in community development activities is clear. Furthermore, closer working with organisations such as the Rural Community Network and the Sub-Regional Rural Support Networks is essential for the NIHE in order to access the wider rural constituency, which is predominantly owner occupied and so less inclined to have dealings with an agency largely identified with social rented housing.

Energy and environmental issues

The growth of interest in the concept and practice of sustainability during the 1990s has seen energy and the environment move much more to the top of current rural housing issues. The NIHE 1996 House Condition Survey showed that 63 per cent of owner occupied rural housing had no cavity wall insulation and 40 per cent had less than the recommended amount of roof insulation. Such factors have led to the NIHE becoming a home energy conservation authority for Northern Ireland. At a broader level, pressures to conserve the built and natural environment, for heritage and tourism reasons, have also grown. This has resulted in calls for greater quality in new build design and more emphasis on the retention of vernacular architecture than was previously the case.

PHOTOGRAPH 6.3 'QUALITY IN DESIGN' RURAL NEW BUILD SCHEME, COUNTY DOWN

PHOTOGRAPH COURTESY OF NIHE

Housing conditions

Rural housing conditions, as measured through unfitness, remain a matter of concern for policy makers. The NIHE's profiling of properties which are in poor repair shows that 'there is a strong association between poor housing conditions located in dispersed rural locations occupied by owner pensioner households, typically on incomes of less than £10,000 per annum' (NIHE, 1999: 23). This situation requires both a targeted and a sensitive approach. But targeting is difficult as the current mandatory grant scheme allows limited scope for the promotion of a more focused grants approach. A move towards a discretionary grants system would provide greater flexibility, although, on the downside, this could also provide an excuse for government to cut back on grant expenditure. The need for a sensitive approach to isolated elderly homeowners again emphasises the requirement for the NIHE to build closer links with those communities living in rural localities. The additional issue of re-using empty homes is gaining greater profile as the impact of constraints on new development grows. Because the reasons for empty homes are often non-housing-related, a multi-agency approach again seems the optimum solution.

PHOTOGRAPH 6.4 IMPROVING HOUSING CONDITIONS THROUGH RENOVATION GRANT AID

PHOTOGRAPH COURTESY OF NIHE

Demand for and provision of affordable rural homes

Identifying demand has traditionally centred on the use of waiting lists for social housing. This approach has long been seen as flawed in rural areas and the NIHE has acknowledged that 'need is not necessarily registered for those requiring accommodation beyond the larger settlements due mainly to a judgement that additional public sector accommodation will not be provided there' (NIHE, 1991: 33). This led to the introduction of latent demand tests which sought to identify hidden need primarily through newspaper advertising. The completed tests were, however, somewhat piecemeal in their distribution and lacked a consistent procedural approach. Furthermore, the tests have focused largely on demand for social renting (the least popular rural option) and have not catered for other tenures. The NIHE has acknowledged that there remains a need for a consistent rolling programme of testing to ensure that hidden demand for all tenures is identified.

The establishment of demand requires translation into housing provision. To date, such a responsiveness has faced two problems. Firstly, demand itself is often not enough because limited resources mean that this demand must manifest itself as an urgent need for social housing when measured against the NIHE Housing Selection Scheme. This looks at an individual's housing circumstances but, while appropriate for deciding who should actually obtain available property, the emphasis on identifying urgent need to justify house provision is weighted against rural areas where such need is more dispersed. The idea of developing housing schemes as regeneration instruments as opposed to being solely a response to urgent need requires further exploration.

A second and related difficulty concerns land availability. While this has not been a major limitation in rural areas in the past, and was effectively dismissed by the Department for Regional Development (2000) in its response to the panel report on the Public Examination into *Shaping Our Future*, there is now anecdotal evidence to suggest that land prices in some areas are putting sites beyond the reach of social housing providers. This situation must be monitored and consideration may need to be given to initiatives similar to the operation of the rural housing enabler schemes in England, whereby specific officers work with communities and developers in facilitating site identification and housing provision. An alternative approach may be to amend planning policy to allow for rural exception sites similar to what prevails in England and Wales. These allow planning permission to be granted on an exceptional basis for housing schemes where there exists an identifiable lack of affordable housing to meet local needs.

FUTURE STAKEHOLDER CHALLENGES

As suggested earlier from a housing perspective, it is the inter-action between government and the NIHE which has led to implementation of policies affecting rural communities. These three stakeholders of government, communities and the NIHE have specific challenges to face within the rural housing policy arena.

Government

The devolved administration in Northern Ireland must actively address the integration of government activities in rural areas across Northern Ireland. While the Department of Agriculture and Rural Development (DARD) has attempted to do this, its primary role has historically been dealing with farming, fishery and forestry matters. So often the rural development element of DARD (and previously DANI) has seemed to be the poorer relation and, apart from some localised projects, it has had limited effect in influencing rural development matters across housing, transport, education, and health. These issues of social development are largely left to individual departments. While an interdepartmental rural committee does exist at present, there is no overarching and comprehensive strategic framework for this group to follow. If, as seems likely, European rural funding diminishes after 2006, the need to bring together government departments' efforts and expenditure on rural areas will increase. A Northern Ireland Rural White Paper would represent a welcome response to this state of affairs. A coordinating function within the Office of First and Deputy First Minister would provide clout and an impetus for the integration and monitoring of various departmental activities in rural areas. In this respect, it is worth noting that the Department for Social Development is specifically charged with urban regeneration and, given the inevitable overlaps, it would seem more appropriate if both urban and rural regeneration were the responsibility of a single department.

Rural communities

The local accountability of devolved government creates a greater opportunity for rural communities to have their voice heard. Apart from planning issues and to a lesser extent property unfitness, there has not been any outcry on housing matters from rural Northern Ireland. It is difficult to say whether this is because rural communities are satisfied with their housing circumstances, or whether such matters are felt to be beyond their sphere of influence, or whether the link between housing and rural regeneration is not readily apparent. Whatever the cause, this situation is likely to change. The reality is that Northern Ireland is beginning to replicate housing circumstances elsewhere in the UK and in the Republic of Ireland. Problems of affordability are emerging for rural communities, particularly in the Belfast Travel to Work Area as the commuting belt spreads ever more widely. The increase in second homes in some coastal areas is also creating housing pressure, while fragile communities in more isolated areas have their own housing-related regeneration needs. Again experience elsewhere suggests that these emerging factors will lead rural communities to realise that housing provision is pivotal to their continuity. It is notable, for example, that the Scottish Executive is responding to the demands of both pressured and fragile communities through programmes such as Rural Partnership for Change and Initiatives at the Edge (Scottish Homes, 2000). The challenge for rural communities is to respond to these changing housing and governance circumstances so as to influence housing outcomes.

The Northern Ireland Housing Executive

As well as the operational matters mentioned earlier in this chapter, the biggest rural challenge facing the NIHE is to promote its relevance to rural Northern Ireland. There is, arguably, a perception in rural communities that the NIHE's function is almost exclusively that of a social landlord, dealing with its estates. This may partly explain why rural community groups beyond these estates do not seek to address housing issues. The perception arises, in part, because social renting has traditionally been the NIHE's core business. Its main physical presence in rural areas is in the form of a District Office network whose resources are weighted heavily towards landlord matters. Regrettably in many rural areas, the individual NIHE estate is often seen as 'different' from the surrounding rural community, and so the likelihood of the wider rural constituency becoming involved with the NIHE is lessened. In order to address rural housing issues in predominantly owner occupied rural areas, a concerted effort is required by the NIHE to enhance the promotion and delivery of a comprehensive housing service involving all tenures at local level. Such an effort to change mindsets is, perhaps, a bigger challenge than the specific housing and regeneration challenges the NIHE is likely to face in the years ahead.

CONCLUSION

Housing is a central challenge in rural places, whether the problem is defined as one of affordability or fragility. Such problems cannot be resolved by housing agencies working alone. Other government agencies and departments have roles to play. Rural communities should recognise and articulate their housing needs, and agencies such as the NIHE should facilitate this through developing greater links with these communities. In this chapter the background exploration of the NIHE's work in rural areas and the case study of the Crossroads initiative illustrate how one aspect of the rural challenge can be addressed. The analogy of a country crossroads is a reminder that without proper signposting, rural policies can lead in different directions. An overarching government *rural strategy* is required so that the public, private, community and voluntary sectors are all travelling together towards the same destination!

ENDNOTE

The views expressed in this chapter are those of the author and are not necessarily those of his employer, the Northern Ireland Housing Executive.

REFERENCES

Commission of European Communities (1988), *The Future of Rural Society*, Brussels.

Connolly, M. (1990), *Politics and Policy in Northern Ireland*, London: Phillip and Allen.

Department of the Environment and Ministry of Agriculture, Fisheries and Food (1995), *Rural England: A Nation Committed to a Living Countryside*, London: HMSO.

Department of the Environment for Northern Ireland (1996), *Building on Success: Proposals for Future Housing Policy*, Belfast: HMSO.

Department for Regional Development (2000), *Shaping Our Future: Towards a Strategy for the Development of the Region: Report of the Panel Conducting the Public Examination.* Belfast: HMSO.

HMSO (1990), *Report of the Select Committee on the European Community: The Future of Rural Society*, London: HMSO.

Hood, M. (2000), *Empowering Rural Communities: Involving Residents in Rural Regeneration*, paper presented at the conference 'Developing and supporting communities in rural areas', Aviemore, Scotland: Chartered Institute of Housing.

McPeake, J. and B. Murtagh (1993), 'The Rural Housing Problem in Northern Ireland', in M. Murray and J. Greer, (eds), *Rural Development in Ireland*, Aldershot: Avebury.

Northern Ireland Housing Executive (1990), *Rural Housing Policy Review: Leading the Way*, Belfast: Northern Ireland Housing Executive.

Northern Ireland Housing Executive (1991), *Rural Housing Policy: The Way Ahead — A Policy Statement*. Belfast: Northern Ireland Housing Executive.

Northern Ireland Housing Executive (1999), *Places for People: A Rural Housing Policy Review*. Belfast: Northern Ireland Housing Executive.

Phillips, D. and A. Williams (1982), *Rural Housing and the Public Sector*, Fairborough: Gower.

Shucksmith, M., D. Robertson and B.D. MacGregor (1987), *Rural Housing in Scotland: Recent Research and Policy*, Glasgow: University of Glasgow.

Shucksmith, M. (1990), *Memorandum in House of Lords Report the Select Committee on the European Communities: The Future of Rural Society,* London: HMSO.

Scottish Homes (1993), *Rural Update: News on Rural Housing from Scottish Homes*, Edinburgh: Scottish Homes.

Scottish Homes (1998), *Tackling Rural Housing: Policy Statement 1998*, Edinburgh: Scottish Homes.

Scottish Homes (2000), *Scottish Homes: News on Scottish Homes Activities Across the Region*, Spring edition, Edinburgh: Scottish Homes.

Young, M. and G. Lemos (1997), *The Communities We Have Lost and Can Regain*, London: Lemos and Crane.

CHAPTER 7

DEALING WITH THE CONSEQUENCES OF A DIVIDED SOCIETY IN TROUBLED COMMUNITIES

Brendan Murtagh

INTRODUCTION

As Ireland profoundly demonstrates, power cannot be conceived outside a geographical context. Social power requires space, its exercise shapes space, and this in turn shapes social power... As such, a cultural landscape can be visualised as a powerful medium in expressing feelings, ideas and values, while simultaneously being an arena of political discourse and action in which cultures are continuously reproduced and contested. (Graham, 1997: 4)

This chapter is concerned with the contested nature of rural places, the socio-spatial effects of territoriality and policy responses to ethnic fracturing since the imposition of Direct Rule in 1972. Direct Rule brought with it a planning style that emphasised technical and bureaucratic values. In the desperate attempt to manage the economic, social and, most importantly, political crises of the late 1960s and early 1970s, the professionalising of policy processes, policy makers and law became a central project for the UK government. The 'cultural meaning, value system and power relations' which Graham attaches to the use and development of land were either ignored or simply denied by a policy regime determined to parade its objective independence, technical excellence and reliance on normative methods. This culturally blind approach produced distinctive planning and policy outcomes that rarely factored in the causes or consequences of ethnic division into decision-making processes. Whilst this helped to insulate planners and planning from accusations of discrimination and bias, it left unchecked a series of dynamics connected to a divided society in rural Northern Ireland. These included seismic shifts of Protestants from border areas, enclaved villages and communities in terminal decline, differential rates of community development and capacities between Protestants and Catholics, a fractured land market, and increasing social distance that undermined the fabric of rural communities bound historically by the common pursuit of agriculture. The chapter contends that these are issues that should represent mainstream concerns for land use planners, as well as policy makers and practitioners engaged in rural regeneration.

The analysis commences by rehearsing briefly some of the mainly ethnographic accounts of the processes and effects of ethnic segregation and how this is reproduced in rural areas both spatially and socially. Empirical evidence from a case study of mid-County Armagh is then used to illustrate the scale, reality and planning costs of segregation in a rural setting. But the main part of the chapter is concerned with the response of policy makers to these conditions and contradictions. This is especially important as both global and local currents are forcing public officials to re-inspect the meaning of segregated space for their core professional values as well as practice.

Thus in relation to the former, the restructuring of agrarian economies from productivist to post-productivist farming systems has produced new forms of exclusion that have stretched the methodological and substantive boundaries of rural planning and development across developed countries. Within Northern Ireland, the legislation embedding the Good Friday Agreement has produced some of the most formidable and rigorous equality policies in the world. These have generated the follow-on requirement to evaluate the distributional effects of public policy and its programmes and decisions on people of different religion, race, gender and those with disabilities. Policies must also contribute to the overarching task of Targeting Social Need (TSN) and in this sphere both equity and social need have produced uncertainty, challenges and important opportunities for rural planning and development. There are also some unresolved contradictions in equality policies and these are explained in the context of the case study evidence. The chapter concludes by suggesting that a concern for rural diversity, social need and fair treatment offers the discipline of land use planning in particular, the scope to contribute positively to rural change, the project of peace and Northern Ireland's uncertain transition to post-conflict stability.

TROUBLED PLACES

The description and analysis of rural divisions in Northern Ireland have originated from largely ethnographic research. The concentration of urban space lends itself to quantified description, spatial mapping and measures of dissimilarity. But in rural areas the boundaries to social and spatial identities are less visible and appreciably more blurred. The importance of the agricultural economy for both religions and the way it cuts across traditional notions of ethnic identity in labour sharing, market exchanges and sub-letting of land is part of the explanation (Dawson, 1997). And so, more explorative and qualitative methodologies, applied to a range of case study environments, have characterised a distinctive tradition in the analysis of rural conflict and separation.

In the early 1950s, Rosemary Harris emphasised the frequent and positive nature of contact between neighbours in the small County Tyrone village of 'Ballybeg'. However, she also highlighted the existence of segregated arenas where religion and social institutions reproduced exclusive patterns of behaviour and community networks. In her description of shopping patterns in the village she pointed out that 'the advantage offered by one shop over its rivals had to be very considerable before a Protestant owner could attract Catholic customers and vice-versa' (Harris, 1972: 6). Leyton's (1975) study of the small

Protestant rural community of 'Perrin' observed that its inhabitants 'see their village as a bastion of Protestant morality and Protestant virtue' (Leyton, 1975: 11–12) but highlighted that, in other areas experiencing high levels of violence, Protestants emphasised their political rather than their religious identity. Similarly, in their analysis of a small border village which they called 'Daviestown', Hamilton et al (1990) highlighted the damaging consequences for community relations of a prolonged paramilitary campaign in the area, especially by 'arousing suspicion and fear and leading to an almost total polarisation and lack of understanding between Catholics and Protestants … The violence had strengthened the constraints which had always existed, leading to increased social segregation and polarisation' (Hamilton et al, 1990: 54–55).

But, Donnan and McFarlane (1986) warned against an overemphasis on religion and ethnic identity in explaining the strength and nature of community interaction in rural areas. For example, they pointed out that kinship patterns were important in land inheritance and that neighbours, regardless of their religion, were frequently involved in sharing arrangements between farmers. In her work, Harris (1972) highlighted the common identity produced by attachment to locality and the pride created by belonging to a community with a sense of place and history. Finally, Donnan and McFarlane pointed to the significance of local social structures and hierarchy based on influence, wealth and social class, which cut across kinship, religious or community bonds. Thus, they concluded that it is difficult to say whether kinship, social class or religion is the determining variable in explaining social relations generally and inter-group contact in particular:

If people are continually switching from one identity to another, from situation to situation, it becomes problematic to assign primacy to any single identity. Nevertheless, at particular times, in particular places, with particular people, some identities may be consistently more weighted than others. (Donnan and McFarlane, 1986: 895–6)

Dawson's (1997) study of North Ards in County Down demonstrated the efforts made by Protestants to keep land within the family, the farming sector and ultimately the same religion. He highlighted the sense of isolation experienced by Protestants in the area using vocabulary more common to the urban genre:

> Dismal visions are symbolised by the imagery of the enclave. To the north and east is the sea which divides the area from Great Britain. To the west are the hills which barely hold back the city sprawl. To the south is the bogland beyond which lies the land that hosts what is a growing, increasingly prosperous and in some eyes, hostile Catholic population. (Dawson, 1997: 49)

In his analysis of land transfers between Protestants and Catholics in the Glenravel ward of North Antrim between 1958 and 1987, Kirk pointed out how Protestant and Catholic farmers accepted lower values for land by selling it within the ethnic group. Table 7.1 shows that 8 per cent of the 529 sales in this period were from Protestants to Catholics and only 4 per cent from Catholics to Protestants. A total of 43 per cent of sales were within-Protestant sales and a further 40 per cent within-Catholic sales. Accordingly, he concluded that 'group interests are best served by the existence of social closure with an absence of land transfer across the religious divide' (Kirk, 1993: 334).

TABLE 7.1 LAND TRANSFERS BY RELIGION IN GLENRAVEL WARD, 1958–1987

Flow	Acres	% Acres	Number	% Number
Protestant to Protestant	4460	55	226	43
Catholic to Catholic	2171	26	211	40
Protestant to Catholic	840	10	41	8
Catholic to Protestant	429	5	23	4
No religion	333	4	28	5
Total	**8233**	**100**	**529**	**100**

Source: T. Kirk (1993), 'The Polarisation of Protestants and Roman Catholics in Rural Northern Ireland: A Case Study of the Glenravel Ward, County Antrim, 1956–1988', unpublished PhD thesis, 496.

Poole and Doherty (1996) have analysed shifts in the population of towns with a population of 5,000 or over in Northern Ireland and have provided particular insights into population change in the border region. Of the twenty towns whose change was examined between 1911 and 1981, fifteen experienced an increase in the Catholic share of their total population. They conclude that 'in consequence, Protestants adjust to the threatening Catholicisation of their town by moving house just enough to ensure that they continue to live in the same kind of local environment as before' (Poole and Doherty, 1996: 248) and also note that this behaviour was greatest in the band of towns close to the border with the Republic of Ireland.

Thus an understanding of population shifts in Northern Ireland goes beyond conventional rural-urban interaction. Stockdale (1991), for example, in an analysis of the process of counter-urbanisation has identified Armagh District and Newry and Mourne District as experiencing the highest levels of rural population growth. She argues that this can be related to a relaxation in planning controls from the late 1970s, personal residential preferences and improving economic alternatives to agriculture. The result is that previous pockets of isolated growth were more generally consolidated by the latter part of the 1980s to produce several major axes of growth, especially in the mainly Catholic areas that skirt the border with the Republic of Ireland. The relationship between ethnicity and behaviour-related spatial outcomes subsequently prompted the completion of a major research project in rural Northern Ireland which is discussed below.

A TROUBLED PLACE: DIVISION IN COUNTY ARMAGH

This analysis draws on research carried out in mid-County Armagh for the Northern Ireland Community Relations Council and includes quantitative surveys and interviews with policy makers and planners (Murtagh, 1999). Figure 7.1 shows the case study area, which in 1991 had a population of 77,538 people. Of this total, 44 per cent were in the north sector, some 16 per cent were in the south sector and 40 per cent were in the middle or interface zone. The research was especially concerned with the processes of change in the interface zone, which is located between the mainly Protestant north sector and mainly Catholic south sector, and sought to explore the effects of segregation in this more contested locale.

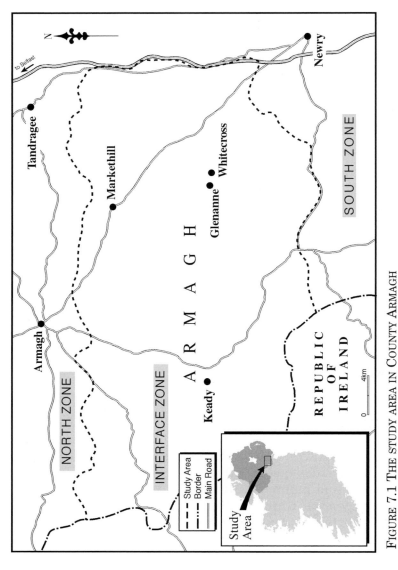

FIGURE 7.1 THE STUDY AREA IN COUNTY ARMAGH

174

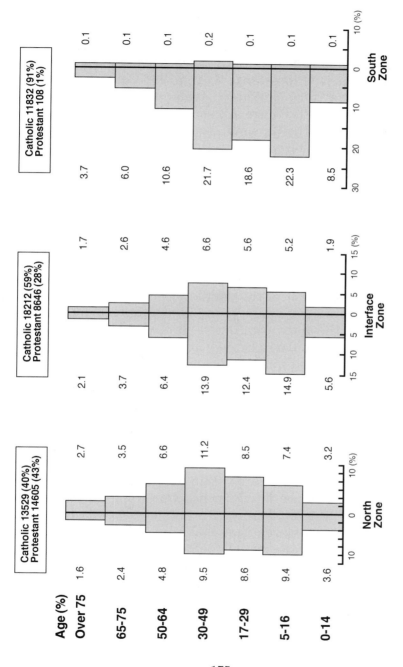

FIGURE 7.2 POPULATION STRUCTURE IN THE COUNTY ARMAGH STUDY AREA ZONES, 1991

Immediate differences in the population characteristics of the two religious groupings became apparent when average household size and age structure was examined. In the interface zone, the average household size was 3.7 persons for Catholics and 3.0 persons for Protestants. At the 1991 Census the overall household size for Northern Ireland was 3.2 persons (Shuttleworth, 1992). Figure 7.2 shows that in the north zone, Protestants and Catholics were, overall, in relatively even proportions, although there were greater numbers and proportions of Catholics in the younger age cohorts. Thus, in the north zone, 13 per cent of the population aged 16 and under was Catholic compared with 11 per cent for equivalent Protestants. Moreover, the Protestant population was slightly older than the Catholic population with only 4 per cent of Catholics aged 65 years and over compared to 6 per cent for Protestants.

In the interface zone, 59 per cent (18,212) of the population was Catholic compared with 28 per cent (8,646) for Protestants. More than 20 per cent of the population were young Catholics (under 16 years old), while young Protestants made up just 7 per cent of the total population. Indeed, older Protestants aged over 50 years outnumbered young Protestants aged under 16 years. The reverse was the case for the Catholic population, where 12 per cent of the population was over 50 years of age. This has profound implications for demographic growth in that the Catholic population has greater long-term potential for renewal, while the Protestant population is aging relative to Catholic trends. In the south zone only 1 per cent of the population was Protestant and marks a decline in the proportion of Protestants living in the area from 19 per cent in 1971. The corresponding increase for Catholics was from 67 per cent in 1971 to 91 per cent in 1991.

Of the thirty-two wards that make up the study area as a whole, only seven were 'mixed' (defined by having Protestants and Catholics in a proportion of between 30 per cent and 70 per cent in each ward). The impact of small area changes in the religious balance of the population is illustrated, for example, by the small town of Keady. Between 1971 and 1991 the proportion of Catholics rose by 10 per cent from 79 per cent to 89 per cent, whereas the Protestant population declined from 9 per cent to 3 per cent. The reverse was the case in Tandragee, for example, where the Protestant population increased from 46 per cent to 64 per cent in the same period, while the proportion of Catholics declined from 16 per cent in 1971 to 13 per cent in 1991. The dominant demographic trend seems to have been a proportional increase in the Catholic population in the south zone and a broadly comparable increase in the Protestant population in the northern part of the study area.

These macro demographic changes both reflect and reproduce patterns of segregation in local communities. They are especially felt in the interface zone where population sorting has created new lines of division, hardened existing cleavages and left some communities isolated or enclaved. While rural areas may lack the visible drama of urban peacelines, the effects of territoriality and segregation can be just as divisive. This is illustrated in an analysis of Glennane and Whitecross, two villages one and a half kilometres apart in the east of the interface zone They are approximately seven kilometres north-west of Newry and nine kilometres south-east of Armagh City. In 1991 Glennane was predominantly Protestant and had a population of 140 persons whilst Whitecross was predominately Catholic and had a population of 170 persons.

A census survey conducted in each village highlighted that Whitecross was 96 per cent Catholic while Glennane was 92 per cent Protestant. One respondent to the survey from Whitecross commented that 'we have probably found ways of not meeting and mixing', thus highlighting the importance of avoidance as a tactic in sub-culture preservation and development. This lack of contact was borne out by the quantitative data which found that almost two-thirds of people in Whitecross said that they never visit Glennane. On the other hand the picture is slightly more complex for Glennane, as residents were more likely to travel through Whitecross to access other transport and service centres. Notwithstanding this necessity, some 29 per cent of respondents said that they never visit Whitecross.

Figures 7.3 and 7.4 map the activity of residents of each village when shopping for comparison goods, convenience goods and services such as visiting the doctor or going for entertainment. The diagrams show that the residents of Glenanne mainly looked north to largely Protestant towns such as Armagh, Markethill and Portadown for their shopping needs. It is interesting that more people travelled to Markethill for these goods than Newry, despite the latter's more dominant functional status and offering a wider number, range and quality of services than Markethill. When the activity profile for Whitecross was examined an almost reverse image emerges. Here, the population was drawn south to the mainly Catholic towns of Newry, Keady and even across the border to Dundalk. Glenanne's troubled history, in part, explains its vulnerability. In 1996, ten Protestant workmen from the village's factory were shot by Republican paramilitaries and this, in turn, followed a number of farmhouse killings of Catholics by Loyalist paramilitaries. The British Army base, just outside the village, was bombed in 1983, three soldiers were killed and the base was later closed. In 1995 the local primary school also closed, making it difficult to attract or retain families and adding to an already delicate demographic profile. A year later the village post office closed and the Orange Hall was destroyed in a fire. As local institutional capacity disassembled, maintaining a critical mass of population in Glenanne has become difficult. Sustainability has a distinctive resonance when communities are struggling to survive in contested ethnic space. The prospects for reversing decline and building a viable population structure are intimately wedded to ethnicity, religion and territory, and, unless these are factored into locality analysis and planning, future prospects look bleak.

In short, differential demographic changes and capacities, activity segregation, fear, uncertainty and population exit all characterise the reality of locality change and management. But, after a period of policy ambivalence, a number of factors are causing a necessary rethink of the meaning of ethnicity for rural planning and development. These policy adjustments are explored in the next section of this chapter.

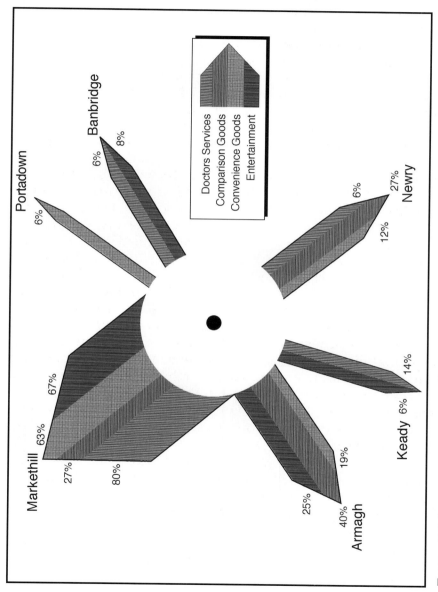

FIGURE 7.3 ACTIVITY ANALYSIS FOR GLENANNE

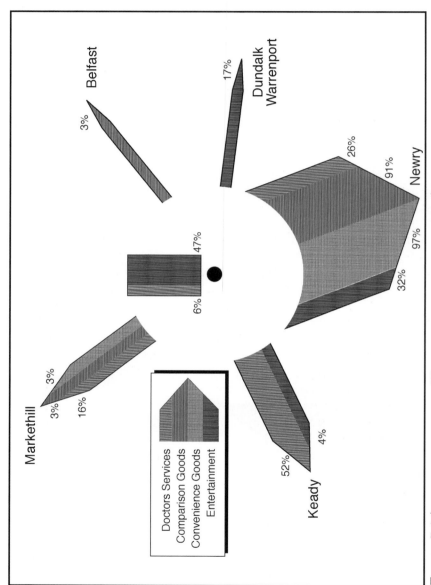

FIGURE 7.4 ACTIVITY ANALYSIS FOR WHITECROSS

PEACE, EQUALITY AND SOCIAL NEED IN RURAL AREAS

Post-industrialisation, globalisation and the unpredictable nature of places have challenged planning and its traditional reliance on quantitative methods and positivist projections of the future. Greater uncertainty characterises the management of spatial change and thus new methodologies, different forms of governance and multiple interests, including women, racial minorities and the poor, are being embraced by public servants struggling to respond to deep and volatile crises in a range of advanced capitalist societies (Healey, 1994). In Northern Ireland, these currents have been given a distinctive momentum by the peace process, Targeting Social Need (TSN) and the equality agenda.

Article 2(i) of the Good Friday Agreement dealing with *Rights, safeguards and equality of opportunity* committed the UK government to make rapid progress with 'a new regional development strategy for Northern Ireland, for consideration by the Assembly, tackling problems of a divided society and social cohesion in urban, rural and border areas' *(The Agreement*, 1998: 19). The Regional Strategic Framework *Shaping Our Future* thus needed to embrace these broad political concerns and, for the first time, make explicit the connection between rural planning and ethnic division. The third Strategic Planning Guideline (SPG 3) in the draft strategy aimed 'To foster development which contributes to community relations, recognises cultural diversity, and reduces socio-economic differentials' (Department of the Environment for Northern Ireland, 1998: 32). This translated to the adoption of a dual approach that aimed to promote residential integration where possible, whilst at the same time recognising the desire of some people and communities to live apart. This reality would be underpinned by the provision of better access for enclaved communities, breaking down physical barriers and supporting the development of shared spaces accessible to both Protestants and Catholics. However, when the draft strategy discussed specific planning objectives related to rural areas, there were no references to ethnic division as a cause or consequence of change in this arena. This omission is thrown into even sharper focus when it is considered that *Shaping Our Future* highlighted the overarching principles of TSN and equality in the formulation and design of the strategic framework and argued that these twin priorities should transcend spatial development programmes.

Targeting Social Need has been the third public expenditure priority in Northern Ireland since the late 1980s and can be read within the continuous and diverse response of the UK government to the Northern Ireland crisis, specific manifestations of Republican discontent and attempts to steer the state to political stability (Murtagh, 1998). The approach was given added impetus by the Good Friday Agreement and aims to bend mainstream resources towards unemployed people, specific groups such as Travellers and disabled people, and 'disadvantaged areas with high levels of unemployment, poverty and poor environmental conditions' (Central Community Relations Unit, 1998: 3). Promoting Social Inclusion has become an integral element of that approach and aims to produce innovative ways of responding to stubborn rates of poverty and unemployment, especially where they are spatially concentrated. Each government department has been tasked with the preparation of an Action Plan that sets out how it is proposed to deal with these obligations. Thus, for example, Table 7.2 summarises the key elements of the New TSN Action Plan for the Rural Development Division of the Department of Agriculture and Rural Development (DARD). The overall objectives of the Rural Development Programme (2000–2006) are set out, together with desired outcomes from implementation. The main elements include developing the capabilities of rural communities, area based actions and community regeneration projects that will be supported by the EU Single Programme for Agriculture and Rural Development.

But, what is less clear is how these aspirations are to work themselves through in highly contested areas, where differential rates of development are producing distinctive futures for Protestant and Catholic communities and where social need cannot be disentangled from the precarious ethnic geography of places such as mid-Armagh. In fact, it is not clear how the objectives of New TSN can be reconciled with the policy emphasis on equality. In short, the pursuit of development programmes targeted at social disadvantage produced by ethnic segregation may require an inequitable distribution of resources between different spatially concentrated religious communities.

TABLE 7.2 NEW TSN ACTION PLAN FOR THE RURAL DEVELOPMENT
DIVISION, DEPARTMENT OF AGRICULTURE AND RURAL DEVELOPMENT

Element	Action
Social need to be tackled:	Economic and social disadvantage in rural areas.
Desired outcome:	To stimulate the economic and social revitalisation of rural areas of Northern Ireland, with a particular focus on the most disadvantaged rural areas of Northern Ireland, through partnership between the public, private and voluntary sectors.
TSN Objective:	To ensure that disadvantaged rural groups can avail of the post-1999 Rural Development Programme.

Source: DARD (1999), *New TSN Action Plan*, p. 5.

The Northern Ireland Act 1998 aims to put into law the commitments of the Good Friday Agreement and the government's White Paper *Partnership for Equality*. Section 75 of the Act makes provisions for all government departments and agencies to prepare Equality Schemes to be submitted to a newly established Equality Commission for Northern Ireland (ECNI). Section 75 of the Act reads:

A public authority shall, in carrying out its functions relating to Northern Ireland, have due regard to the need to promote equality of opportunity —

a. between persons of different religious belief, political opinion, racial group, age, marital status or sexual orientation;

b. between men and women generally;

c. between persons with a disability and persons without; and

d. between persons with dependents and persons without.

Equality Schemes should set out how policies and programmes impact on these groups and the steps to be taken to ensure that any negative or unintended consequences do not adversely affect each category. They should also set out systems for monitoring and recording impacts, staff training and dealing with complaints. Schemes should be subjected to a wide public consultation before being submitted and approved by the Equality Commission. The Equality Commission was established in 1999 and brings together separate organisations dealing with religious, racial, gender and disability discrimination. Related to the preparation of the Schemes is a requirement to evaluate key policies using Equality Impact Assessments. These should assess the effects of programmes and initiatives on the groups identified in Section 75, the measures that might mitigate any adverse effects and consideration of alternative policies that might better achieve the promotion of equality of opportunity (Equality Commission for Northern Ireland, 1999).

The draft Equality Scheme for the Department of Agriculture and Rural Development was published in July 2000 in response to Equality Commission guidelines (DARD, 2000). The Scheme evaluates the impact of each policy and programme against four criteria:

a. Is there any evidence of higher or lower participation or uptake by different (legislatively defined) groups?

b. Is there any evidence that different groups have different needs, experiences, issues and priorities in relation to the main policy area?

c. Is there an opportunity to better promote equality of opportunity or good relations by altering policy or working with others in government or the community at large?

d. Have consultations in the past with relevant representa-
    tive organisations or individuals within groups indicated
    that particular policies create problems that are specific
    to them? (DARD, 2000, section 3.2).

In regard to rural development, Equality Impact Assessments
will be conducted not only on the new Rural Development
Programme, but also PEACE II (Natural Resource and Tourism
Measure), the Transitional Objective 1 Programme relating to
Rural Regeneration, LEADER + and INTERREG III. In its
draft Equality Scheme document, the Department for
Agriculture and Rural Development indicates that each of these
identified programmes will have an impact on the four criteria
set out above. But again, the Scheme contains few details about
how any inequities will be responded to, or how those with a
brief for rural planning and development will acquire the skills
needed to evaluate inequality and construct appropriate policy
and operational responses.

This agenda highlights the value of what Bollens (1999) has
dubbed an 'equity' role for rural planning and development
practitioners. He argues that it is possible to adopt one of four
alternative stances in areas of ethnic conflict (Table 7.3).

TABLE 7.3 POLICY ROLES IN AREAS OF ETHNIC CONFLICT

Strategy	Tactics
Neutral	Address the symptoms of ethnic conflict at individual level
Equity	Address symptoms of ethnic conflict at ethnic group level
Resolver	Address root causes of conflict
Partisan	Maintain or increase disparities

Source: Adapted from S. Bollens (1999), *Urban Peace-building in Divided
Societies,* p. 24.

Setting aside the perversity of a partisan strategy, the 'equity'
approach represents a departure from the 'neutral' positions
adopted by government planners in the previous thirty years,

but, as Bollens makes clear, it addresses the symptoms of conflict at the group or ethnic-religious level. He argues that this provides a limited basis upon which to engage the root causes of alienation, fear and decline that can be recognised in places such as Glenanne. The reality is that places similar to Glenanne and Whitecross produce very different policy imperatives and demand distinctive responses in terms of equality and social need. A benign attempt to equalise resources or opportunities might, thus, preclude a clear analysis of the processes, not the consequence, of rural change. In this scenario, blanket policies may limit the scope to sensitise strategies to the particular needs of individual communities experiencing decline as a result of their precarious position in contested ethnic space. A 'resolver' stance, on the other hand, assumes the adoption of problem-centred approaches and implies that what might be applicable in one area or community might not be suitable in another. An inclusive approach to problem scanning may better suit the complex interplay between rural change, population exit and territorial closure identified above in mid-Armagh. Specifically, a resolver-centred approach means having the confidence to rely on a mix of methods and consultative processes that might help to build alternative routes out of deprivation and disadvantage for enclaved communities. Practitioners in this context could embrace some of the interest mediation skills developed in other conflict situations and apply dispute resolution techniques that speak directly to the contested nature of areas, and consider how they can recover ethnically as well as economically. A strategy for regeneration that recognises the distinctive problems of Protestant Glenanne and its lack of capacity to engage mainstream rural development resources would fit within TSN policy and, presumably, the emphasis in equality legislation on restoring imbalances in opportunity, in this case for people living in an enclaved village. This offers nothing short of a radical agenda for rural planning and development.

But, there are significant issues surrounding the construction of such an approach. Key questions include, whether it would be read as equitable by the Catholics of Whitecross with their own economic problems, whether it could be legislatively challenged under other aspects of the Northern Ireland Act on the basis of resource distribution, and whether and with whom the mix of skills exist to put such a response together? An involvement in rural planning and development along these lines is fraught with difficulties and apparent contradictions, but translating the values of social justice and equality of opportunity into practice could help to make policy and practice more relevant to and less detached from, the hard realities of ethnic geography and how it is produced and consumed.

CONCLUSION

The brief discussion in this chapter of *Shaping Our Future*, and the New TSN Action Plan and draft Equality Scheme for the Department of Agriculture and Rural Development suggests that policy responses to ethnic segregation are firmly located at the strategic and aspirational level. There seems to be little detailed articulation of broad policy concerns in operational practice, how new competencies implied for rural managers will be acquired, or how equality and New TSN policies fit together when complex choices and sectarian trade-offs seem inevitable. The raft of responses to the Northern Ireland conflict have produced a plethora of policies and initiatives and, it could be argued, reflect an increasingly desperate attempt by the UK government to manage crisis and embed peace. The Good Friday Agreement spoke to a wide range of constituencies in an attempt to be inclusive and sellable. But it also produced a range of priorities that appear at times to be contradictory or, at least, where the connections between them have only been weakly thought through. This is especially the case in the relationship between targeting social need and equality, as the former will inevitably involve responding to the distinctive needs of one community or the other, especially given the high rates of spatial segregation which exist across Northern Ireland.

It is hardly surprising then, that these issues have been couched in aspirational language rather than in the fine grain of operational policy or decision-making criteria. Mixing ethnicity,

187

equity and social need into rural planning and development is a difficult task and requires a range of competencies that are not the core priorities of, for example, the mainstream planning profession. The required skills of land use planners preparing the Regional Development Strategy for Northern Ireland, as prescribed by the Royal Town Planning Institute, were conceived in and refined for very different (and mainly urban) circumstances than those in rural places such as mid-Armagh. Reliance on procedural and technical values offers little prescriptive guidance when dealing with wicked problems of ethnic conflict and poverty.

But it is vital that planners acquire and develop new skills in the analysis of ethno-spatial change and its effects, and that mainstream planning opens up to the range of ethnographic methodologies which might assist with understanding the effects of segregation and life in rural enclaves. Developing consultation methods sensitive to the needs of single-identity communities, dispute resolution techniques and conflict mediation approaches all have a role to play in this sphere and can contribute to the better management of troubled places. Monitoring and evaluating the effects of policies on a range of interests and groups requires a broader interpretation of impact assessment than merely the effects of planning decisions on the condition or quality of the environment. Flexible and adaptive approaches to communities in social need, whilst monitoring and adjusting for the distributional effects of policies on different religions, races, genders and people with disabilities, offers a major opportunity for planning to contribute to the effective renewal of marginal rural areas. Such an agenda has important implications for planning education and how graduates are equipped with the necessary combination of skills to make a valued contribution to the mediation of competing interests, the closure of social distance and the shared concern for peace in Northern Ireland.

REFERENCES

Bollens, S. (1999), *Urban Peace-building in Divided Societies,* Boulder, Colorado: Westview Press.

Central Community Relations Unit (1998), *New TSN,* Belfast: CCRU.

Dawson, A. (1997), 'Identity and Strategy in Post-productionist Agriculture: A Case Study from Northern Ireland, in H. Donnan and G. McFarlane (eds), *Culture and Policy in Northern Ireland,* Belfast: Institute of Irish Studies.

Department of Agriculture and Rural Development (1999), *New TSN Action Plan for the Department of Agriculture and Rural Development,* Belfast: DARD.

Department of Agriculture and Rural Development (2000), *Draft Equality Scheme for the Department of Agriculture and Rural Development,* Belfast: DARD.

Department of the Environment for Northern Ireland (1998), *Shaping Our Future: Draft Regional Strategic Framework for Northern Ireland,* Belfast: HMSO.

Donnan, H. and G. McFarlane (1986), 'You Get on Better with Your Own: Social Continuity and Change in Rural Northern Ireland', in P. Clancey, S. Drudy, K. Lynch and L. O' Dowd (eds), *Ireland: A Sociological Profile,* Dublin: Institute of Public Administration in association with the Sociological Association of Ireland.

Equality Commission for Northern Ireland (1999), *Guide to Statutory Duties: A Guide to the Implementation of the Statutory Duties on Public Authorities Arising from Section 75 of the Northern Ireland Act 1998,* Belfast: ECNI.

Graham, B. (1997), *In Search of Ireland,* London: Routledge.

Hamilton, A., C. McCartney, T. Anderson and A. Finn (1990), *Violence and Communities,* Coleraine: Centre for the Study of Conflict, University of Ulster.

Harris, R. (1972), *Prejudice and Tolerance in Ulster: A Study of Neighbours and Strangers in a Border Community,* Manchester: Manchester University Press.

Healey, P. (1994), 'Discourses of Integration: Making Frameworks for Democratic Urban Planning', in P. Healey, S. Cameron, S. Davoudi, S. Graham and A. Madani-Pour (eds),

Managing Cities: The New Urban Context, Chichester: John Wiley and Sons.

Kirk, T. (1993), 'The Polarisation of Protestants and Roman Catholics in Rural Northern Ireland: A Case Study of the Glenravel Ward, County Antrim, 1956–1988', unpublished PhD thesis, School of Geosciences, Queen's University, Belfast.

Leyton, E. (1975), *The One Blood: Kinship and Class in an Irish Village,* Newfoundland: Memorial University.

Murtagh, B. (1998), 'Planning for Anywhere: Housing Policy in Northern Ireland', *Housing Studies,* vol. 13, no. 6: 833–839.

Murtagh, B. (1999), *Community and Conflict in Rural Ulster,* Coleraine: Centre for the Study of Conflict, University of Ulster.

Poole, M. and P. Doherty (1996), *Ethnic Residential Segregation in Northern Ireland,* Coleraine: Centre for the Study of Conflict, University of Ulster.

Shuttleworth, I. (1992), 'Population Change in Northern Ireland, 1981–1991: Preliminary Results of the 1991 Census of Population', *Irish Geography,* vol. 1, no. 25: 83–88.

Stockdale, A. (1991), Recent Trends in Urbanisation and Rural Population in Northern Ireland, *Irish Geography,* vol. 24, no. 2: 70–80.

The Agreement (1998), agreement reached at the multi-party talks, Belfast.

CHAPTER 8

CIVIL SOCIETY, SOCIAL CAPITAL FORMATION AND LEADER 2

Mark Scott

INTRODUCTION

Bottom up approaches to rural development are essentially concerned with managing change, mediated through active local communities. This suggests that the ability to be effective in this arena and to realise a rural vision is dependent on the concept of *learning communities*, whose focus is on created assets rather than solely endowed assets. Although a significant diversification of the local economic base represents development, so also does the creation of additional capacity for positive change such as new investment resources or new local structures to make decisions and to take organisational action (O'Cinnéide and Keane, 1990). Fundamental to this process is the formation of social capital.

This chapter examines the creation and utilisation of social capital in rural Northern Ireland through the EU LEADER Programme. The chapter commences with a brief exploration of the concept of social capital and its relationship with civil society and local development. This is followed by a short introduction to the LEADER programme. The remainder of the chapter considers three aspects of social capital formation within this operational context: building networks; developing future know-how through collaboration; and the combined collective capacity to influence action. The discussion draws on extensive qualitative research involving semi-structured interviews with LEADER 2 participants.

CIVIL SOCIETY AND LOCAL DEVELOPMENT: THE ENGAGEMENT OF
SOCIAL CAPITAL

Civil society is frequently advanced as an alternative form of
mediation to replace the activity of mass parties, corporatist
organisations, and interest groups which have characterised
politics in Western countries for most of the past century.
According to Friedmann (1998):

Civil society refers to that part of social, as distinct from
corporate life that lies beyond the immediate control of the
state. It is the society of households, family networks, civic
and religious organisations and communities that are bound
to each other by shared histories, collective memories and
culturally specific forms of reciprocity. (252)

Democratising a socially responsible framework for civil society
involves the creation of dialogic spaces capable of stimulating
pluralist engagement (Giddens, 1994). Out of such discourse
can come what Gaffikin and Morrissey (1999) have termed a
'creative disturbance' of ideas which unsettle conventional
canons and generate fresh agendas. Increasingly, the role of
social capital formation is central to debates concerning civil
society.

Social capital is a phrase which has gained much currency in
academic and political circles and is defined by the World Bank
(2000) as: 'the norms and social relations that enable people to
coordinate action to achieve desired goals'. Its most influential
advocate is Robert Putnam (1993; 2000) and for whom social
capital refers to features of social organisation, such as the
trust, norms and networks that can improve the efficiency of
society by facilitating coordinated actions and cooperation for
mutual benefit. Putnam argues that strong traditions of civic
engagement are the hallmarks of a successful region and, moreover, that stocks of social capital tend to be self-reinforcing and
cumulative. Successful collaboration in one sphere builds the
trust that can facilitate future collaboration in another area of
endeavour. Putnam argues that voluntary cooperation is easier

in a community that has a substantial stock of social capital in the form of norms of reciprocity and networks of civic engagement. In this way, through interaction and collaboration, trust can reach sufficient levels to allow for reductions in transaction costs. Thus, for example, Flora (1998) suggests that social capital can improve the efficiency of other forms of capital such as financial/manufacturing capital, human capital and environmental capital. Similar to other forms of capital, social capital is productive and makes possible the achievement of certain ends not attainable in its absence.

Flora and Flora (2000) suggest that social capital is a long-term characteristic of a spatial community and varies very much from place to place. The characteristics of high social capital situations are listed by Frazer (1999) as including: strong networks of neighbours and extended families; a strong community infrastructure, such as community groups, playgroups and religious organisations; high levels of civic participation; good communication; a positive self-image; and a positive external image. Moreover, social capital thrives when individuals within a social system interact with one another in multiple roles over a period of time (Flora, 1998). Therefore, it would appear that for successful local development to take place, these characteristics should be harnessed or strengthened through a rural development process. Indeed, as Murray (2000) contends:

> strong participatory citizenship, whereby people are involved in planning and in implementation, in facilitative leadership roles and in creating better futures for their own communities, is inextricably linked to the existence of social capital networks of engagement. (101)

The LEADER programme and the related work of Local Action Groups offer a useful illustration of a collaborative process which has drawn on and enhanced social capital in rural Northern Ireland during the 1990s.

LEADER IN NORTHERN IRELAND

The LEADER programme (Links between Actions for the Development of the Rural Economy) was introduced in 1991 and represents a venture by the European Commission's DGVI (Agriculture) to initiate a participatory approach to rural development. LEADER reflects a growing consensus in Europe concerning what community-led rural development is and how it should best be promoted. It embodies the essential elements of a bottom-up approach, which include an endogenous development emphasis, a territorial focus involving the preparation and implementation of local development programmes geared to local requirements, the creation of public-private-voluntary sector partnerships, and the genuine involvement of local people by mobilising them as resource for rural development (Moseley, 1995, 1997). The support for LEADER, therefore, demonstrates the realisation within the European Commission that rural development should be regarded as 'development *by* and *of* the local community, not just *for* it' and that decisions are more likely to 'stick' if they are taken locally and reflect a community consensus (Moseley, 1997: 202).

LEADER 1 was implemented in Northern Ireland by the Rural Development Council, which awarded financial support to a range of local projects. LEADER 2, in contrast, which covered the period 1994 to 1999, was much more extensive and comprised a larger budget and wider participation. A total of fifteen LEADER Partnerships or Local Action Groups (LAGs) were established in the region (Figure 8.1), each with a partnership board, professional staff, a strategy, and a budget ranging from £250,000 to £1 million. The LAGs tended to concentrate on a local economic development role in rural areas, with small and medium-sized enterprises, rural tourism and the exploitation of agricultural products being the most common themes supported. In addition, the LAGs have been involved in stakeholder-based consensus-building processes and have fused technical knowledge and local experience with action outcomes.

FIGURE 8.1 DISTRIBUTION OF LEADER 2 LOCAL ACTION GROUPS IN NORTHERN IRELAND

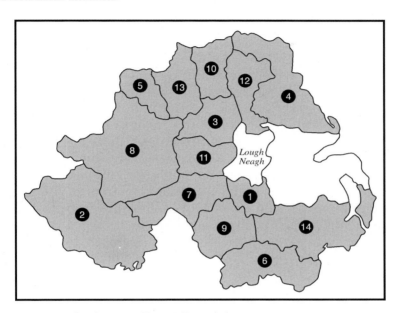

1	Craigavon Rural Development
2	Fermanagh LAG
3	Magherafelt Area Partnership
4	North Antrim LEADER
5	Rural Area Partnership in Derry
6	South Down/South Armagh LAG
7	South Tyrone Area Partnership
8	West Tyrone 2000
9	Armagh District LAG
10	Coleraine LAG (COLLAGE)
11	Cookstown LEADER
12	Lower Bann LAG
13	Roe Valley LEADER
14	Rural Down Partnership
15	(not shown on map) – Canal Corridor Partnership

The chapter now considers the extent to which these LAGs have harnessed or developed social capital through a combination of collaborative processes.

BUILDING NETWORKS

Participation in local development

LEADER groups involved the wider community in local development by initially including people in the preparation of a local strategy and then funding a suite of projects. Overall, the results achieved have been mixed in terms of success. A tightly compressed timetable for submitting operational plans to the Department of Agriculture for Northern Ireland (DANI) was a serious disadvantage for the groups, as was the lack of community infrastructure to engage in strategic debate in many of the areas. This often led to a narrow involvement, focusing on administrative and professional elites without wider consultation. In some instances an operational plan was prepared even before a partnership board had been established. In these instances, a major opportunity was missed to develop a vision for the rural area based on a participatory approach to strategic planning. However, other LAGs, such as North Antrim and South Down/South Armagh, by drawing on their established community group constituencies, were able to involve a wide range of community interests. But this tended to focus on groups which were already organised and which were in a position to contribute.

Some imaginative arrangements to engage local people in strategic planning were developed. For example, Armagh District LAG animated new community groups and business interests by facilitating participation in village action plans and involvement with the Armagh Business Centre. Both these methods opened the communication lines between the District Council and the community and private sectors. Coleraine LAG introduced community group role-playing scenarios in its strategic planning process. In each case the realisation of new lines of communication and new skills contributed to local ownership of the strategies.

The second method of involving people in local development was through the funding of projects. At the outset DANI had determined that the ceiling for grant aid by LAGs would be in the range of £20,000–£30,000. Funding at this low level would thus provide for a spreading of resources to a large number of project promoters. Thus, by the end of 1999, over 2000 projects had received commitments for funding (Department of Agriculture and Rural Development, 2000), varying, for example, from forty projects under the auspices of Lower Bann LAG to some 170 projects by North Antrim LEADER. This approach, which could be described as 'scatter-gun', was marked by a very wide spread of projects and possibly too small an amount of money to have a lasting impact. However, compared to LEADER 1 in Northern Ireland, which operated a flagship approach and gave £4 million funding to fifteen projects, there is little doubt that the LEADER 2 method has extended the spatial coverage of rural development participation. The exploration of potential linkages across such a spread of projects has been investigated by West Tyrone LAG as a way to create clusters of development and indirectly to also add to the social capital base of a local area.

Local networks and horizontal interaction

Local networks and horizontal links have been strengthened through the involvement of key stakeholders on LEADER boards. In terms of representation, the practice of a three-way partnership between a District Council, local business and the community/voluntary sectors has emerged as the general model, with the additional involvement of statutory and key local agencies as appropriate. LEADER boards have thus provided a forum for communication between multiple interests in rural areas and, interestingly, were doing this before the advent of the EU Special Support Programme for Peace and Reconciliation which led to the setting up of District Partnerships. In some instances the basic partnership model was extended quite considerably by an effective sub-group structure. North Antrim LEADER, for example, attracted over forty additional stakeholders to membership of sub-groups, thus involving almost sixty people, including board members, in local decision making.

Networks have also been extended through the relationship of LAG with other local programmes such as those led by the

District Partnerships, Area-Based Strategy Groups, and District Councils. The joint management of local programmes, shared board members between the programmes, and interaction between the managers of local initiatives have been notable features of this collaboration. This horizontal interaction has led to the funding of joint projects between the programmes and has helped direct potential promoters to suitable funders. A significant limitation to this effort, however, has been the absence of a common local vision to provide a shared point of reference between local programmes and to clarify the distinctive roles for each to play.

Inclusion

As discussed above, the LAG boards generally established three-way cross-sectoral partnerships. Nonetheless, there were noticeable deficiencies in the structure of their memberships. These included a low rate of female participation and low levels of representation by trade unions and environmental interests. Young people and those groups who are experiencing rural disadvantage, such as the unemployed, were also largely absent.

In terms of the distribution of funding, the majority of LAGs relied on a 'commit and spend' philosophy that often resulted in funding being given to individuals who were already in a position to help themselves. To target those most in need some LAGs developed an alternative programme-led delivery approach which, when combined with animation of the target groups, proved an effective method to relate funding more closely to local community needs.

Trust and respect

A key feature of many of the LAGs has been the nurturing of new trust relationships within the board setting. This has taken two forms. Firstly, cross-sectoral dialogue has helped to break down the barriers of mistrust among representatives, particularly those experienced between the community/voluntary interests and District Councils, and also to a lesser extent with the private sector. The evidence suggests that there has been a shared commitment to work together. As O'Donnell and Thomas (1998) argue, partnership in this form is necessary because no party can achieve its goals without a significant degree of support from the others.

In the context of Northern Ireland, the opportunity for cross-community dialogue between Catholics and Protestants, Nationalists and Unionists has been as important as cross-sectoral interaction. Although this has largely taken place within the dominant local economic development discourse, it has provided a significant step in building new relational resources of mutual respect. This has profound implications for creating social capital of the bridging type.

DEVELOPING FUTURE KNOW-HOW THROUGH COLLABORATION

Mutual learning

Know-how for change can live on among participants even after a group disbands and, therefore, can help to institutionalise coordinated action in the long run (Innes et al, 1994). In order to do this it may be necessary for local stakeholders to acquire new knowledge and skills. A significant consequence of collaboration within LEADER boards has been the enhanced opportunity for members to learn from each other. This mutual learning often led to behavioural changes both within the board and among participants in some of the programmes. Within the board, for example, members reported 'new ways of working' and the changing 'styles of discussion' by some of the other sectoral representatives. This is summed up by the following two inter-view extracts:

I've learnt how to interact more, with community groups and different sectors, but also with other District Councils, and working with councils on other ideas ... This first contact with other councils was often through LEADER. (Councillor)

I think we've learnt from the councillors — we *do* benefit from their experience. But they've learnt from us [commu-nity groups] too. They've learnt to tread carefully and they can see that they are answerable to members of the community. They are used to the 'argy bargy' of the council chamber. But there's no 'argy bargy' in LEADER. We have to work in cooperation. (Community group representative)

Communication and interaction increasingly allowed for shared understanding of the local area by LAG members. Often, for the first time, board members were able to develop a more 'complete picture' of the existing situation, rather than simply a sectoral perspective. This has led to an improved identification of local needs and opportunities and, in some instances, to the creation of a multi-dimensional analysis that was absent in the original operational plan. These benefits of interaction and the corresponding behavioural changes have helped to develop new skills within LAGs such as negotiating, bargaining and problem solving.

Behavioural changes have also emerged among beneficiaries in LEADER programmes. In the farming sector, for example, projects have emerged for exploiting niche markets through joint business planning and collective purchasing and marketing. These projects had not been included in original operational plans but had emerged during a constant communicative process. The participating farmers developed a sense that innovative solutions are increasingly needed and that these could include cooperation with those previously viewed locally as competitors. Furthermore, board members without farming knowledge became more aware of realistic alternatives to conventional farming, which in the past may have only included simplistic notions around agri-tourism.

LAG BOARD CAPACITY

The early phase of LEADER 2 in Northern Ireland was characterised by a compressed timetable for LAGs to form a partnership board and to prepare a local strategy. This was unfortunate, as the planning exercise could itself have been developed as a learning experience to acquire new skills among the board members. However, although this opportunity was not grasped, board members and indeed other rural stakeholders have indicated that know-how has been developed:

> The board has come a long way. We are working better as a board, getting used to it, and we are a lot more confident. (Community group representative)

> I think people have learnt a lot from the process of partnership. It took some of the less experienced a good while to catch up, maybe six months to a year. But this last year there has been a marked difference — they're having a good impact. (International Fund for Ireland representative)

Changes in the levels of performance *vis-à-vis* identified implementation gaps provide a useful insight into improved LAG capacity. Very often these adjustments comprised a budget review, a strategic review or a change in delivery approach, with the latter two of more significance. The strategic reviews were usually undertaken by the board and manager, without the assistance of outside consultants, and thus were an indication of the increased confidence and, indeed, leadership of the groups. Generally, there was a perceived improvement in the revised plans compared to the original consultant-driven operational plans, with this shift towards a more participatory strategic planning approach suggesting the development of some necessary skills at the board level. Changes in mode of delivery among some of the LAGs, from a reactive, application-led approach to a proactive, programme-led approach can be regarded as a further illustration of improved capacity.

Individual capacity within the LAG board

A marked difference in capacity was evident among the participating board members, with some well experienced in local government or community development initiatives, and others new to local development. These differences in capacity had important consequences for interaction within the LAG board. At the beginning of the LEADER programme, some of the less experienced personnel expressed great difficulty in becoming involved in discussions or grasping the complexity of the issues. Those with experience and know-how tended to dominate meetings. However, over the course of the programme, there was a substantial improvement in the individual confidence of those previously inexperienced, as one research interviewee commented:

> I really want to stay involved with LEADER after LEADER 2 has been completed — well, there's a few reasons why. Firstly, I'm a woman, and at the moment there is no other woman representative on the board. But mainly I want to stay involved because now that I've built up knowledge of what's happening, I don't want to stop. I'm now in a position to make a positive contribution. (Community group representative)

Certainly, in many cases, there was a high level of technical expertise among those members of LAG boards with backgrounds in business, government or the voluntary sector. However, this does not necessarily imply that these individuals also possessed the necessary skills in negotiation and collective problem solving. As one interviewee commented:

> I thought I had the right skills, with quite a lot of experience working in council. But partnerships are different. I had to learn how to interact more with different interests. (Councillor)

This suggests an awareness that board members need to develop know-how, not only in the substantive area of rural development, but also in how to participate effectively in a partnership setting.

THE COMBINED COLLECTIVE CAPACITY TO INFLUENCE ACTION

The combined capacity to influence action is created through the formation of alliances and agreements that provide mutual gain and increase the possibility that proposals will be adopted

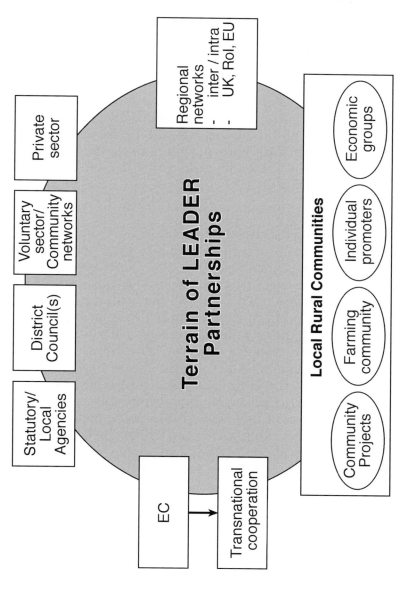

FIGURE 8.2 THE TERRAIN OF LEADER PARTNERSHIPS

Source: Adapted from F. Gaffikin and M. Morrissey (1998), 'Why Partnerships?', Border Crossing Project, unpublished report.

and implemented (Innes et al, 1994). One approach to examining the capacity of the LAGs to influence action would be to evaluate the impact of the projects supported by LEADER and to calculate the additionality of the programme outcomes. However, many projects have yet to mature or, at the time of writing, are still at an implementation stage, suggesting that an outcome evaluation is not yet possible. An alternative approach to assessing ability to influence action would be to examine the *terrain* within which the LEADER groups have been operationalised and to assess how the LAGs have added value to local development. Figure 8.2 offers a schematic of this:

A number of features can be identified that demonstrate the added-value of LEADER 2.

* *Networking*

This has been a strong feature of LEADER in Northern Ireland, with LAGs involved in intra-regional and European networking. The former has been facilitated by the Northern Ireland LEADER Network (NILN), established by the LAGs in 1996. Managers generally described NILN as particularly useful at the beginning of the programme as it provided a forum for the professional staff to regularly meet, to resolve early difficulties, and to engage in the transfer of ideas. The NILN has also provided lobbying support on a collective basis to DANI, for example, in relation to the future direction of rural development in Northern Ireland. This joint voice is perceived as considerably increasing the influence of LEADER groups in the policy arena. The inter-regional networking within the UK has, perhaps, been less successful. Financial difficulties led to the UK LEADER Network (UKLN) being established as late in the programme as 1998. A major role of the UKLN has been in relation to rural development post-1999 and lobbying the EC through the preparation of position papers. At the European level, the networking function has been provided by the LEADER Observatory, which provides an information role and disseminates best practice through conferences, publications, and the Internet. No other local development programme in rural areas in Northern Ireland has had this networking feature, which has helped

LEADER groups to make connections across Europe and to reduce the isolation of many rural areas.

• *Transnational cooperation*
Although LAG managers often expressed difficulties in relation to establishing transnational cooperation projects, this aspect represents a clear added-value of LEADER in Northern Ireland. However, it would seem that the full potential of this activity has yet to be fully realised in that projects have developed as 'show case' initiatives, rather than addressing a specific need or function. But transnational cooperation has also encouraged LAGs to develop cross-border links with LEADER groups in the Republic of Ireland. For example, the West Tyrone LEADER group has formed a cross-border partnership with its counter-part in County Donegal. This has allowed the Tyrone-Donegal Partnership to secure additional funding from the International Fund for Ireland and INTERREG.

• *Beneficiaries*
The principal focus of the Northern Ireland Rural Development Programme through to 2000 has been on community groups and community-based projects. Although LEADER groups have also funded community groups, their emphasis has more generally been on individual promoters. This has allowed for a broadening of the rural development perspective in Northern Ireland to include the development of links with the farming community. However, few of the LAGs have targeted capacity building at individuals or specific economic groups in relation to enterprise training, animation of cross-border tourism oper-ators, or business planning for farmers.

• *Target area*
The explicit rural focus of the LEADER groups, which excluded involvement in the cities and regional towns, indicates an added-value of the programme. LAGs have extended the geographical scope of rural development activity beyond the five target areas of disadvantaged rural communities, and have operated much more widely.

- *Inter-district council relations*

Six of Northern Ireland's LEADER 2 groups have operated on an inter-District Council area basis, with these LEADER boards providing a forum for councillors and officers from neighbouring districts. In some instances this has led to the development of further initiatives. For example, Lower Bann LEADER company has drawn on the support of three District Councils and has established an international four-way partnership with local authorities in Buffalo (USA), Niagara (Canada) and County Offaly (Republic of Ireland). This partnership has been dubbed 'the Atlantic Corridor', with the aim of providing access points in Europe for US and Canadian companies. The important point here is that although the LAG board has been managing the project, LEADER has not been a source of funding.

CONCLUSION

LEADER groups in Northern Ireland have been able to create considerable social capital resources for effecting rural development actions. The organisational partnership approach has facilitated mutual learning through multi-sectoral and cross-community discussion, which has led to an increasingly shared understanding of local contexts and commitments to collaborative work. On occasions this has opened up fresh possibilities in new relational settings.

In dealing with social capital formation, this chapter has concerned itself with an important *process* of rural development. Yet much of the evaluation work carried out on the Northern Ireland Rural Development Programme has been concerned with demonstrating visible quantifiable returns, in particular value-for-money job creation. This focus on the end products of rural development fails to recognise that successful programme outcomes are inextricably linked to effective processes, and that these processes of rural development can, in turn, have important local impacts. This underlines the need for a wider perspective of appreciation in regard to rural planning and development outcomes and which recognises process-related goals, such as social capital creation. A total quality approach requires a new responsiveness to organisational capacity.

REFERENCES

Allen, J. (1998), 'Community Conflict Resolution: The Development of Social Capital within an Interactional Field' paper presented at the conference 'Social Capital — Bridging Disciplines, Policies and Communities, April 20–22, Michigan University.

Amdam, J. (1995), 'Mobilisation, Participation and Partnership Building in Local Development Planning: Experience from Local Planning on Women's Conditions in Six Norwegian Communes', *European Planning Studies*, vol. 3, no. 3: 305–332.

Amin, A. and Thrift, N. (1995), 'Globalisation, Institutional "thickness" and the Local Economy', in P. Healey, S. Cameron, S. Davoudi, S. Graham and A. Madani-Pour, (eds), *Managing Cities, The New Urban Context*, Chichester: John Wiley and Sons.

Department of Agriculture and Rural Development (2000), *LEADER II in Northern Ireland, A Measure of Success*, Belfast: DARD.

Flora, C. and J. Flora (2000), Building Social Capital, Social Capital Let's Talk, *The World Bank's E-mail Discussion Group on Social Capital*, accessed at www.worldbank.org /poverty/scapital/sctalk/talk29.

Flora, J. (1998), 'Social Capital and Community', paper presented at the conference 'Social Capital — Bridging Disciplines, Policies and Communities', April 20–22, Michigan University.

Frazer, H. (1999), 'What it Takes Today to Build Communities', paper presented at the conference 'Building Successful Communities', May 24–25, NICVA.

Friedmann, J. (1998), 'Planning Theory Revisited', *European Planning Studies*, vol. 6, no. 3: 245–253.

Gaffikin, F. and M. Morrissey (1998), 'Why Partnerships?', Border Crossings Project, unpublished report.

Gaffikin, F. and M. Morrissey (1999), *City Visions: Imagining Place, Enfranchising People*, London: Pluto Press.

Giddens, A. (1994), *Beyond Left and Right: The Future of Radical Politics*, Cambridge: Polity Press.

Healey, P. (1997) *Collaborative Planning: Shaping Places in Fragmented Societies*, London: MacMillan Press.

Hughes, J., C. Knox, M. Murray and J. Greer (1998), *Partnership Governance in Northern Ireland*, Dublin: Oak Tree Press.

Innes, J., J. Gruber, R. Thompson and M. Neuman (1994), *Coordinating Growth and Environmental Management Through Consensus Building*, Berkeley: University of California.

Innes, J. (1996) 'Planning Through Consensus Building', *Journal of the American Planning Association, Autumn*, 460–471.

Keane, M. (1998), 'The Changing Role of Statutory Agencies in Rural Development post-1999', *Pleanáil, The Journal of the Irish Planning Institute*, No. 14: 117–128.

Low, M. (1999), 'Their Masters' Voice: Communitarianism, Civic Order, and Political Representation', *Environment and Planning A*, vol. 31: 87–111.

Moseley, M. (1995), 'The LEADER Programme 1992–94: An Assessment of a European Area-based Rural Development Programme', unpublished paper, Cheltenham and Gloucester College of Higher Education.

Moseley, M. (1997), 'New Directions in Rural Community Development', *Built Environment*, vol. 23, no. 3: 201–209.

Murray, M. (2000), 'Social Capital Formation and Healthy Communities: Insights from the Colorado Healthy Communities Initiative', *Community Development Journal*, vol. 35, no. 2: 99–108.

O'Cinnéide, M. and M. Keane (1990), 'Applying Strategic Planning to Local Economic Development', *Town Planning Review*, vol. 61, no. 4: 475–486.

O' Donnell, R. and D. Thomas (1998), 'Partnership and Policy Making, in S. Healy and B. Reynolds (eds), *Social Policy in Ireland: Principles, Practice and Problems*, Dublin: Oak Tree Press.

Porter, M. (1996), 'What is Strategy?', *Harvard Business Review*, November–December: 61-78.

Putnam, R. (1993), 'Making Democracy Work: Civic Traditions in Modern Italy', Princeton, New Jersey: Princeton University Press.

Putnam, R. (2000), *Bowling Alone: The Collapse and Revival of American Community*, New York: Simon and Schuster.

Schon, D. (1991), *The Reflective Practitioner: How Professionals Think in Action*, Aldershot: Arena.

Voluntary Activity Unit (1996), *Monitoring and Evaluation of Community Development in Northern Ireland*, Belfast: Department of Health and Social Services.

World Bank (2000), accessed at www.worldbank.org/poverty/scapital/index.

CHAPTER 9

LEARNING COMMUNITIES: PARTICIPATORY PLANNING AT THE LOCAL SCALE

Nick Mack and Rachel Naylor

INTRODUCTION

A widespread feature of contemporary rural development practice is the contribution of local people to the creation, planning and implementation of ideas which build on local physical, social and cultural resources. Furthermore, it is now an established convention that participation should be as inclusive as possible and should draw different people with their varied backgrounds into a process of development. In this way, people can become stakeholders with benefits for social cohesion and local resources can be mobilised more effectively and equitably. This chapter introduces an approach towards enabling citizenship called the 'learning community'. It outlines the tools used to facilitate participation and learning and reviews the experience thus far of a pilot project being undertaken by the Rural Development Council[1] with a cluster of communities in County Down.

---

1   The Rural Development Council published a workbook titled *Learning Communities* in 2001. This is designed to assist community facilitators who are working with communities to identify local needs and produce action plans for addressing these needs.

LEARNING COMMUNITIES AND CULTURAL CAPITAL

The learning community approach to rural development seeks to draw people into a strategic planning process which is empowering, inclusive, builds a sense of community and has continuity. It requires considerable reflection and collaboration in order to influence local action and wider decision making. The concept is grounded in an appreciation of the value of cultural capital which extends beyond local traditions, festivals or arts activities, important as these are to enhancing community identity and confidence. Cultural capital comprises collective knowledge and know-how, and ranges from technical knowledge to the informal knowledge by which people live in the particular context of their communities and surrounding areas. What is known and how it is known and shared are central to this perspective.

Cultural capital is important in distinguishing the rural as a part of local and regional development. Rural products and services, for example, are inextricably linked to their places of origin and to the cultural contexts surrounding them in terms of practice, husbandry, attitudes, history, meaning and intent. Cultural resources can be used to forge new territorial identities and can be significant for gaining political-administrative recognition. Territorial identity can also encourage communities, businesses and official bodies to rally around a shared sense of place and possibility and to provide purpose and self-confidence to bring about a positive process of development. Cultural capital can thus be regarded as an important ingredient in the formation of bonding and bridging social capital through its capacity to deepen mutual understanding and trust at the local level. In short, the learning community approach seeks to cultivate the exchange of knowledge and collective learning through enhanced collaboration within and between neighbouring communities, and among strategic players.

THE APPROACH

The learning community approach invites people living in a community into a process of dialogue comprising an exchange of experiences, feelings, ideas and views. This is designed to lead towards a meaningful, rooted and broadly owned strategic planning process that can support the production of a *community-owned* development plan, as opposed to one drawn up and owned by a community *group*. The principal areas of enquiry are the knowledge of people in the community about their community, along with perceived needs and potential. The added value of this effort is that the plans produced by communities within a territory can be drawn together to identify common issues and actions, thus moving the dynamic towards the scale of a learning region. Accordingly, collaborative action within communities can combine with external working linkages to create new strategic alliances.

THE STAGES AND TOOLS

The learning community model has several key features, commencing with the establishment of a core or a host group which can assist with assembling participants for discussion groups, co-facilitating groups, arranging venues and materials, organising a community conference, initiating inquiry groups, publicity, implementation of the survey, writing up the action plan, articulating the plan to key players and, eventually, launching the plan.

A follow-on animation phase in each community can see photography, vox pops[2], video and diaries employed to gather opinions, ideas and experiences. This animation process essentially uses arts-based tools to maximise the diversity of participants, to exchange information and to reduce the effect of barriers to participation. These barriers often include the *gravitas* of the process itself and a frequent reliance on questionnaire surveys and public meetings as the only means of gathering opinions. These limit the articulation and exchange of more emotional or felt experiences and thus reduce the depth and meaning of local dialogue. A key aim in using the arts-based tools is to create the space, support and opportunity for

---

2   Vox pops are written, video or audio-taped responses to one or two pertinent questions about the community.

participants to reflect on their own experience of life in the community and to become more aware of it as something which can be questioned and assessed rather than passively accepted. These tools give significance to local experience and knowledge. They enhance the reflective process of stepping back from what is known and re-appraising it, and they help to highlight those cultural resources within the community which are distinctive and interesting. They also help people to articulate and exchange ideas in different ways. And of course, animation gives valuable publicity about the strategic planning process and can encourage the involvement of others.

Community websites were gradually developed as an additional tool during the action research project for use during the animation stage and thereafter. The websites provide a continuous update on the planning exercise, the opinions raised, and photographs taken. They provide another interactive forum for the exchange of views and enable participation to take place when it is convenient to do so. The sites can remain as a knowledge base for the community and can be expanded to include local information, research findings and the action plan. The dialogue forum can also continue. The aim is to facilitate a way in which the community can talk among itself and, by not registering with search engines, a global technology can be used to the advantage of the local.

Following this energising phase there is a need to facilitate the community to take stock of the positive and not so positive aspects of the current situation and to begin the process of generating ideas for action. The key mechanism here has involved the setting up of discussion groups, each of which is allocated a specific theme to deal with, for example, transport, community health, the local economy and the countryside. The intention is that discussion groups should be as informal as possible. Techniques such as a 'talking wall'[3] can draw on insights collected during the previous animation phase and will encourage

---

3   A talking wall is an ideas-generation and mind-mapping technique and uses post-it notes in response to a series of questions. These are attached to a large sheet of paper and sorted into common themes.

creative brainstorming of issues and ideas. A two-stage exercise first maps out the issues and then links these to potential actions.

Finally, a community conference can usefully bring together the analysis of these discussion groups and develop the issues and ideas into a full action plan. The participants work on an equal basis as co-contributors on behalf of the community as a whole, and all discussion is practically focused, with the expectation of it being acted upon. The intention is to design a strategy which contains a variety of projects of different complexity, along with lobbying or partnership-building actions. The important outcome of the community conference process is that agreed actions are adopted by the most appropriate group, club, or association within the community to take further forward. Potential actions lacking agreement or sufficient information can be revisited at a later stage or, alternatively, inquiry groups may be formed to explore the relevant situation in more depth. The conference should also identify the most appropriate statutory or development support agency for each proposed action and should seek to assemble specific project teams. There is merit in establishing a community development forum at the end of the conference which will maintain contact and common purpose across project teams, groups and other players. However, such a forum should not be condemned to drifting into an exclusive and hierarchical committee role and should be a champion for continuous community involvement.

A CASE STUDY OF THE LEARNING COMMUNITY IN BALLYNAHINCH, DRUMANESS AND SPA

Ballynahinch is a historic market town with a population of approximately 5,200 and a Protestant majority. Drumaness is a nearby former linen mill village and is predominantly Catholic. Spa is a crossroads commuter settlement neighbouring Ballynahinch and is mainly Protestant. The three communities have a mix of private and social housing and are characterised by an expanding population, local agricultural, retail and light industrial employment and commuting to work. Some residential areas and all schools are single identity and while there are social tensions relating to sectarianism, there is also a wealth of community regeneration activity. This combination of dispersed geography and social division presented key challenges in terms of communicating a development process and dealing with social exclusion. But it also presented an opportunity to move forward in terms of building inclusion and local learning.

In order to pilot the learning community approach, the Rural Development Council (RDC) in early 1999 contacted the Ballynahinch–Drumaness–Spa (BDS) Community Group in its capacity as a key gatekeeper and facilitator in the area. The community development worker agreed to work in partnership with the RDC, and a small grant was made available to assist the planning process. The worker immediately set up a core group of volunteers from within BDS who were interested in taking this initiative forward. The goals of the project were defined as:

- drawing up a clear and inclusive community action plan for the area;
- maximising ownership, support and interest across the communities in the development of the plan;
- ensuring opportunities for all sections of the community to contribute to the preparation of the plan;
- identifying clear and understandable roles for the implementation of the action plan for all local organisations who wished to become involved;
- deploying the exercise to inform statutory physical planning for Ballynahinch, Drumaness and Spa within the context of a new Area Plan;
- devising suitable indicators to enable an annual review of progress against the provisions of the plan as well as ongoing community planning activity.

A wide-ranging community questionnaire survey was designed and executed by the BDS Community Group, with assistance from the RDC and Queen's University. Seven discussion groups were convened, involving more than 200 people, and topic sessions were included with senior citizens, mothers of toddlers, a youth group, a community–police liaison committee and a housing interest group. Participants from statutory agencies and other key players were kept informed of progress but were not directly involved in the discussion groups, as it was felt that this might inhibit the articulation of the community viewpoint and shift the balance of power during the dialogue. Disposable cameras were provided to young people, who captured their own view of life in BDS and who went on to provide captions as a commentary on the images during a facilitated discussion evening. The photographs and captions were subsequently made into a display for discussion at the community conference.

The approach taken to the focus groups was flexible. In some cases participants were invited to discuss the issues in the evening at a shared venue. For example, the housing interest group was invited to the Ballynahinch sports centre and both transport and childcare facilities were offered. In other situations, the facilitators went out to talk to groups of participants who would have found it difficult to give up time in the evening. Short time slots frequently meant that additional sessions were necessary. All facilitation and recording were provided by community development workers from neighbouring groups through a local community network.

Participants indicated that they enjoyed the discussion groups which made use of mind-mapping exercises and anonymous voting by sticky dots. Conversations focused on the main issues affecting them and the identification of action points. There was considerable appreciation for how much they had learned about what was happening in their local area and about the differing perspectives of others. Some of the participants initially queried whether the community had the legitimacy to discuss and draw up action points and were surprised by the prospect that what they were doing could make a difference. But over time a sense of common purpose and responsibility was nurtured and the anxieties of those not familiar with such a role in the community were allayed.

Representatives from most of the discussion groups attended the community search conference. Refreshments, transport and childcare were provided. The same facilitators used previously also facilitated the conference and were coordinated by a central facilitator. A large room was used as the venue, around the edges of which were displayed the original flip-chart sheets recording the deliberations of the discussion groups and the reflection-based photographs and captions. These served to present and remind participants of work achieved thus far and, again, no public officials were in attendance.

An informal atmosphere was fostered throughout the conference and at the beginning people were reminded that they were the experts on their own situations. The main thematic areas were signalled as comprising childcare and health, the environment and consultation, traffic and parking, community safety and community facilities. After an 'ice-breaker', the conference proceeded with a short presentation on the main issues associated with these topics. Participants were then asked to move to one of five tables. Each table was designated for one issue. A facilitator sat at each and recorded the action points, the indicators of progress and the desirable timescales decided upon. The results from the survey were also distilled into the five main themes and provided as additional information at each of the theme tables. At time intervals, participants were invited by the coordinating facilitator to move to other issue tables which they felt they could contribute to. Throughout the conference, the facilitators worked to achieve balanced 'air time' and focused dialogue.

At the end of the search conference, each facilitator reported back on the main action points and timescales, together with the perceived community group, business interest or statutory body with relevance to implementation. Some of the action points also involved the establishment of inquiry groups to research further into particular issues. These were discussed by the participants, slight changes were made and were compiled as an action plan by BDS Community Group. This was published a few weeks later in April 2000 at a launch event attended by these public agencies and other key players. A summary of the main points from the plan is presented in Table 9.1.

One especially innovative feature of the planning process was the creation of a website which was introduced to encourage greater participation by young people and those living in the surrounding countryside. The planning website was widely publicised, in particular through secondary schools in the area, where all children have the opportunity to learn Internet skills. It was anticipated that many farm families would also have ICT facilities. But in order to assist people without home, school or business access, a computer and telephone line were provided in the public library and free access was offered via the Internet to the website. Training was given to the librarians on how to connect with the site and to support other first-time users. The BDS website evolved from a simple welcome page and a request for comments to be added to the page by way of a community dialogue. Regular screening ensured that nothing offensive was included. Some of the photographs were scanned in, with captions, to stimulate discussion as well as interest. Finally, an online version of the questionnaire was designed and added to the site for two weeks. The site was sponsored by one of the free website hosting companies and constructed using straightforward office software. The process was very much a self-taught learning exercise and over fifty visits were recorded to the site during the last two months of the planning exercise.

TABLE 9.1 SUMMARY OF THE MAIN ACTION POINTS OF THE BALLYNAHINCH–DRUMANESS–SPA COMMUNITY PLAN

Consultation and participation:
1. encourage collective community discussion through a conference every eight to twelve months;
2. statutory agencies should form more coherent approaches to action and include public participation in planning, involving young people;
3. the community should develop an ongoing forum for issue raising with statutory agencies, the District Council, business, etc., and maintain the website as a dialogue point.

Community safety:
1. reduce vandalism to cars, street crime, destruction of property, assaults by young people through increasing community policing, education on these issues and parenting classes;

2. reverse perception of Ballynahinch as a no-go area on a Saturday night through persuading the media to reporting in a less sensational way;
3. reduce joy-riding and illegal driving through forming an enquiry team to talk to Courts about sentencing policy, police traffic branch, etc.
4. raise awareness and profile of Community–Police Liaison Committee programme;
5. deal with drink and drugs abuse through checks on age of drinkers by licensees and other measures.

Traffic and transport:
1. increase use of car parks and more car parking spaces for use by disabled persons;
2. improve road safety through measures to reduce speeding and increase pedestrian crossing points;
3. improve public transport through changing timetables, increasing routes, introducing frequent minibuses.

Community facilities:
1. inform community about community group committee membership meeting times and aims, to avoid secrecy and encourage openness;
2. improve and make safe places to walk in Ballynahinch and Drumaness;
3. hold events in Ballynahinch Square involving the community in planning.

Environment:
1. initiate zero tolerance of litter through more bins and investigating of traffic wardens also becoming litter police;
2. prevent flooding by listening to the community reports of where and when it happens.

Childcare and health:
1. improve ease of getting appointments at the doctor's surgery, the attention and time given to patients and the attitude of surgery staff through a meeting with surgery staff and the appointment of a community representative on the surgery committee;
2. get part-time crèche at the shops by approaching the supermarket manager;
3. secure more affordable childcare through encouraging schools to set up a nursery.

CONCLUSIONS

The experience gained from this learning community approach to rural development allows for the identification of a number of insights with relevance to future practice in this sphere of activity. These are set out in this final section of the chapter.

- *Continuous and creative promotion of the process is vital to its success*
In BDS, press releases on progress were published regularly and the website was launched with a press conference in Ballynahinch library. Posters were displayed in multiple venues and included doctors' surgeries, shops and the mobile library vans which travel out to Drumaness and Spa. Bookmarks were printed to promote the website and were made available in the BDS office and leisure centre. They were presented in library books borrowed from the mobile and per-manent libraries. Information letters were sent out to schools and community groups. An *ex post* evaluation suggests that branding the learning community project with its personal logo would also have helped with promotion.

- *There is a need to create space for all community citizens, and particularly those who may be more marginalised, to express their views initially*
Thus BDS did not involve the statutory players in the production of the plan but rather opted to keep them appraised of progress. This information sharing could with hindsight have been improved on, to build interest and support for the plan at a later stage.

- *A website has potential to be a key part of the participatory planning process*
To ensure maximum impact, a website needs to be created and publicised from the start of the process. However, in BDS the website was launched late in the process and thus there was insufficient time for it to gather momentum. It is crucial to keep the website regularly updated to promote dialogue, but this can prove time-consuming. There is, therefore, the need for a

member of the core group, who is interested in ICT, to be charged with this task. A more sophisticated use of the software and close monitoring of the use of the site could help adjust the direction of publicity.

- *Continuity, momentum and focus must be maintained*
There is a need to remind participants at every stage that their work is part of a process. In BDS there was a tendency for people to get so involved in their area of interest and discussions that the connections to the wider process were often missed. In other words, that part of the process at that moment became an end in itself. But at the same time, it is important that people feel they have achieved something at the conclusion of each stage. The challenge is to get the correct balance between participation and closure.

- *The core group needs to consist of a wide cross-section of the community who are involved in the planning of the process from the start and who stay with it*
In BDS much of the workload was passed over to the community development worker with knock-on implications for the overall effectiveness of the process and the capacity of the worker to cope.

- *There is a need to make the process both long-term and capable of influencing wider decision-making processes*
There are threats to the future of initiatives similar to BDS due to the short-term nature of funding for community groups and projects in Northern Ireland. Thus, for example, the future of the BDS Community Group development worker and office is uncertain and, unless there is ongoing financial support, the impact of the learning community effort will be diluted. However, the commitment of the BDS Community Group committee members can ensure that the process does not halt and indeed many elements of the action plan have been incorporated into funding bids. Small community interest groups have also agreed to take on parts of the action plan and at the public launch key statutory players expressed interest in looking at

those parts of the action plan that the community has suggested they take on board.

In conclusion, the ethos of the learning community approach places a greater emphasis on improving knowledge and the sharing of knowledge. It tries to build local citizenship and to re-focus attention away from a singular emphasis on grant chasing to building understanding and appropriate action. Such action at the very least can change the way a community or area is understood, both internally and externally. A solid foundation is necessary for inclusive and sustainable development, and this must involve a re-appraisal of the balance between social, cultural and economic capital formation. The learning community approach provides some tools to meet this challenge.

CHAPTER 10

COMMUNITY-LED REGENERATION IN SMALL TOWNS AND VILLAGES: THE CRISP INITIATIVE

Michael McSorley and Alistair McKane

INTRODUCTION

Regeneration is an integral part of rural planning and development and is given a prominent profile within the new Northern Ireland Regional Development Strategy. A raft of policies are supportive of revitalisation in declining settlements in order to make them more attractive places in which to live and work. It is a policy imperative to involve local communities, the private sector and District Councils in this activity. However, this commitment to overcoming the stagnation of small towns and villages is relatively recent and was formalised for the first time within the 1993 Planning Strategy for Rural Northern Ireland. For professional planners this was welcome recognition of the need for rural planning to address the issue of rural deprivation. Until then, planning policy had largely focused on urban issues, was essentially regulatory and involved the control of development through land use zoning in Area Plans. The rural content of these plans tended to place an emphasis on protection of the environment and were somewhat indifferent to the spiral of decline affecting smaller towns and villages evident at a wider scale throughout Western Europe. The growth of car ownership, easily accessed urban supermarkets and the closure of small rural schools combined with the economic and housing choice dominance of the larger towns as catalysts for that change. In Northern Ireland these local problems were compounded by the effects of over two decades of serious unrest, which deterred the continuation of living above shops, discouraged private investment and tourism, and exacerbated despair and apathy among local people.

The opportunity to respond to these bleak conditions actually goes back to 1990 when, following an approach by the Department of the Environment, the International Fund for Ireland launched a new funding programme designed to offer community groups in the most disadvantaged areas the opportunity to kick-start regeneration. This chapter outlines the operation of the Community Regeneration and Improvement Special Programme (CRISP) and, following discussion of a number of case studies, identifies important lessons for rural planning and development practice.

THE INTERNATIONAL FUND FOR IRELAND

The International Fund for Ireland (IFI) was constituted under the 1985 Anglo-Irish Agreement, Article 10 of which states that 'the Irish and British governments should consider the possibility of securing international support for the economic and social development of those areas of both parts of Ireland which have suffered most severely from the consequences of the instability of recent years'. The IFI was formally established the following year as an independent international organisation and, with contributions from the United States, the European Union, Canada, New Zealand and Australia, the value of cumulative approved projects and administration costs by 2000 was some £403 million. The stated objectives of the Fund are to promote economic and social advance, and to encourage contact, dialogue and reconciliation between Nationalists and Unionists throughout Ireland. Its geographical remit covers Northern Ireland and the six border counties of the Republic of Ireland, ie. Cavan, Donegal, Leitrim, Louth, Monaghan and Sligo. The Fund is overseen by a seven-member board and is served by an advisory committee of officials appointed by the two governments. Government departments and public bodies are involved as administering agencies, with local contact points being provided by a team of development consultants. From the outset the IFI has adopted a programme approach to the disbursement of its resources across a wide spread of activities (Table 10.1).

TABLE 10.1 INTERNATIONAL FUND FOR IRELAND PROGRAMMES AND BUDGETS, 1986–2000 (UK£'000)

Activity	Cumulative approved projects and administrative costs
Regeneration of deprived areas	105,755
Community capacity building:	
Communities initiative	20,868
Wider horizons	43,998
New initiative	1,339
Economic development:	
Business enterprise and technology	87,438
Tourism	48,864
Urban development	54,624
Flagship	18,024
Investment companies	22,105
Total	**403,015**

Source: International Fund for Ireland (2001), *2000 Annual Report and Accounts*, Belfast and Dublin, 49.

Especially prominent, in terms of budget, is the commitment to the regeneration of deprived areas. While the targeting of need consistent with the spatial extent of designated disadvantaged areas informs all IFI programme commitments, support is also provided in a category of its own for special regeneration projects. In Northern Ireland these include, firstly, the Community

Economic Regeneration Scheme (CERS) introduced in 1989, which has been focused on the larger deprived urban areas. Some twenty-two projects with a total investment of over £34 million have been assisted. Secondly, there is the CRISP initiative, introduced in 1990, and which up to September 2000 has supported sixty-seven schemes in smaller settlements at a total investment of nearly £53 million. In the Republic of Ireland the IFI assists a Border Towns and Villages Programme designed to promote economic regeneration and cross-community cooperation.

THE CRISP INITIATIVE

Communities eligible for CRISP funding have to be within designated disadvantaged areas, which have been defined on the basis of electoral wards marked by persistent high levels of unemployment, low standards of living and poor environmental conditions. The scheme is restricted to small towns and villages with populations ranging from around 300 up to a maximum of 10,000 people. Projects supported should be able to respond to an identifiable need not being met by the private sector, be economically viable, and be able to repay any loan finance, create jobs at a reasonable cost and generate local income, and be consistent with measures contained within a wider strategy for local development. The starting point involves the development consultants of the IFI working in partnership with the Department of the Environment's CRISP project officers to establish new or strengthen existing development associations. These associations need, as far as is practical, to be cross-community and command a broad base of local support. Members must be prepared to commit the necessary energy and time in quite a long-term regeneration process. Each group must also contain business skills and is required to register itself as a company limited by guarantee, or a cooperative company in order to take forward its scheme.

CRISP schemes have combined a number of elements. Firstly, there has usually been a core economic project with funding being made available on a 50–50 basis from the IFI and the

Department to construct new or renovate derelict properties in the settlement, thus bringing them into beneficial use in a way which is consistent with the needs or the potential of the local community. In the earlier years, funding was awarded up to 100 per cent of the capital costs of the approved projects, with a 20 per cent clawback over ten years at a favourable interest rate. This regime has since been replaced by a maximum grant of up to 80 per cent. Project preparation and implementation is led by the local community group with the aid of the IFI and the Department's project managers and, before approval, a rigorous independent appraisal is carried out to determine viability.

A second element of CRISP has commonly been an environmental improvements scheme to address townscape appearance. Common practice has been to retain landscape architects to work with the community on the identification of enhancement proposals. These can include the installation of new street lighting, the removal of overhead cables, new street furniture and signage, new footpaths and traffic calming measures. This work is perceived as a useful confidence-building measure for local residents that the future can be better, and as a lever to draw in private sector investment.

The third element of CRISP has comprised Urban Development Programme expenditure which has given grant aid to the owners of derelict or vacant property to facilitate the renovation or the construction of new commercial premises. Again in the early years of CRISP the rate of support was as high as 75 per cent of approved expenditure, though during the interim this has decreased. A modest amount of additional funding has been made available for disbursement through the community company for ancillary minor works, for example, the repainting of building façades or the replacement of shop signs.

And finally, funding has also made provision for the time-limited employment of project workers to help with overall project management. Since devolution under the Good Friday Agreement, the operation of the programme and the broader regeneration remit has transferred from the Department of the Environment to the Department for Social Development.

THE OPERATION OF CRISP

The overall outcome of CRISP is that in the space of about ten years, a total of sixty-seven towns and villages (Figure 10.1) have had projects approved, of which more than forty-six are nearing completion at a cost of over £40 million, with the IFI contributing some £24 million. They vary from premises which provide new space for business development, to tourist facilities, to mixed-use centres accommodating a variety of retail, community and residential uses. Some of these projects have, on an individual basis, created forty to fifty jobs while others have had substantial local revenue consequences. What all of them have in common, however, is that they are providing services and facilities which would not otherwise have been made available. They have created community focal points and physical landmarks, thus helping to breathe new life and confidence into rural areas.

One of the positive effects of CRISP has been that it has directly encouraged the formation of new working relationships between local communities, District Councils, regional government and its agencies. For instance, because the core property project (or Community Economic Regeneration Scheme), has provided up to 80 per cent of capital costs, the balance of the finance has had to be sought from other sources. Typically this has come from the combination of a District Council grant, commercial borrowing and local community fund-raising. Magherafelt District Council provides a good example. It has a large number of disadvantaged wards and has received CRISP designations for Draperstown, Maghera, Bellaghy, Tobermore, Upperlands, Swatragh, Desertmartin, and Castledawson. As a sign of its commitment to the process of community-led economic development, the Council's contribution to each of these schemes has ranged from £40,000 to £60,000. Magherafelt District Council is, however, not unique in its support for regeneration schemes and other Councils play equally active roles. As a co-funder, each District Council is involved as a partner with the development group, IFI and Department in the planning and implementation stages.

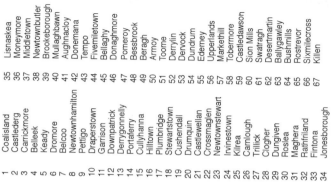

1	Coalisland	35	Lisnaskea
2	Castlederg	36	Moneymore
3	Carrickmore	37	Middletown
4	Belleek	38	Newtownbutler
5	Keady	39	Brookeborough
6	Dromore	40	Mullaghbawn
7	Belcoo	41	Aughnacloy
8	Newtownhamilton	42	Donemana
9	Pettigo	43	Tempo
10	Draperstown	44	Fivemiletown
11	Garrison	45	Bellaghy
12	Downpatrick	46	Donaghmore
13	Derrygonnelly	47	Pomeroy
14	Portaferry	48	Bessbrook
15	Cullyhanna	49	Beragh
16	Hilltown	50	Armoy
17	Plumbridge	51	Toome
18	Stewartstown	52	Derrylin
19	Cushendall	53	Dervock
20	Drumquin	54	Dundrum
21	Castlewellan	55	Ederney
22	Crossmaglen	56	Upperlands
23	Newtownstewart	57	Markethill
24	Irvinestown	58	Tobermore
25	Kilrea	59	Castledawson
26	Carnlough	60	Sion Mills
27	Trillick	61	Swatragh
28	Clogher	62	Desertmartin
29	Dungiven	63	Ballygawley
30	Roslea	64	Bushmills
31	Maghera	65	Rostrevor
32	Rathfriland	66	Sixmilecross
33	Fintona	67	Killen
34	Jonesborough		

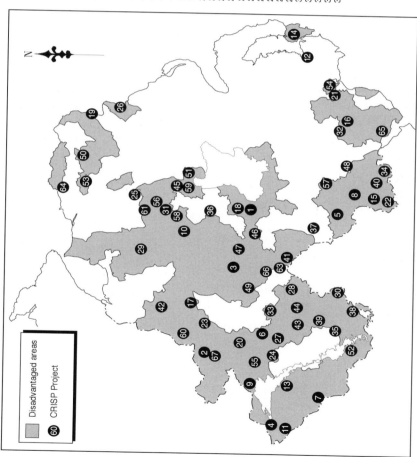

FIGURE 10.1 THE DISTRIBUTION OF CRISP SCHEMES IN NORTHERN IRELAND

The commencement process has ideally involved each community group carrying out an analysis of local needs and assets, setting objectives, and devising a strategy. For example, in the case of Toome an overall plan to regenerate the village was formulated with the support of Antrim Borough Council. The process involved a series of public meetings and in-depth consultations with local interests. The agreed strategy was devised around three elements: a mixed-use centre to accommodate a range of services lacking in the village, a tourism scheme to exploit the potential of the River Bann and Lough Neagh, and the provision of industrial floorspace. To date, Toome's community group (known by the acronym TIDAL, i.e., Toome Industrial Development Amenities and Leisure) has completed Toome House with funding under CRISP. It houses a variety of retail, office and community uses. Construction work on the industrial site, at the time of writing, is under way by the private sector. Meanwhile, the tourism project is working towards the provision of improved fishing facilities. The activities of TIDAL also provide a good illustration of effective fund-raising. As part of the 20 per cent self-funding of Toome House, TIDAL raised over £57,000 from the local community. Two-thirds of this was in the form of loan-stock over a four-year period, the contribution being repayable by the community group to individual contributors.

But over the period since CRISP was introduced, funding from other sources has become available. The result is that community groups have been able to bring forward additional projects and enhance existing schemes. Portaferry Regeneration Ltd, for example, which has delivered three projects with CRISP funding (a visitor hostel, workspace and a boat-berthing facility), was one of the first development groups to receive funding from the Department of the Environment under the EU Special Support Programme for Peace and Reconciliation. This project comprised the refurbishment of derelict stables, which are now let by the community company to Ards Borough Council as a tourist information centre. Similarly, Castlewellan Regeneration Ltd, which previously had redeveloped derelict property to provide a residential conference centre with CRISP funding, has since completed the refurbishment of town centre premises into a tele-centre suite with related offices through EU Peace and Reconciliation funding.

The National Lottery is also active in providing financial support to community groups. For example, its Charities Board is enabling the Bellaghy and Upperlands CRISP groups to add the provision of a substantial element of community space to their plans. More recently the Heritage Lottery Fund has introduced its Townscape Heritage Initiative (THI) to Northern Ireland. This gives assistance to the restoration of buildings of architectural merit in Conservation Areas. Thus, for example, Downpatrick Property Trust received CRISP funding to redevelop derelict property in Irish Street in 1994, letting it as charity shops. The company was subsequently successful in a round one bid to THI in 1998 and has embarked on plans to refurbish other derelict buildings in the vicinity. Indeed, of the thirteen schemes approved in the initial THI rounds of 1998 and 1999, CRISP community groups have been especially prominent. In this context it is worth noting that, whereas in Great Britain the THI is channelled through local authorities, the Heritage Lottery Fund is implementing the initiative in Northern Ireland through the voluntary sector. The capacity-building input of CRISP has been a significant factor in giving community groups this lead role.

A TALE OF TWO TOWNS — NEWTOWNSTEWART AND LISNASKEA

Newtownstewart is a small town of some 2,000 people located in the west of County Tyrone. The town had suffered a number of terrorist bomb attacks and, despite Conservation Area status, it had by the late 1980s many derelict and rundown buildings. A local development association was established in 1989, and through a preliminary audit process it identified the town's location on the main Omagh to Derry trunk road, the proximity to some excellent fishing and canoeing waters, the nearby opportunities for hunting offered by the Baronscourt Estate and the character inherent in the old town centre as collectively creating an opportunity to establish tourist accommodation. An appropriate development site, comprising a derelict police station and an adjacent terrace of four derelict houses, was selected because of its trunk road and river frontage location. These buildings had formed a particularly uninviting prospect on the southern entrance to the town for many years. Thus the benefits which would accrue to the town were not only from the environmental improvement and direct jobs created, but also from the spin-off effects of more visitors to the town's shops, pubs and restaurants. In addition, the development association would have its confidence and capability increased.

The core economic project comprised six high-quality self-catering apartments, a caretaker's flat, a restaurant leased to a private entrepreneur and a small unit leased to Strabane District Council for use as a museum and tourist information point. The scheme was constructed on time and within budget and has consistently exceeded average occupancy rates for tourist accommodation in Northern Ireland despite its peripheral location outside the established tourist areas. Acceptance into the CRISP programme also brought with it an Environmental Improvements (EI) scheme for the town centre, a painting scheme and some assistance with the initial costs of management and marketing. Unusually, the development association assumed direct responsibility for the EI scheme, selecting and appointing professional consultants, letting the contract and supervising the work. Because of its Conservation Area status, the EI work had of necessity to be carried out to an extremely high standard, and this led to some tensions with the wider community, for example, in the improvement of the aesthetic appearance of the streetscape and safety for pedestrians versus the loss of car parking space. Frequent, well-attended and strongly debated public meetings led to an acceptable compromise and the main street today gains much praise for the quality and sensitivity of its treatment. Additionally, a substantial uptake of the grant-aid available to the private owners of derelict buildings saw several key properties improved and the final element of the original CRISP scheme, the painting spruce-up, is close to completion.

Encouraged by its initial success, the development association turned its attention to industrial enterprise. A potential key tenant seeking workspace in the locality was identified, and funding from Department of Agriculture and Rural Development and the International Fund for Ireland was obtained to construct a major building on the edge of the town. Having achieved its economic and environmental goals, the development association then partnered with the Newtownstewart Community Association to assemble a cocktail of funding for the construction of a much-needed community and leisure facility in the town. Located on a derelict site adjacent to the Grange Court tourist accommodation complex, the new facility provides indoor games/facilities and a shared meeting space for the town's inhabitants. In both concept and appearance it complements the adjacent CRISP project.

But not content with these achievements, the development association has recently addressed a key limitation of the tourist accommodation. The initial six flats provided thirty-two bed spaces, but this was insufficient to take a coach party. In an innovative joint marketing venture with a similar community group in Ballyshannon, County Donegal, the Newtownstewart Development Association obtained funding from INTERREG and the District Council to construct an additional six apartments providing specially adapted space for disabled visitors. The new accommodation also provides increased opportunity for two-centre river and sea fishing holidays with Ballyshannon.

While this project as a whole, in the opinion of the authors of this chapter, is worthy of the highest accolade, such a long-running and complex scheme has not been without its problems. There have been delays, and relational difficulties have, at times, been experienced. But tensions within any community are inevitable and there are always begrudgers with the 'it will never work' and 'you are wasting your time' comments. But the patience and expertise of the group, coupled with the experience and commitment of the main funders have meant that these have been successfully overcome. Such a programme has put huge strains on the time and patience of the voluntary board members who are ultimately responsible for the project.

But the benefits to Newtownstewart are many: an improved and enhanced town centre, new industry and tourist infrastructure, some jobs and greater encouragement to trade in the town, a new leisure building, and a stronger, more assertive partnership rather than rivalry between the local community groups.

In Lisnaskea, County Fermanagh, the problem and solutions were somewhat different. Located some twelve miles south of Enniskillen, Lisnaskea possessed a thriving number of small, privately run businesses, disadvantaged by the lack of suitable premises and the ability to employ sufficient staff to provide efficient administration. The community development association had long identified the need for new workspace and had tried in vain for several years to identify a site within the relatively tight limits of the statutory town plan. However, after working with the CRISP project team and the Divisional Planning Office of the Department of the Environment, which was preparing a new Area Plan, the group identified suitable land. This was subsequently zoned for industrial development. With funding from CRISP, the new centre provided 12,000 square feet of industrial space, part of which included a special care centre for the disabled and has been fully let since completion.

Unlike Newtownstewart Development Association, the Lisnaskea group retained the services of the Department of the Environment's Landscape Service to design and implement its EI scheme. This had mixed success because, although the quality of the design was excellent, the geographical remoteness of the implementing agency, based in Belfast, led to an extremely lengthy implementation process and generated frustration within the group at the lack of local control over the process. In addition, a major area of dereliction had been identified in the town centre. This was noted as a potential Comprehensive Development Area and was left to the Department of the Environment's Planning Service to take forward. But, as with any such scheme, the legal complexities meant that it took a long time to reach implementation stage. Frustration in the community increased at the apparent slow progress towards addressing what was regarded as an urgent issue.

However, much speedier progress was made with an INTER-

REG funded extension to the Enterprise Centre, providing an additional 7,500 square feet of workspace (again, full on completion) and a Department of Agriculture and Rural Development–INTERREG promoted wildfowl reserve at Lough Head, a short distance from the town. In an interesting case of turning adversity to advantage, the development association had originally planned to construct a marina close to Lough Head and to canalise the river to bring cruisers on the Erne waterway into the town. Prevented from doing so by Area of Special Scientific Interest and RAMSAR site designations, the group agreed to capitalise on this by utilising the area as a visitor attraction.

The benefits to Lisnaskea of the CRISP scheme and the associated follow on, as with Newtownstewart, have been significant: up to forty jobs, twelve new and expanding businesses, a new daycare facility, a new visitor attraction, and a considerable environmental enhancement. From the development group's point of view, it has been a story of success tinged with frustration at the apparent inability of different parts of government and statutory authorities to all work at the same speed. Issues perceived locally as extremely important and urgent have not always been appreciated as such by remote government departments which are often dealing with competing demands for attention. However, effective liaison by local project teams did much to ameliorate such difficulties.

CONCLUSION: EMERGENT LESSONS FROM THE CRISP EXPERIENCE

Prior to the introduction of CRISP, there had not been an equivalent effort at small town and village regeneration in Northern Ireland. Consequently, there was no metaphoric road map and no ready answers to the numerous problems that would be encountered along the way. Mistakes were made in that some early projects were too ambitious and some environmental improvement schemes too small to have any real impact. But overall, the various formal assessments carried out in recent years have commented favourably on the initiative. Independent evaluations of CRISP have attested to the contribution of the programme in stimulating economic activity, improving business confidence and developing partnerships. They also highlight the work of community groups working voluntarily on a cross-community basis for the public good and the benefits of their work in holding communities together. For example, a report by KPMG et al (1998) found that:

- 94 per cent of the anticipated employment of CRISP schemes had come into existence;
- CRISP projects would not have proceeded without funding support; and
- CRISP projects overwhelmingly regarded the main benefits of their schemes as economic, while also demonstrating the effectiveness of communities working together.

A further report by PricewaterhouseCoopers (1998) has echoed these conclusions.

In terms of the lessons learnt it is clear, firstly, that many of the most successful CRISP schemes are those which combine social and community dimensions with the economic elements. Thus, schemes in Garrison and Derrygonnelly, for example, while primarily commercial in emphasis, contain daycare centres for the elderly and pre-school playgroup facilities. The inclusion of these components allows each scheme to reach out to a much wider cross-section of the local community, while the provision of additional jobs in the service sector is equally worthwhile. A reasonable level of flexibility in the programme has meant that many schemes, while being primarily economic in focus, have been able to contain important social and community features. Indeed, following a conspicuous lack of success in letting first-floor office space in many small villages, the traditional activity in such locations of commercial uses on the ground floor was combined with self-contained living accommodation overhead.

Secondly, many of the economic projects have been marginal in terms of profitability and indeed if they were not so, then the private sector would already be involved. Accordingly, they have required continuous hard work by the local community groups to achieve success, and ongoing monitoring by the funders to address management problems. However, most have been repaying their loans, have achieved their original objectives, and enjoy the support of local people. But CRISP was never perceived as providing the only response to the problems of these rural communities. Rather, it was regarded as a kick-start to a much deeper process of regeneration, and thus the long-term benefits and some longer-term difficulties around the viability of early schemes are only now beginning to filter through.

Thirdly, the eligibility for CRISP funding on the basis of designated disadvantaged areas led to some towns and villages being located across a line on a map and, therefore, being excluded. However, the introduction of a Community Property Development Scheme (CPDS) for non-disadvantaged towns and villages has mitigated this issue and provided an acceptable alternative. Randalstown, for example, was not eligible for CRISP assistance but its central area has benefited from CPDS investment. In addition, the selection criteria tended to create an artificial distinction between urban and rural. Some villages were considered to lack a coherent morphology and were deemed ineligible for CRISP, despite local perceptions of these being villages. Furthermore, a preference in planning policy terms was often given to village centre sites over more countryside locations, although the latter could have been more economically viable, being cheaper to purchase and more accessible.

Fourthly, the difficulties encountered have included greater bureaucracy as well as the dominant role given in decision making to the economic appraisal process, which can begin to affect the composition of projects away from what the local community may perceive as being necessary to what they perceive as having the best chance of satisfying government economists. Moreover, the marketplace in terms of funding agencies and programmes has become more complex and crowded. There are differing priorities and requirements, and charting a path through this administrative maze to identify and secure appropriate funding for particular projects can prove a daunting challenge for rural community groups. There is the added danger of overloading the community sector to the extent where it can no longer cope on a voluntary basis, and the time of volunteers is so taken up with community development that it impacts adversely on home and family life. Many of the community groups have found it difficult to recruit and retain the involvement of young people and are, therefore, becoming tired and less willing to take risks and engage in new projects.

And finally, it is clear that CRISP is in the vanguard of the bottom up approach. It champions local solutions for local problems, with planners taking their brief from the community, and delivering a strategic response in line with government policy and objectives. A decade of regeneration work demonstrates that rural planning and development in Northern Ireland has achieved something significant. Planning should not be condemned to act as a regulatory activity in that it can and does need to make things happen. The CRISP initiative is powerful evidence of the achievements possible when planners work in partnership with others and with adequate resources to deliver on local regeneration.

ENDNOTE

The views expressed in this paper are those of the authors and are not necessarily those of the Department for Social Development and the International Fund for Ireland.

REFERENCES

Department of the Environment for Northern Ireland (1999), *The CRISP Story,* Belfast: Regional Development Office.
International Fund for Ireland (2001), *2000 Annual Report and Accounts*, Belfast and Dublin.
KPMG, Colin Stutt Consulting, Northern Ireland Economic Research Centre (1998), *Assessment of the Impacts of the International Fund for Ireland 1987–1997*, Belfast and Dublin: International Fund for Ireland.
PricewaterhouseCoopers (1998), *Review of Urban Regeneration Policy*, Belfast: Department of the Environment for Northern Ireland, Regional Development Office.

FIGURE 10.1 TOOME HOUSE, TOOME, COUNTY ANTRIM

FIGURE 10.2 RESTORATION BY DOWNPATRICK PROPERTY TRUST, IRISH STREET, DOWNPATRICK, COUNTY DOWN

FIGURE 10.3 CRISP CORE ECONOMIC PROJECT, NEWTOWNSTEWART, COUNTY TYRONE

CHAPTER 11

PLANNING AND DEVELOPMENT NETWORKS IN THE BORDERLANDS OF IRELAND

Jonathan Greer

INTRODUCTION

Economic and social disadvantage in the borderlands of Ireland has been a longstanding problem but remains an issue which still requires a resolution in modern Ireland. One of the main difficulties in tackling the economic and social needs of the Irish border region is that political issues regularly take precedence. Cross-border cooperation has continuously been seen within the context of constitutional positions, particularly that of Northern Ireland, and embroiled in political debates over North-South relations. As a result, both the UK and Irish governments have failed to seriously address disadvantage in the region, as planning and development have largely been driven by political, rather than strategic issues (O'Dowd, 1994).

However, notwithstanding the disappointing performance at the macro-level, a range of local cross-border partnerships has been established to combat the acute economic and social problems of this largely rural territory. With aid and assistance from the UK and Irish governments and the EU in particular, partnerships in the border region have emerged as development stakeholders and have increasingly recognised that shared problems must be addressed by working together.

However, within the last two decades partnership initiatives have developed in a rapid and at times *ad hoc* manner which is creating a complex and confusing picture, distorting strategic development. Indeed, the plethora of partnerships in the border region is well documented by Birrell (1999) who, in acknowledging the active role played by local authorities in this area, categorises local authority cross-border initiatives into a number of groups including: formal area networks; joint projects; twinning/visits and exchanges; and wider networks. Within these categories the most longstanding, spatially extensive and formal partnership arrangements are the local authority cross-border networks.

Over the last twenty-five years three networks, the North West Region Cross-Border Group (NWRCBG), the East Border Region Committee (EBRC) and, more recently, the Irish Central Border Area Network (ICBAN), have been formed by local authorities to develop cross-border economic opportunities. The concept of dealing with shared problems and opportunities has been at the core of the local authority networks. These have sought to implement integrated strategic action plans for agriculture and rural development, tourism, infrastructure, and town regeneration. The purpose of this chapter is to analyse the local authority networks with a view to assessing their progress in developing cooperative linkages and addressing the economic and social problems of the border region.

The discussion commences with a brief review of the background to cross-border cooperation within the spheres of planning and development and highlights the difficult environment in which the local authority networks operate. Their role is then examined, giving specific attention to their contribution as actors in the economic and social development of the border region. The narrative draws on interviews carried out with key informants who are familiar with this network arena. The chapter concludes by discussing the future contribution of these networks to cross-border development.

THE BACKGROUND TO CROSS-BORDER DEVELOPMENT

In the first thirty to forty years after the border was confirmed in 1925, few contacts were made at an institutional level between the two governments of Northern Ireland and the Republic of Ireland. In the 1940s and 1950s both jurisdictions, largely developed in isolation as the Free State Government established a strongly Catholic ethos, remained neutral in the Second World War and became an independent Republic in 1949. The Stormont Government, on the other hand, was content to limit contact with the rest of the island of Ireland and instead maintain stronger links with Great Britain. During these years, the divergence of policy approaches in education, health and economic development had a detrimental effect on the economy of the border region. People tended to live back to back with communities looking to their respective capital city as the centre of activity, rather than fostering cross-border economic opportunities (Busteed, 1992). The border counties thus became economically deprived, being characterised by a narrow range of employment opportunities, dominated by small scale farming, high levels of unemployment, under-employment and out migration (O'Dowd et al, 1994: 35).

It was only in areas of immediate common concern that linkages were established. Officials from the North and the South met regularly, for example, to administer and maintain the railway system and to manage a project to regulate drainage in the Erne basin (Stephens and Symons, 1956). Other cross-border links were developed by the two governments in 1952 when the Foyle Fisheries Commission was established to regulate and monitor the number of fish in the river, to control water pollution, regulate fishing licences and implement drainage schemes (Foyle Fisheries Commission, 1996).

The 1960s, in contrast, could be described as a more progressive period for North-South cooperation. The first steps towards developing greater North-South cooperation were initiated by Seán Lemass when he was elected Taoiseach in 1959. Lemass negotiated the Anglo-Irish Free Trade Agreement (AIFTA) with the UK government in 1965. This sought to set in place a system of tariff reductions which would result in free trade between the two countries by 1975 (Lee, 1989). The AIFTA was the first step towards improving North-South economic relations by putting the necessary structures and procedures in place so that open trade could be freely facilitated across the island as a whole. The agreement, therefore, marked a turning point in the economic significance of the Irish border (House, 1990).

Moves towards greater cross-border economic cooperation between Northern Ireland and the Republic of Ireland were quickly dampened, however, with the outbreak of the 'Troubles' in August 1969. The rise of terrorist violence in the early 1970s created a politically unstable environment and quickly polarised the two main communities in Northern Ireland, Nationalist and Unionist. Against this background the UK and Irish governments became concerned with maintaining the security situation rather than deepening the economic and political cross-border relations which had been nurtured in the O'Neill and Lemass era (Lyne, 1990).

In 1972 the accession of the UK and the Republic of Ireland to the European Economic Community (EEC) created a new forum within which cross-border contacts could be rebuilt. The EEC highlighted the socio-economic problems of Northern Ireland and in particular the problems which Northern Ireland and the border region faced by being located on the periphery of Europe. Socio-economic problems were given special attention as it was felt that 'the desire for peace was closely linked to living conditions and employment' (Moxon-Browne, 1992). Through the Regional Development Fund the EEC, with the UK and the Irish governments, commissioned a number of studies to review the problems of peripherality in the border region and to recommend areas for possible North-South cooperation.

The first of these was embarked on in 1976 and examined cross-border communications in the Derry-Donegal area. The study advanced a number of recommendations for capital projects and service improvements that could be implemented by government authorities and agencies working on a cross-border basis. The proposals ranged from harmonisation of road standards, to the improvement of public transport, postal and telecommunications services (Peat, Marwick et al, 1977: 10).

This was followed in 1979 by the Erne Catchment Study whose principal themes were arterial drainage and tourism. It was concluded that the effective management and development of the catchment area in these sectors could best be achieved on a cross-border basis (Brady et al, 1979). These reports from the late 1970s culminated with the publication of the Irish Border Areas Report in 1983 which commented that:

> These areas ... amongst the most economically and socially deprived in Europe, have the additional disadvantage of being cut in half by a frontier that hampers normal economic development. (Economic and Social Committee of the European Communities, 1983)

The scope for cross-border cooperation was given further impetus with the signing of the Anglo-Irish Agreement in 1985. The Agreement acknowledged that both the UK and Irish governments would jointly manage the conflict in Northern Ireland. This gave the Republic of Ireland a voice in Northern Ireland's affairs by establishing an Intergovernmental Conference,

> concerned with Northern Ireland and with relations between the two parts of Ireland, to deal on a regular basis with political matters, security and related matters, legal matters and the promotion of cross-border cooperation. (Lee, 1989: 456)

But by the beginning of the 1990s significant changes were also taking place at the European level to facilitate and promote cross-border trade. The Single European Market was introduced in 1992 with the freeing of border controls on the movement of people, vehicles and goods. Within Ireland, however, there was an increased security presence along the border as a result of terrorist violence. Military operations and the erection of fortifications at that time, according to O'Dowd, took precedence over any fresh momentum for cross-border cooperation,

> In times of heightened conflict, notably in the last twenty-five years, the British Army has sought to assert the sovereignty

of the UK at the border by establishing fortifications, check-points and a systematic policy of road closures. The long struggle over the re-opening and re-closing of the roads reveals the primacy accorded by the British government to assertion of state sovereignty over the wishes of the local inhabitants and over programmes supported by the same state to improve cross-border infrastructure and communi-cations (O'Dowd et al, 1994: 29).

Nevertheless, cross-border developments were still progressed through the Anglo-Irish Secretariat. The Secretariat provided a basis for formulating areas of joint coordination and pro-grammes of expenditure. Cooperation was then formalised at the European Union (EU) level with the introduction of the INTERREG programme in 1990, aimed at assisting border regions overcome their special problems, not least adjustment to the Single European Market. Although INTERREG sought to stimulate cross-border cooperation in Ireland, the programme did encounter a number of operational difficulties. One of the criticisms, for example, of the first round of funding for 1991–1993 was that only a few projects were actually imple-mented on a cross-border basis. The programme tended to focus more on stand-alone projects implemented on each side of the border, but which were justified as having a developmental effect on the region as a whole.

The aims of INTERREG 2 retained the fundamental objectives of addressing the problems of peripherality. However, more emphasis was placed on generating partnerships between Member States and across their regional and local authorities in line with the principle of subsidiarity. To this end, the Commission indicated that proposals for border areas should be formulated within a coherent and integrated strategy. Their merit would be assessed against criteria which included the contribution of the strategy to cross-border cooperation and the degree of involvement of regional and local authorities. Support was subsequently given to projects related to the themes of agriculture/fisheries/forestry, human resource development, environmental protection and regional development. Latterly, the European Union Special Support Programme for Peace and Reconciliation has sought to bolster cross-border development, not least in the sphere of business expansion.

FIGURE 11.1 LOCAL AUTHORITY NETWORKS IN IRELAND

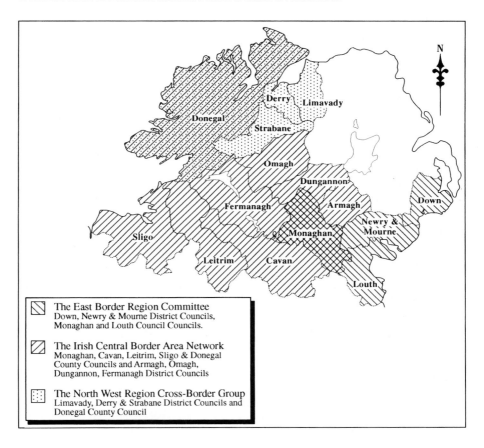

THE EXPERIENCE OF THE LOCAL AUTHORITY CROSS-BORDER NETWORKS

The late 1970s saw the establishment of the East Border Region Committee (EBRC) which is a partnership of Down District Council, Newry and Mourne District Council, Louth

County Council and Monaghan County Council. The North West Region Cross-Border Group (NWRCBG) comprising Donegal County Council, Strabane District Council, Derry City Council and Limavady Borough Council also dates from that time. The INTERREG 1 programme contributed to the funding of a central secretariat. This support continued under INTER-REG 2 by which time a third network was established. The Irish Central Border Area Network (ICBAN) was set up in 1995 and consists of Omagh District Council, Dungannon and South Tyrone Borough Council, Fermanagh District Council and Armagh City and District Council in Northern Ireland along with Sligo, Donegal, Leitrim, Cavan and Monaghan County Councils in the Republic of Ireland (Figure 11.1). Each of the networks has established formal partnership arrangements with committee and executive structures. The sections below consider how well each network is working on a collective basis, strategic development and the facilitation of strategic action, and the tension between regionalisation and centralisation.

Working together

One of the main challenges faced by each of the local authority networks has been the need to establish a common approach among their respective participants. The longstanding absence of trust has made it difficult at times to reach out to others who are perceived to be different. For example, the NWRCBG has struggled to avoid political matters impacting on the relationships between partner councils. On a number of occasions tensions have flared up within the group and have created a strained environment for the network to operate in. Indeed, as a direct result of political problems one Council, which at the time was Unionist-controlled, left the network for a short period. The border areas have suffered heavily from the Troubles and the consequent tension and fear did have the effect of polarising the two communities in the region. This in turn has created unease among participants with the frustration felt by one Unionist councillor interviewee illustrative of that situation:

It is always one hell of a barrier when you are working on a cross-border basis and then you lift the paper one morning to find that there was £1 million worth of damage in Armagh or Enniskillen. The Troubles created tension and difficulties for Unionists working in cross-border bodies. You always think 'I am knocking my brains out trying to get funding for a cross-border region and there is £1 million up in smoke under my nose'. That takes away from your enthusiasm I have to say. As a Unionist Councillor I have always felt that you are climbing a slippery slope, you make progress, you work your tail off and you stick your neck out, and then some terrorist incident happens and you are pulled back down again.

The difficulties involved in working together in partnership arrangements have been made even more problematic because of different priorities. From the inception of the EBRC, for example, questions have been raised over the participation of Monaghan County Council and, in particular, Down District Council, which is not located on the border. The EBRC has found it difficult to formulate projects which are applicable to the whole sub-region and from which the Monaghan and Down Councils can gain equal benefit. Close proximity and common economic and social problems, on the other hand, have allowed Newry and Mourne District Council and Louth County Council to establish a central axis within the network in regard to joint projects and linkages. At times this has created tension when projects are proposed which are beneficial to two or three councils but funding contributions are needed from all four councils. This network has been able to produce brochures promoting economic development, but very few solid projects have been brought forward of relevance to all the partners. Additional tensions have surfaced because of councillors representing their own local interests. This has resulted in organisational fragility making it difficult for the networks to embrace more neutral decision-making processes in regard to planning and development matters.

Strategic development

Given the problems of operating within a contentious political environment and reconciling different partner priorities, it is not surprising that the networks have generated limited visible outcomes. For many years the networks have tended to focus on producing tourist brochures, lobbying central government to introduce new policy measures and implementing a number of *ad hoc,* local-scale and under-resourced projects. Essentially the networks were content to adopt a reactive approach to cross-border cooperation, resulting in piecemeal development. More recently, however, the networks have progressed to formulate sub-regional strategies which mark a watershed in their evolution. These strategies have forged a common purpose among the partner councils, set out specific objectives and made the long-term aims much more clear to all partners. In addition, by concentrating attention on economic and social issues, these strategies have avoided wider political debates, thus assisting Unionist and Nationalist councillors to better interact, build trust relations and work together.

Despite this, the networks have not been able to attract block funding to implement strategic actions. The strategies and projects that have been proposed have often been perceived as too ambitious and for this reason the partnerships have clashed with central government departments. On other occasions the perception of limited input from local stakeholders has raised questions of strategy ownership and implementation commitment. The local authority networks have had to learn that they are operating within the ambit of national government policy. First and foremost there are jurisdiction matters to consider and the realities of competing priorities between government departments and agencies on each side of the border. Strategies have been dissected by these public bodies in their search for conformity with overarching policies. As a result only a limited number of specific and often modest actions have been deemed applicable for funding. The process of scrutiny given to one such strategy has been described by a civil servant as follows:

In INTERREG we have up to forty government agencies North and South who assess projects and make executive decisions on where the money goes. This happens at a departmental level and is very centralised in terms of governance North and South. The integrated plan went into INTERREG and the various government departments, but as it raced down into the atmosphere towards planet INTERREG it broke up. The Northern Ireland Tourist Board and Bord Fáilte were looking at the tourism bit, the Departments of Agriculture were looking at the agricultural section and the Departments of the Environment, in a disaggregated way, were also looking at discrete bits of an overall plan without seeing the totality of the plan. It became the parts rather than the sum, some elements of the strategy were funded and some were not. The strategy did not survive being put through the mangle grinder of INTERREG.

In addition, the strategies formulated by the local authority networks were refused EU funding by the two governments on the basis that they were developed in isolation from one another. Because each network focused on its own, relatively small sub-region, the strategies and projects, if implemented, would have duplicated services or have had a detrimental effect on the environment, economy and tourist potential of other parts of the entire border region. In effect the networks were competing against one another and not devising a coherent strategy for the whole of the border corridor.

Facilitating strategic action

Following the failure of the North-West Strategy to receive funding, the North West Region Cross-Border Group adopted an extensive consultation process to take into account the views of other stakeholders in the region. It embarked on a facilitative approach to encourage greater involvement and participation among government departments, along with the private, voluntary and community sectors. This moved the network away from formulating local authority wishlists towards strategic actions which are integrated, relevant to the region and complementary with government policy.

At a wider level the cross-border networks have now shifted from the former emphasis on projects to a more programme-based approach. Previously the networks had formulated projects on an *ad hoc* funding-led basis which created problems of duplication and lack of coordination. Under the programme approach, however, the networks have now identified themes for development which are closely related to those formulated in the strategies. Indeed, the networks have established sub-groups working towards developing specific programmes identified in their strategies, which has allowed them to bring wider interests on board and become enablers of development.

The cross-border partnerships have learned from previous practice and there is a recognition that they must cooperate to formulate an effective cross-border strategy. To this end, the networks have developed distinctive integrated area plans for each of the three sub-regions, which in turn are located within a comprehensive strategy for the whole border corridor (KPMG and Colin Stutt, 1999). The networks have adopted a dual approach to development by working on an individual basis for those issues which need to be addressed at the sub-regional level, and cooperating to implement actions which need to be addressed on a border corridor basis. In this way, the networks have been able to meet the requirements of the INTERREG programme by working to a coherent regional and integrated strategy which treats the border region as a 'single geographical unit' with internal diversity. The networks have also joined the Association of European Border Regions (AEBR) which seeks to provide technical assistance and promotion of cross-border cooperation among internal and external border regions of the EU. Under the AEBR the networks have secured deeper linkages throughout the Irish borderlands and have also have been able to share in the experiences of other cross-border groups in Europe.

Centralisation versus regionalisation

There has long been a perception among the local authority networks that they have been held back by central government departments in order to prevent extended decentralisation. For instance, since the inception of the East Border Region Committee various schemes concerning economic development, tourism and agriculture have been promoted and although Ministers and officials of the Northern Ireland Office and the Republic of Ireland government have met with this partnership, they have declined to participate in the formulation of strategies or provide financial assistance. At a wider scale the failure to achieve greater functional responsibility has created frustration within the partnerships and running tensions with government departments on each side of the border. However, in recent years this uncomfortable situation has eased somewhat and space has been created for the networks and central government to work together more closely. Following the setting up of the County Enterprise Boards in the South and the funding given to District Partnerships in the North under the EU Special Support Programme for Peace and Reconciliation, both governments are beginning to appreciate that devolved programmes can be successfully implemented. As one interviewee from the Department of Finance in Dublin explained:

> The Department of Finance and Personnel in Belfast at present is a reflection of how the Department of Finance in Dublin was ten to fifteen years ago in terms of the central control we used to have. The other departments were in fear of us because we dictated everything, we held the purse strings and they could not spend without getting our authority. I can see the Department of Finance and Personnel going through the very same change that the Department of Finance has experienced. They are on a very similar evolutionary path to us but they are a little bit behind. It is fascinating the way they are evolving and to see the way the Programme for Peace and Reconciliation has

been introduced. The devolution under the peace programme horrified civil servants because of the extent of control that was passing down. They could not believe it could operate without being brought up before the Court of Auditors. But gradually there has been an acceptance that it does seem to be working. I think it is experience and evolution on the basis of experience which has changed perceptions. Meanwhile, the cross-border bodies are also evolving and becoming more strategic and proactive and we are now more positively disposed towards helping them and getting them going. The frustrating thing is that, looking back, it seems to have been a necessary evolutionary process that all concerned had to go through.

FUTURE CROSS-BORDER DEVELOPMENT AND THE LOCAL AUTHORITY NETWORKS

The experience of the local authority networks suggests that too much attention has been given to the *ad hoc* project-based approach at the local scale. Formulating projects without the framework of an overall strategy has increased dependency on external funding, introduced short-term initiatives and led to duplication and lack of coordination. Over the past fifteen years this pattern of development has been repeated across the Irish border region as a plethora of partnership arrangements involving the public, private, and voluntary and community sectors has emerged under funding initiatives from the International Fund for Ireland, Co-operation Ireland, and EU programmes such as INTERREG, the Special Support Programme for Peace and Reconciliation and LEADER. As a result, a complex and confusing picture of partnership gover-nance has emerged which has distorted development in the border region and, according to Birrell (1999), indicates a lack of awareness or detailed information on the nature and extent of cross-border cooperation.

There is a need, therefore, for greater strategic coordination at the macro level to improve partnership performance and cross-border development in Ireland. The operation of the North-

South Ministerial Council (NSMC) and cross-border bodies[1] under the 'Good Friday' Agreement affords a major opportunity to formulate the necessary strategic framework which can oversee partnerships, allocate funding and provide advice and management guidelines. The structuring of planning and development at this macro level could ensure that the partnerships' focus is more sharply on long-term strategic goals that are complementary to government policy. Moreover, this would facilitate greater linkages between government departments in the North and the South and in turn attune strategies to promote the border region in a more engaging way. The failure of the new Northern Ireland Regional Development Strategy to embrace an imaginative vision for the Irish borderlands is ample evidence of a neglect that should not continue. A strategic framework, formulated under the auspices of the NSMC, however, would constitute a symbolic and practical reconfiguration of planning and development activity by elevating its status to trans-national significance.

Notwithstanding the need for this macro-level response, a balance must be achieved by energising local planning and development efforts. This role can be fulfilled by the local authority networks, which have emerged as facilitators and enablers for development. The networks have travelled along a sharp learning curve, transforming themselves from organisations with no focus to partnerships which are marked by a strategic, proactive confidence. The networks can become

---

1. The North-South Ministerial Council (NSMC) brings together those with executive authority, North and South, to work together by agreement on matters of mutual interest. Those participating on the Council are mandated by, and remain accountable to, the Assembly and the Irish Parliament. Six implementation bodies have been identified to put decisions by the Council into effect on a cross-border or all-island basis. The six implementation bodies are: Inland Waterways; Food Safety; Trade and Business Development; Special EU Programmes; Language (Irish and Ulster Scots); and Aquaculture and Marine Matters. Areas for cooperation in the cross-border bodies include aspects of: Transport; Agriculture; Education; Health; Environment; and Tourism.

important actors for development by establishing thematic participatory partnerships, acting as a voice for their region and linking with the NSMC to formulate and implement an integrated strategy for the border corridor. Indeed, in the effort to improve vertical coordination, the networks have already undertaken the necessary groundwork by engaging in a mutual learning process with central government. By acting together, the NSMC and the local authority networks can adopt a more structured approach to planning in the borderlands and the island of Ireland to steer development and investment beyond the dominant growth centres of Belfast and Dublin.

More particularly, given that EU programmes are a subject area for one of the implementation bodies established under the 'Good Friday' Agreement, the networks are well placed to become more directly involved in the formulation and implementation of border region development. Historically, the networks have had no direct say in the allocation of EU funds, but by working alongside the two governments in the new cross-border body, they have the capacity to administer programmes related not least to social inclusion. By adopting a participative approach involving the voluntary and community sectors, the networks can initiate a true 'bottom up' approach to help address social and political exclusion, improve local decision making, and rebuild civil society.

Finally, the role of the networks as facilitators for development in the border region could in the longer run be extended and strengthened by the outcomes of the mooted reorganisation of local government in Northern Ireland. From 1972 local authorities have been operating under a range of limited powers such as licensing of entertainment and environmental health, leisure provision, street cleaning, refuse collection, maintenance of cemeteries and aspects of economic development (Knox, 1999). As a result, this has created a mismatch of functions and constrained economies of scope. However, the reorganisation of local government may well return authority for roads and planning, and expand functions in the areas of economic development, tourism and community services (Birrell and Hayes, 1999), which will further empower the networks and increase the potential for cooperation and multi-sectoral development. Any reduction in the number of local authorities in Northern Ireland presents a further opportunity for the networks to expand their membership and scale of spatial operation.

CONCLUSION

By becoming facilitators for development, the local authority networks have demonstrated a more mature and responsible approach to planning. The networks have moved on from solely lobbying central government and developing short-term projects to engaging the public, private, voluntary and community sectors in formulating and implementing regional strategies. The challenge for the networks is to maintain and extend this participatory approach to local development, while forging closer links with the NSMC. The networks have the potential to promote economic and social development, improve public service delivery, transfer skills and experiences, and bring different political persuasions together to improve relations within the Irish borderlands.

REFERENCES

Birrell, D. (1999), 'Cross-border Cooperation between Local Authorities in Ireland', *Local Governance,* vol. 25, no. 2: 109–118.

Birrell, D. and A. Hayes (1999). *The Local Government System in Northern Ireland*, Dublin: Institute of Public Administration.

Brady Shipman Martin and PA International (1979), *The Erne Catchment Area Study*, report prepared for the governments of the UK and Ireland and the Commission of the European Communities.

Busteed, M. (1992), 'The Irish Border: From Partition and Confrontation to Cooperation?', *Boundary Bulletin*, no. 4: 13–17.

Economic and Social Committee of the European Communities (1983), *Irish Border Areas Information Report*, Brussels.

Foyle Fisheries Commission (1996), *Annual Report 1996.*

House, H. (1990), 'The Border That Wouldn't Go Away: Irish Integration in the EC', *New York School Journal of International and Comparative Law*, vol. 11, nos 1 and 2: 229–247.

KPMG and Colin Stutt (1999), *Border Corridor Strategy and Integrated Areas: Plans for Border Corridor Groups*.

Knox, C. (1999), 'Northern Ireland: At the Crossroads of Political and Administrative Reform, *Governance*, vol. 12, no. 3: 311–329.

Lee, J.J. (1989), *Ireland 1912–1985*, Cambridge University Press.

Lyne, T. (1990), 'Ireland, Northern Ireland and 1992: The Barriers to Technocratic Anti-partitionism', *Public Administration*, vol. 68, no. 4: 417–433.

Moxon-Browne, E. (1992), 'The Impact of the EC', in B. Hadfield (ed.), *Northern Ireland: Politics and the Constitution*, Milton Keynes: Open University Press.

Dowd, L. (1994), *Whither the Irish Border? Sovereignty, Democracy and Economic Integration in Ireland*, Belfast: Centre for Research and Documentation.

O'Dowd, L., J. Corrigan and T. Moore (1994), *The Irish Border Region: A Socio-economic Profile*, Belfast: Department of Sociology and Social Policy, Queens University.

Peat, Marwick, Mitchell and Co., and Stokes, Kennedy, Crowley and Co. (1977), *Cross-Border Communication Study for the Londonderry and Donegal Area*, report prepared for governments of the UK and Ireland and the Commission of the European Communities, Belfast and Dublin.

Stephens, N. and L. J. Symons (1956), 'The Lough Erne Drainage Scheme', *Geography*, vol. XL, no. 1: 123–126.

SECTION FOUR:
RETROSPECT AND PROSPECT

CHAPTER 12

Interpreting the Rural in Northern Ireland: Place, Heritage and History

Brian Graham

INTRODUCTION

The geographer Yi-Fu Tuan (1991) argues that regions may have no existence outside the consciousness of the writers and artists who create them and who, through the power of their work, may persuade others to accept their imaginings. Central to such constructs is the vexed question of landscape and its multiplicity of meanings. As Simon Schama (1995: 61) contends, 'once a certain idea of landscape, a myth, a vision, establishes itself in an actual place, it has a peculiar way of muddling categories, of making metaphors more real than their referents; of becoming, in fact, part of the scenery'. Such ideas are central to any interpretation of the meaning of rurality in the fractured and dissonant world of Northern Ireland. The shaping of place through the interplay of representations of the past and their contemporary meanings helps define the disputed meanings of its oral (and written) identities. The general aim of this chapter is to explore this nexus of contestation and to examine the ways in which the rural in Northern Ireland has been portrayed in literature, academic work and heritage, as we seek to define both who we are and the meaning of the place we inhabit.

'Heritage' now shares the fate of 'environment' as a term so abused and debased that its meaning is often lost. It is seen here as a socially constructed negotiated knowledge, set within specific social and intellectual circumstances. A heritage is thus a time-specific and conscious iteration of particular interpretations of knowledge, conceived for particular circumstances and to support particular interests. It follows, therefore, that its meanings can be altered as texts (including the landscape) are re-read in changing times and circumstances. Consequently, if heritage comprises the meanings attributed in the present, and for present reasons, to history and historically situated place, it is inevitably the case that such knowledges are also fields of contestation (Graham et al, 2000).

David Lowenthal (1985, 1996) argues that the past validates the present by conveying a set of timeless values and unbroken lineages and by restoring what are perceived of as lost or subverted values. In their evocation of the West as the repository of the soul of Ireland, poets and writers such as W.B. Yeats and J.M. Synge, and artists like Paul Henry, sought to create an 'authentic, quintessential Irish identity, encoded in a landscape different to the industrialised, modernised landscapes of contemporary Britain' (Whelan, 1993: 42), the source of Yeats's 'filthy modern tide'. Indeed, Yeats may be the supreme example of an artist creating a deliberate symbolic landscape allegory of identity, a mythology that became a fundamental iconography in the nascent nationalism of the Irish Free State.

There is nothing uniquely Irish about such intellectual constructs of place. Archetypal national landscapes that draw upon geographical imagery and particular readings of memory and myth are typical of Anderson's (1991) 'imagined communities' of nationalism, comprising people defined by cultural and political networks and bound by territorial frameworks. As Crooke (2000), for example, shows in her study of the creation of the National Museum of Ireland, national narratives are invented and imposed on representations of place, their legitimacy validated by particular readings of the past. Nationalism, like other forms of identity, creates discourses of inclusion and exclusion — who qualifies for membership and who does not. If heritage, therefore, is defined as the meaning of the past in the present, it is implicated in the interplay between power, politics and identity. Landscape provides one of the most potent illustrations of this point.

To geographers, 'landscape' has assumed different meanings at different times. For Paul Vidal de la Blache and, somewhat later, Carl Sauer, it was indicative of a harmony between human life and the milieu in which it was lived. Such ideas underpinned the Annales School of *Géohistoire*, and its concerted attempt to map and explain the complex reality of human life by reference to local and regional studies. For Fernand Braudel, in particular, any social reality had to be referred to the space, place or region within which it existed. The spatial basis of *Géohistoire* was the *pays*, literally an area with its own identity derived not only from its physical geography, but also from the ethnic and linguistic divisions imposed on a region by its history.

Such ideas found a powerful resonance with Estyn Evans, perhaps the most influential twentieth-century geographer of Ireland. Mediated through the ideas of H.J. Fleure, Evans was drawn to the concept of regional synthesis that shaped Vidal's and Braudel's geographies (Graham, 1994). For Evans, regions were not just the 'product of a symbiotic union of people and places', but also the 'consequences of the shifting relationships between people and people' (Livingstone, 1992: 285). Thus geography was 'the common ground between the natural world and cultural history' (Glasscock, 199: 87). The epitome of this discourse was to be found in Evans's masterpiece, *Mourne Country* (1951), a perfect miniature to illustrate Tuan's point about the creation of place through writing.

Contemporary geographers, however, regard landscapes less as places shaped by lived experience, and defined by material artefacts, than as primarily symbolic constructs. They can be interpreted as texts that interact with social, political and economic institutions and can be regarded as signifying practices 'that are read, not passively, but, as it were, re-written as they are read' (Barnes and Duncan, 1992: 5). Nevertheless, it has to be remembered that these representations are situated, that is, the view comes from somewhere and the representations are tied to particular relationships of power between peoples (Seymour, 2000). For Cosgrove (1993: 8), cultural landscapes are 'signifiers of the culture of those who have made them', but it is also the case that such hegemonic interpretations can be subverted by alternative readings that reflect, for example, gendered and ethnic dimensions to identity.

The situation is also rendered more complex by the simultaneous role fulfilled by cultural landscapes as economic capital. Heritage is not merely about identity and belonging, because heritage places are also locations of economic consumption. Cultural heritage, both tangible (material) and intangible (folklore, language, mythology, tradition), is the most important resource for tourism in Ireland. That market, however, is highly segmented and consumed at varying levels of intensity by different types of tourist. Tourism can be parasitic upon cultural heritage, which is often consumed at an inconsequential and stereotypical level, and, if taken to extreme, the economic commodification of the past will so trivialise it that, arguably, the result can be the destruction of the heritage resource which is its *raison d'être*.

In drawing upon such ideas to explore the interpretation of the rural in Northern Ireland, this discussion has four specific objectives. In the first instance, it addresses the portrayal of the rural in literature and geography and examines why certain representations have dominated over others. A second concern lies with the resonances of these representations for the shaping of rural identities in a society that lacks any coherent overarching representation of place. Thirdly, some attention is given to the ways in which the rural is represented through heritage policies, particular attention being given to the Ulster Folk and Transport Museum. Finally, the discussion considers the interaction between heritage and rurality in Northern Ireland, as the advent of the post-productivist countryside defines an entirely new parameter for 'rural' that overlies but does not eradicate the traditional arena of ethnic contestation, claim and counter-claim.

THE PORTRAYAL OF THE RURAL IN NORTHERN IRELAND

Patrick Duffy (1997: 69) makes the important point that overarching the idealisation of the West in artistic and literary representations of Ireland is the myth of the rural, 'a narrative which has echoes of a more universal allegory of the communality and practical tranquillity of the rural idyll in the face of the ever-expanding urbanisation'. Yeats's literary movement 'glorified the rural aesthetic as the authentic source of Irishness', creating a romantic nostalgia that still permeates traditional representations of Irish nationalism, the 'Celtic Tiger' notwithstanding. Duffy observes, however, that many other Irish writers — Frank O'Connor, Patrick Kavanagh, John McGahern, Edna O'Brien — while not altogether immune to the mysticism of Arcadia, invoke a more claustrophobic and oppressive reality that suffocates the individual, for whom the only apparent escape lies in migration to the city.

In Northern Ireland, however, the historical processes of urbanisation, but more potently the overriding, endlessly intractable, dilemma of contested ethnic identity and sectarianism, subsumes the rural as it does everything else. In stark contrast to the Republic of Ireland, the North remains, in the words of John Wilson Foster (1991: 281), 'a place yet to be imagined by the majority of its inhabitants'. For Foster, landscape is 'a cultural code that perpetuates instead of belying the instabilities and ruptures' (1991: 149). But it is also one of the few domains that 'seems on occasion to join the sects' (1991: 159). Foster argues that regionality — a continuity of identity vested in place — might provide an overarching sense of belonging for all the peoples of Northern Ireland living in their finely detailed ethnic heterogeneity. While A.T.Q. Stewart (1977) uses the analogy of the 'narrow ground' in his analysis of two 'interlocked' communities, Carlo Gébler (1991) is perhaps more realistic in his metaphor of two ostensibly separate standing trees, which, beneath the surface, share hopelessly intertwined root systems. In this image, we can visualise the close-wrought intimacy of the sectarian divides of rural Ulster (see Murtagh, 1998), the ethnic geography endlessly defying generalisation as neighbouring villages and townlands proclaim their allegiance through a panoply of flags, halls and paramilitary trappings (including a burgeoning landscape of memorialisation of their recent dead).

One of the primary cultural factors demarcating Northern

Ireland from its southern neighbour is that it has never evolved that sense of an invented landscape which might help unify its population in a shared communal sense of identity. Foster (1991: 294) argues that Ulster people have suffered from the 'twin psychological colonialisms of Irish nationalism and British nationality that have falsified their consciousness and diverted them from the true task of self-realisation'. In this proclamation of the strength and necessity of a primarily indigenous synthesis of identity vested in Ulster place, we can detect a marked resonance with the ideas of the Ulster poet John Hewitt. Indeed it is perhaps in a poetry characterised by a sense of place — in the work, among others, of Hewitt, Seamus Heaney, Derek Mahon, Paul Durcan, Tom Paulin and Gerald Dawe — that rural Ulster is most clearly portrayed in all its complexities of contested identities.

Foster (1991: 120) sees Hewitt as a townsman drawn to an uncongenial countryside and a planter drawn to a 'native culture that is, at root, equally uncongenial'. Perhaps, as others have suggested, he was grappling with the classic dilemma of those who cannot fall back on religion to define the Irishness in their identity. Instead, Hewitt turned to the landscape — and particularly the rural world — as a medium of uniting native and settler. He depicted a regional landscape of singular geographical coherence, one which conveyed an historical and traditional continuity of identity to its peoples. It was not the militaristic Ulster of unionism, 'the land of the heroes of the Somme and the generals of England's war' as Vance (1990: 228) sourly describes it. Rather Hewitt 'ventured out of the stockade into unsurveyed territory where planter writ does not run' (Foster, 1991: 159). But as some among his many critics have observed, Hewitt's vision of an integrating regionalism was no more than a pious hope, Ulster having no regional cultural model that might compare, for example, with Frédéric Mistral's Provençal *Félibrige*. Nonetheless, there is a notable contemporary resonance between Hewitt's commitment to regional identity and the broader debate on sub-state regionalism in Europe. The nation-state is a fragile and contingent entity under pressure from above through the forces of globalisation, and from beneath as the regional cultural diversity temporarily subsumed by nationalism in the eighteenth and nineteenth centuries becomes aligned with contemporary political impulses expressed through devolution and other forms of regional autonomy.

Hewitt's ideas and poetry share too many similarities with the geography of Estyn Evans. Both canons are imbued with a conceptualisation of regionalism that equates to the *pays* of *Géohistoire*, Hewitt's relationship with the Glens of Antrim bearing distinct similarities to that of Evans with the Mournes. Significantly, both *pays* are readily defined rural refuges. The pamphlet *Ulster: The Common Ground* (1984) contains perhaps the most explicit account of Evans's culturally diverse and regionalist view of Ulster. He saw the hidden closed-in drumlin lands of south Ulster as a Protestant landscape, occupied by a people of limited vision and imagination, marooned in their 'psychic stockade', to use Foster's graphic phrase (1991: 159). In contrast, there is the other tradition of Ulster — the open, naked bogs and hills, the lands of the poetic and visionary in the Ulster soul. Evans believed that such diversity could be reconciled as a single theme with many variations, the very personality of Ulster deriving from the unique fusion of many such small and different *pays*. He recognised, of course, that the landscape and material heritages were also a potent source of dissension and conflict, but argued that we must live with and exploit them as a 'total inheritance irrespective of formal creeds' (1984: 8).

The difficulty here is that Evans's search for a common ground largely eschews urbanisation but also the intangible heritage of religion, politics and social conflict. Instead the 'common' is defined by material heritage, its variations evocative of the finely differentiated physical environments of Ulster. The core values were of the common people and their attachment to the land that they had helped to make, a land, however, that is far older than all human cultures. Evans held to the ethnographic tenet that peasant cultures represented the repositories of true social values and that Ireland, as a whole, preserved 'to a remarkable degree the customs and social habits of the pre-industrial phase of western civilisation' (Evans, 1942: 6). This reading differed radically, however, from traditional Irish nationalism which also emphasised the primacy of the rural. Evans was concerned to demonstrate the vibrant diversity of the rural world, the very traits subsumed by the monolith of the Gaelic myth. Any unity of purpose could emerge only from that geographical heterogeneity.

THE IMPORTANCE OF RURAL IDENTITIES

For Evans, the personality of the region — whether it was Mourne, Ulster or Ireland — lay in the landscape, which, in turn, 'inhered ultimately in the personality of a region's people' (Campbell, 1996: 243). In privileging the local, he, therefore, admitted to the inevitability of friction and dissonance and would have applauded the idea that Ireland is 'a plurality of continuities, interlocking, full of complexity' (Ó Tuathaigh, 1991: 67). It is this concern with the eclectic and the ordinary (Evans's ethnological outlook led him instinctively to eschew the documents of the powerful and rich), with local particularity in the context of universal process, that lends contemporaneity to Evans's ideas as we struggle to redefine the meanings of identity and place in the face of forces of globalisation, the network society and time-space compression.

In this context, some cultural theorists contend that the deconstruction of the 'out of many one' ideology of nationalism in which belonging is defined by its territorial limits, means that place is no longer important in defining the meaning of belonging as identities become increasingly fragmented and fractured. Conversely, however, it can be argued that place does matter but that it is a place of multiple layers of identity (Graham and Hart, 1999), a porous place constructed out of multiple social relations (Massey, 1995). Thus social and cultural diversity within place is the norm, the assumed heterogeneity of the nation-state the aberrant.

Northern Ireland, nonetheless, displays distressingly unconstructed attitudes to the definition of place, which, like power, is seen as a zero-sum. In other words, 'nationalist' notions of space and place imbue the mindsets of both unionists and republicans, and underpin what should be the long-discredited tribalism of two communities. This is directly analogous to Benedict Anderson's 'imagined communities' of nationalism and shares in the self-same delusions and limited narratives of communality and fraternity that make it possible 'for so many ... people, not so much to kill, as willingly to die for such limited imaginings' (Anderson, 1991: 7). At root, the Northern Ireland crisis is first about identity and only secondly about politics and its structures. One of the many contradictions of the peace process, however, is that it accords primacy to political solutions, which lack legitimisation precisely because they are dissonant to a people's cultural values.

But why should narratives of place vested in rural landscapes possess any sustained relevance in this context, given that comparatively few Western people today are rural dwellers and many of those that are regard the countryside merely as a financial opportunity for urban investors or a place to live? The bulk of Northern Ireland's population are urban dwellers and many have long been removed from the soil and the intimacy of the *pays* by Ulster's lengthy history of industrialisation. Several reasons can be advanced to explain why the 'rural' is important in identity: it is much less obvious that more traditionally conceived rural identities centred on agriculture and its heritage retain any major significance in the post-productivist countryside. First, unionism's 'other' — republican nationalism — is imbued with rural narratives, even if these bear little relevance to the everyday reality of ordinary lives. Secondly, the major urban areas of the North are so brutally tribalised that, apart from the vital exception of city and town centres, it is impossible to identify common grounds. The countryside, however, with its commonality of material and even intangible culture might, arguably, be a resource of more positive symbols and narratives. The evidence does suggest, however, that it experiences the same distortions of mobility patterns and social contacts that occur in Northern Ireland's urban areas (Murtagh, 1998). Thirdly, as Greer and Murray argue in the Introduction of this book, rurality becomes 'a powerful metaphor for claims related to spatial equity, bottom up development processes, and inter-generational sustainability'. The rural is a world of 'active community interests for whom place, culture and identity are powerful signifiers'.

The post-independence Irish State has derived enormous social cohesion from a nationalist narrative vested in rurality. This deified places essentially defined by Daniel Corkery's vision of a 'Hidden Ireland', in which Irish identity was couched in terms of great antiquity, oppressed by British economic, political and religious discrimination (Cullen, 1988). Located in the 'West', this Gaelic and rural dreamworld defined a cultural landscape that later became seamlessly interwoven with Catholic dogma to define a petty bourgeois state dominated by the shared interests of substantial farmers, local business interests and the Roman Catholic church (McLaughlin, 1993).

In response to this classic example of the 'imagined com-munity' of nationalism, literally defined by a narrative of place, unionist identity in the North became almost entirely political. In general, the unionist view of history reduced the past to little more than a handful of events, usually of sectarian hue. The inconography of unionism was of blood sacrifice and/or Catholic deception, but this was in itself insufficient to establish the legitimacy accorded by a strong narrative of place. Unionist Ulster never shared the indigenous representation of place nec-essary to sustain the 'imagined community', even though the historic province of Ulster, separated from the remainder of Ireland by a host of drumlins and lakes that stretches from Dundalk to Donegal Bay, remains a readily identifiable region. To have done so would have been to compromise the Britishness of Ulster by locating it within Ireland.

The most significant exception to this generalisation was the foundation of the then Ulster Folk Museum at Cultra, Co. Down (it became the Ulster Folk and Transport Museum in 1973). The legislation establishing the Museum was enacted by the Northern Ireland Parliament in 1958. In a House in which debate was normally defined by sectarian rancour between unionists and nationalists, there was little controversy, the Museum being regarded as a benign educational institution which might double as a tourism attraction (Graham, 1996). (The social construction of culture and heritage as negotiated, situated knowledges was not acknowledged.) The legislation owed much to Evans, who had skilfully campaigned for an open-air folk museum based on the Scandinavian model. Following its purchase in 1961, Cultra was opened to the public in 1964.

THE REPRESENTATION OF THE RURAL: THE ULSTER FOLK AND TRANSPORT MUSEUM

Prior to considering the representation of the rurality of Ulster encapsulated by the Folk Museum, it is important to stress that such a narrative does not have to be congruent with everyday life. Rather, it is constructed from a suite of symbols, an iconography to which people can subscribe as a basis for general understanding. Evans would have seen the Folk Museum as an institution indicative of region and environment, reflective of regional identities but not creating them. Nevertheless, as Tuan (1991: 693) acknowledges, geographers can 'create place by their eloquence' and, consciously or no, heritage conveys meaning. Museums, for instance, can be envisaged as tools of social engineering, although, as Crooke (2000) observes, those in Northern Ireland have been reluctant to engage publicly with the question of whose tradition is being collected and why. Still, it is possible to read themes of common inheritance and common identity into the assemblage of material artefacts at Cultra.

As once envisaged, the role of the Museum was 'to illustrate the way of life, past and present, and the traditions of the people of Northern Ireland' (Thompson, 1970: 233). This ostensibly straightforward goal conceals very much more complex under-tones, not least the idea of a common Ulster heritage that might transcend sectarian division, an iconography that stresses the integrative idea of regionalism. Thus Buckley (1988) questions the entire two traditions thesis, arguing that the dichotomy of difference is political rhetoric and that the people of Northern Ireland (Ulster) share a general material uniformity that is divided more by geography and class than by ethnicity. The

271

reconstructed vernacular — both rural and urban — buildings at Cultra and their associated material artefacts can therefore be read as reflecting not Protestantism or Catholicism but the intimate, localised variations of environment that define Ulster, a small place of large mental distances.

The Museum's first director, G.B. Thompson, envisaged the institution in terms of the absence of a cultural identity in Ulster, a community in which political-religious identity had superseded and stifled the emergence of any sense of regional cultural personality. He recognised, however, that the Museum could be read in a negative way, identity being both integrative and divisive. Thompson's successor, Alan Gailey (1990), saw folklife as encouraging a sense of unity in the face of diversity. He believed in interpretation but resisted any notion of immutability in potential readings, preferring the idea of a multiplicity of traditions to the appealing but not readily realised 'common ground' (if that is interpreted in the singular). Gailey subscribed, too, to the notion that the past exists only in the present.

In its presentations, the Folk Museum is something of a hybrid. It does run the risk of freezing time by allocating such a central role to rural traditions. Kirkland (1996), for example, argues that the stress placed on the paradigm of tradition as a redemptive force reminding 'Ulstermen' just what they had in common, in fact merely neutralises what might be seen as distinctive or even dangerous local cultural activities. He believes that the past is thus rendered as an 'established touchstone' and not a narrative of schism and fracture. Even John Hewitt saw it this way, referring in his poem 'Cultra Manor: The Ulster Folk Museum' (Ormsby, ed., 1991: 187) to the 'tidy and white' workshops and cottages and the 'archetypal round pillars' but also to the absence of a 'field for the faction fights'. Given this somewhat sanitised past, it is still the case that Kirkland's unduly literal interpretation overlooks the point that authenticity does not exist, the 'realities' of any museum being shaped by its users' experiences and interpretations. It is undoubtedly the case that the ethnographic paradigm that underpins the folk museum model can elide power, social division, conflict and intangible heritage while privileging, instead, the material world of artefacts. Nevertheless, any representation that points to the importance within Northern Ireland of locality and diversity, of multiple and overlapping traditions (and not merely two) offers a challenging alternative to a reading of binary sectarian fracture.

Consequently, if the representations of rural tradition in the Ulster Folk Museum encourage its consumers to appreciate that differences in places and peoples may be attributable to factors other than ethnicity and sectarianism, then these apparently traditional artefacts show how environment, culture and the very clash between native and planter, which Evans contended provided the dynamic of historical change in Ireland, all contribute to a narrative of complex, minutely scaled local variations. Representations of diversity allied to a recognition of the complex causes of difference are central to any eventual resolution of Northern Ireland's identity crisis.

The problem, however, lies less in the museology than in its consumption. It can be argued that the widespread acceptance of a narrative that deconstructs Northern Ireland into a multiplicity of traditions requires a populist policy that maximises public consumption of the heritage artefacts which constitute one medium for transmitting interpretations that contradict and make fuzzy the simple sectarian model of two traditions. The evidence, however, is disappointing. Partly because local government in Northern Ireland is subdivided into 26 District Councils, each anxious to make its mark, partly because sponsors of heritage projects have found it relatively easy to attract capital for infrastructure and buildings in a grant-driven cultural economy, the province is awash with heritage centres, forest and history parks, big houses, cultural trails and industrial museums. Few, if any, of these generate sufficient income from visitors to sustain their running costs — as was all too graphically illustrated by the forced closure of the interpretative centre at Navan Fort, Co. Armagh, in the summer of 2001. A recent Department of Arts, Culture and Leisure (DECAL) report (2001), identifies over 400 managed heritage facilities which attracted 4.55 million visitors in 1999. As visitor numbers are heavily skewed to a handful of sites (most importantly the

Giant's Causeway, Ulster Museum, Ulster Folk and Transport Museum, Ulster American Folk Park, Tollymore Forest Park and the National Trust property at Mount Stewart), the large majority of these facilities are heavily underused. Nevertheless, one of the recommendations of the DECAL report is the establishment of a network of seven to nine regional museums in Northern Ireland, a very high level of provision for a population of 1.6 million.

Nor does the raft of heritage projects appear to have any measurable role in altering sectarian mindsets, despite the unfortunately largely unresearched emphasis accorded to heritage as a facilitator of education. It is the tradition of sectarianism, both rural and urban, rather than the tradition of the past as a rural idyll, which continues to dominate identity politics in Northern Ireland. 'Polite' heritage like the Ulster Folk Museum is consumed by the politically disengaged, and often at a very superficial level, while the paramilitaries and their political parties conduct their own heritage debates through the medium of the gable-wall mural. Unfortunately perhaps, the ghettos of Belfast and Derry arguably tell us more about identity contestation in Northern Ireland than do all the heritage and folk centres and their artefacts of rural tradition.

THE CONTEMPORARY MEANINGS OF HERITAGE AND RURALITY IN NORTHERN IRELAND

The selling of the rural past dominates Northern Ireland's heritage industry, a characteristic that the province shares with many other relatively remote rural regions in which the economic and political forces restructuring the countryside have swept away much of the past, not least agriculture. The theory of the post-productivist countryside suggests that the new ruralities are urban-oriented in terms of demand and consumer patterns. The countryside is an arena of intricate patterns of social inclusion and exclusion and of internal others (Cloke and Little, 1997), with its own demands of equity, diversity and interdependence (Murray and Murtagh, 2002). One of the difficulties in addressing these processes through community initiatives is the very complexity of that diversity and of the conflicting interests involved that define the rural as contested space.

There are two principal dimensions to the contestation of the rural, actual and potential, in Northern Ireland. First, there is the uneasy mix of motivations involved in rural heritage — tourism, education, entertainment, but also the much more pressing questions of meaning and identity. This multiple use and commodification of heritage is a potent source of what Tunbridge and Ashworth (1996) term 'dissonance', the contestation that ensues from the multitude of messages carried by the same material and intangible forms of heritage.

Secondly, as is largely still also true of the Republic of Ireland, Northern Ireland is marketed officially through its natural landscapes and rural traditions. The countryside is becoming an idealised environment which entrepreneurs seek to commodify as a product. Alternatively, such romanticised representations may be used to sell other products that acquire connotations of quality and desirability from their association with the images held by consumers of rural places. In turn, these images are often created by tourism agencies to promote a country or region abroad. In Ireland, for example, products that mesh with the dominant pre-modern imagery of the West, which is more relevant today as a tourism artefact than a nationalist narrative, are likely to be those with the broadest market appeal in terms of consumer perceptions of quality. In Northern Ireland, there is obviously a competing set of unofficial images and narratives, those of the paramilitaries and their associated political parties. While these latter might appear to be more strictly an urban phenomenon, the countryside remains equally divided and is similarly marked and claimed by the iconography of sectarianism.

Both dimensions of contestation are apparent in the official images, which, with their reliance on stereotyped images of tradition (itself a social construct), are often at variance with the contested nature of contemporary rurality and the diversity of rural life. Rural Northern Ireland is imaged in six principal ways, all of which involve readings, narratives and visual images that relate to but often seem to clash with the idea of renegotiating rurality. In turn, these have varying impacts as the raw materials of local identities. The natural environment provides the first perspective. The most iconic signature image is, of course, the Giant's Causeway, the centrepiece of the Causeway Coast Area of Outstanding Natural Beauty. Together with forest and country parks and lakelands, such natural heritage is essentially a neutral resource to be read in terms of prevailing aesthetic taste rather than sectarianism. The contestation it arouses is concerned with the protection of sometimes fragile physical environments and of reconciling the demands of tourism access with the management of landscapes that continue to be shaped by dynamic physical processes.

The second perspective is that of diasporic identity. This includes the ancestral homes of various presidents of the United States and even a prime minister of New Zealand, John Ballance. Genealogy provides an important adjunct to this form of heritage, which is aimed largely at an external audience. Again this seems an essentially neutral resource, although Brett (1993) reads the Ulster-Scots ethos of the emigrant experience of the Ulster American Folk Park near Omagh as a sectarian representation. Alternatively, it can be seen as an historically valid attempt to display the ubiquity of the tragedy of emigration to all the peoples of Ireland and to challenge the republican claim to a monopoly of oppression.

Thirdly, there are various 'national' and local museums (and soon to be more), heritage and visitor centres, which are repositories for collections of local traditions and folklore. Although the Ulster Museum and the Ulster Folk and Transport Museum have a remit that extends to all of Northern Ireland, most of these are fixed in place and heavily oriented towards material culture. These sites tend to project a claim to neutrality, to an 'objective' emphasis on stepping back in time. But no reading of the past is devoid of present-day meanings and these will act as the filters through which visitors perceive the narratives and representations presented to them. There is very little research on the reception by consumers in Northern Ireland of museum and heritage centre displays, although this is critical to their — again largely perceived — role as conduits of education in a deeply divided society. Nor is there any real evidence to support the value of the localism portrayed by many of these centres. The motivating force is all too often the excessive fragmentation of Northern Ireland into its District Council areas, which often have little historical legitimacy. These are not necessarily identifiable *pays*, localities of the mind, so most Councils have set about creating a sense of local identity based on heritage that in turn might help validate this level of governance. One inevitable result is the duplication of heritage provision.

Fourthly, there is a considerable amount of heritage that relates the stories of Northern Ireland's agriculturally based industries — textiles, brewing, distilling — and the transport infrastructure that linked them to Belfast and Derry. Again, much of this is informed by very local perspectives and some reflects the oldest truism in heritage tourism that a place 'markets what it has'. The difficulty lies not in representing the local but in the ways in which that is defined by the sectarian politics of District Councils. Because of the linkage between heritage provision and local government, it could be argued that the selected heritage is that which best reflects the needs and strengths of the prevalent political parties at the local level.

Fifth is the official heritage of the state and its agencies, principally the National Trust. This embraces historical monuments in state care (most of which are unmanaged sites) — castles, big houses and landscaped gardens and parks. These heritage landscapes are often redolent of power and have been described by Hewison (1987) as theatres for the re-enactment of the past, which are run to showcase the inheritance of an élite. Quite whether the consumers see them in these terms is less clear. Mount Stewart, for example, is one of the most popular rural heritage attractions in Northern Ireland and, somewhat contentiously, a candidate for listing as a UNESCO World Heritage Site.

Finally, there are various forms of themed heritage centres which are best thought of as places of entertainment — open farms, activity centres and the like — which have little meaning in terms of identity but portray, for example, somewhat stereotyped images of the rural to urban populations.

The theme that links these six manifestations of rural heritage is that they largely exclude past and present violence, oppression and ethnic contestation. They tend to portray an idealised place defined by bland historical mythology with a physical environment but no politics, even though many of the facilities are overtly political in origin in that they reflect the aspirations of local government in Northern Ireland. Even class politics are elided and there is little cognisance of rural women or of the very complex patterns of rural social exclusion. All too often, rural heritage presents an idealised world inadequately grounded in an interpretation of the historical archives and compounded by a failure to recognise that those too can be read in different ways. If cultural heritage does play a role in conflict resolution and the deconstruction of binary certainties, then this requires a transformation in the interpretation and representation of the heritage landscape. The priorities of grant-driven finance and localised political sensibilities have not produced a heritage portfolio that addresses the real issues of contested identities in Northern Ireland. Crooke (2001) points to optimistic signs that museums and other heritage facilities are adapting to the demands of the new politics. But what is apparent is that the initiative is being grasped in part by the paramilitary organisations and their political parties who are establishing alternative readings of the landscape. Rural Northern Ireland has always been claimed by sectarian markers but these are becoming more overt as an unofficial landscape of remembrance of the paramilitary dead of the Troubles is created. The memorials and flags, miniature gardens of remembrance and shrines to the notable dead, both of the recent and more distant past that are appearing everywhere in rural Ulster, demonstrate the schism between the official heritage of state and local government and the unofficial heritage of identity. In its often sanitised, idealised representation of the material cultures of the past, the former is simply irrelevant to the realisation that the conflict in Northern Ireland is primarily about identity and that identities are created out of the resources of the past.

CONCLUSION

While some of the issues raised here concerning the representation of place, heritage and history in Northern Ireland are obviously not restricted to the rural domain, there is still a pressing need to rethink the rural and its meaning in heritage. Rural places cannot simply be spaces of consumption for urban populations, but equally they cannot be defined by the protectionist ideology of land use planning. Economic and political forces and processes that extend far beyond its boundaries are transforming Northern Ireland's rurality. But as argued here, the challenge of redefining it from within has largely been shirked. The rural world is a resource that could be interpreted in ways that do not eradicate conflict but might contribute to its diminution. The outcome of a divided and diverse society like Northern Ireland may not be an inclusive form of multiculturalism achieved through processes of consensus. The achievable goal might be no more than a grudging acceptance that the other has a right to his or her own history, reflecting a more general realisation that multicultural societies are often comprised of mutual solitudes.

Rural identities in Northern Ireland do remain apparent and although there is scope for optimism, not least in the ideas of diversity and inclusion, it is also the case that economically driven, state-sponsored representations of rural heritage are often irrelevant to identity and to the fragmentation of belonging in the post-productivist countryside. Nor do they embody the eloquence that might create a region. The brave idea of a common ground vested in rurality and material rural cultures that underpinned the original philosophy of the Ulster Folk Museum is a dead letter unless commonality is interpreted as the numerous strands of difference that make up the diversity of rural Northern Ireland. That the proponents of violence are setting about creating their own identity landscape in rural Ulster underscores the failure of official initiatives in asking the important questions about interpreting the troubled history of rural Northern Ireland. While the landscape of memorialisation to the dead is one of the most significant signs that the fighting is over, it signifies too that the contestation of rural Northern Ireland will continue.

REFERENCES

Anderson, B. (2nd. ed., 1991), *Imagined Communities*, London: Verso.

Barnes, T.J. and J.S. Duncan (1992), *Writing Worlds: Discourse, Text and Metaphor in the Representation of Landscape*, London: Routledge.

Brett, D. (1993), 'The Construction of Heritage', in B. O'Connor and M. Cronin (eds), *Tourism in Ireland: A Critical Analysis*, Cork University Press.

Buckley, A.D. (1988), 'Collecting Ulster's Culture: Are There Really Two Traditions?', in A. Gailey (ed.), *The Use of Tradition*, Cultra: Ulster Folk and Transport Museum.

Campbell, J. (1996), 'Ecology and Culture in Ireland', in E. Estyn Evans, *Ireland and the Atlantic Heritage: Selected Writings*, Dublin: Lilliput Press.

Cloke, P. and J. Little (eds) (1997), *Contested Countryside Cultures*, London: Routledge.

Cosgrove, D.E. (1993), *The Palladian Landscape: Geographical Change and its Cultural Representation in Sixteenth-century Italy*, Leicester University Press.

Crooke, E. (2000), *Politics, Archaeology and the Creation of the National Museum of Ireland*, Dublin: Irish Academic Press.

Crooke, E. (2001), 'Confronting a Troubled History: Which Past in Northern Ireland's Museums?', *International Journal of Heritage Studies*, vol. 7, no. 2: 119–136.

Cullen, L.M. (1988), *The Hidden Ireland: Reassessment of a Concept*, Mullingar: Lilliput Press.

DECAL (2001), *Local Museums and Heritage Review*, Belfast: DECAL.

Duffy, P. (1997), 'Writing Ireland: Literature and Art in the Representation of Place', in B. Graham (ed.), *In Search of Ireland: A Cultural Geography*, London: Routledge.

Evans, E.E. (1942), *Irish Heritage: The Landscape, the People and their Work*, Dundalk: Dundalgan Press.

Evans, E.E. (1984), *Ulster: The Common Ground*, Mullingar: Lilliput Press.

Evans, E.E. (1951), *Mourne Country: Landscape and Life in South Down*, Dundalk: Dundalgan Press.

Foster, J.W. (1991), *Colonial Consequences: Essays in Irish Literature and Culture*, Dublin: Lilliput Press.

Gailey, A. (1990), '"... Such As Pass Us Daily": The Study of Folklife', *Ulster Folklife* 36: 4–22.

Gebler, C. (1991), *The Glass Curtain: Inside an Ulster Community*, London: Hamish Hamilton.

Glasscock, R.E. (1991), 'Obituary: E. Estyn Evans, 1905–1989', *Journal of Historical Geography*, vol. 17, no. 1: 87–91.

Graham, B.J. (1994), 'The Search for the Common Ground: Estyn Evans's Ireland', *Transactions Institute of British Geographers* NS19, no. 2: 183–201.

Graham, B. (1996), 'The Contested Interpretation of Heritage Landscapes in Northern Ireland', *International Journal of Heritage Studies*, vol. 2, no. 1: 10–22.

Graham, B., G.J. Ashworth and J.E. Tunbridge (2000), *A Geography of Heritage: Power, Culture and Economy*, London: Arnold.

Graham, B. and M. Hart (1999), 'Cohesion and Diversity in the European Union: Irreconcilable Forces?', *Regional Studies*, vol. 33, no. 3: 259–268.

Hewison, R. (1987), *The Heritage Industry: Britain in a State of Decline*, London: Methuen.

Kirkland, R. (1996), *Literature and Culture in Northern Ireland Since 1965: Moments of Danger*, Harlow: Longman.

Livingstone, D. (1992), *The Geographical Tradition*, Oxford: Blackwell.

Lowenthal, D. (1985), *The Past is a Foreign Country*, Cambridge University Press.

Lowenthal, D. (1996), *The Heritage Crusade and the Spoils of History*, Cambridge University Press.

McLaughlin, J. (1993), 'Place, Politics and Culture in Nation-building Ulster: Constructing Nationalist Hegemony in Post-Famine Donegal', *Canadian Review of Studies in Nationalism* vol. XX, no. 2: 97–111.

Massey, D. (1995), 'The Conceptualization of Place', in D. Massey and P. Jess (eds), *A Place in the World? Place, Cultures and Globalization*, Oxford: Open University/Oxford University Press.

Murray, M. and B. Murtagh (2002), *Reconnecting Rural People through Authentic Dialogue: Equity, Diversity and Interdependence in the Northern Ireland Rural Development Arena*, Research Monograph, Rural Community Network, Cookstown.

Murtagh, B. (1998), 'Community, Conflict and Rural Planning in Northern Ireland', *Journal of Rural Studies,* vol. 14, no. 3: 221–231.

Ormsby, F. (ed.) (1991), *The Collected Poems of John Hewitt,* Belfast: Blackstaff Press.

Ó Tuathaigh, G. (1991), 'The Irish-Ireland Idea: Rationale and Relevance', in E. Longley (ed.), *Culture in Ireland: Division or Diversity*, Belfast: Institute of Irish Studies.

Schama, S. (1995), *Landscape and Memory*, London: HarperCollins.

Seymour, S. (2000), 'Historical Geographies of Landscape', in B. Graham and C. Nash (eds), *Modern Historical Geographies*, Harlow: Prentice Hall.

Stewart, A.T.Q. (1977), *The Narrow Ground: Aspects of Ulster, 1609–1969*, London: Faber and Faber.

Thompson, G.B. (1970), 'Estyn Evans and the Development of the Ulster Folk Museum', *Ulster Folklife,* vols 15–16: 233–238.

Tuan, Yi-Fu (1991), 'Language and the Making of Place: A Narrative-Descriptive Approach', *Annals of American Geographers,* vol. 81, no. 4: 684–696.

Tunbridge, J.E. and G.J. Ashworth (1996), *Dissonant Heritage: The Management of the Past as a Resource in Conflict*, Chichester: John Wiley.

Vance, N. (1990), *Irish Literature: A Social History*, Oxford: Basil Blackwell.

Whelan, K. (1993), 'The Bases of Regionalism', in P. Ó Drisceoil (ed.), *Culture in Ireland — Regions: Identity and Power*, Belfast: Institute of Irish Studies.

CHAPTER 13

RETHINKING RURAL PLANNING AND DEVELOPMENT IN NORTHERN IRELAND

John Greer and Michael Murray

INTRODUCTION

On 17 September 2001 the Minister for Regional Development, Mr Gregory Campbell, introduced a motion to the Northern Ireland Assembly which called for agreement by the Assembly on the proposed Regional Development Strategy, *Shaping Our Future*. A two-hour debate concluded with a resolution endorsing the strategy, thus bringing to an end a plan preparation process which had commenced in June 1997. This journey of inquiry is marked by a number of prominent milestones:

- the publication of a Discussion Paper in November 1997;
- a Draft Proposals Document in December 1998;
- a Public Examination of proposals in the Autumn of 1999;
- the publication of the report of the Public Examination Panel in February 2000;
- the publication of a response to the Panel's report by the Department for Regional Development (DRD) in April 2000; and
- the submission of final representations from interested parties by the end of May 2000.

Throughout this lengthy period of extensive consultation and discussion, key goals have comprised the need to secure a broad consensus on the future spatial planning framework for Northern Ireland and the need for policy prescription to go beyond land use planning. Intensive interaction between Members of the Legislative Assembly and public officials has secured complete cross-party political support for this twenty-five year strategy and might suggest, therefore, that this ambition has now been realised. Accordingly, it is appropriate that this chapter should commence by describing some of the principal features of *Shaping Our Future* (DRD, 2001). The extent to which the strategy is capable of retaining its hard-won consensus during the years ahead, especially within rural society, is briefly explored. The discussion then re-visits the concept of Integrated Rural Development, which, it is argued, offers a more radical framework for rethinking the future of rural places and society than that posited by *Shaping Our Future*. The chapter concludes by identifying important elements of the way forward for rural planning and development within this more expansive context.

THE NORTHERN IRELAND REGIONAL DEVELOPMENT STRATEGY: *SHAPING OUR FUTURE*

The strategy document runs to over 200 pages and comprises six sections made up of thirteen chapters and appendices. In all, there are some 43 strategic planning guidelines supported by 23 diagrams, in themselves evidence of the complex policy arena within which land use planning is located. The document guarantees a long read to those who persevere but, embedded within the language of inclusiveness, there are some very significant policy directions for the future. This chapter section deals selectively with the following themes:

* the spatial development framework;
* housing provision and land supply;
* the Belfast Metropolitan Area;
* rural Northern Ireland.

The spatial development framework

The strategy at the outset is careful to set out some parameters indicating the scale of possible change over the planning period. Thus mention is made of the need to accommodate a population growth of 105,000 by 2015 and some 150,000 by 2025. The dwellings requirement is estimated at 160,000 by 2015 and 250,000 by 2025, which will be capable of providing for a future population level of 1.835 million. The employment need is set at approximately 100,000 additional jobs by 2015. The number of vehicles on Northern Ireland roads is anticipated to double over the period to 2025.

In working through the implications of these headline data, the strategy adopts 'the promotion of a balanced and equitable pattern of sustainable development across the Region' as an overarching set of values. The text emphasises the complementarity of cities, towns and rural areas and underlines the need to optimise the distinctive contributions of these component areas of Northern Ireland in order to maximise the potential of the region as a whole. The spatial framework is thus constructed around an interconnected suite of elements comprising the regional gateways of Belfast and Derry/Londonderry, urban hubs comprising the regional towns, and link transport corridors of roads and railway as 'the skeletal framework' for future physical development (Figure 13.1).

It is, perhaps, not surprising that this spatial framework should broadly mirror the earlier 1975–1995 Regional Physical Development Strategy in relation to the prominent role of the cities and regional towns. The relegation of Magherafelt, Ballymoney and Ballycastle to second tier status in the urban hierarchy is, however, a departure from the previous framework when, having regard to the then newly constituted District Council areas, it was perceived as only proper that each administrative area should have a designated District Town within a single tier of regional growth centres. A further similarity with the previous spatial framework is the prominent recognition given to the strategic natural resource endowment of rural areas which, when conjoined with an extensive green

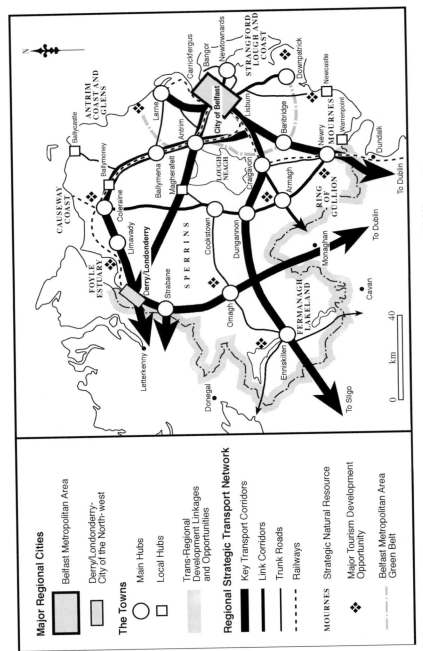

FIGURE 13.1 THE NORTHERN IRELAND SPATIAL DEVELOPMENT STRATEGY, 2025

Source: Adapted from Department for Regional Development (2001), *Shaping Our Future.*

belt for the Belfast Metropolitan Area, sends a strong signal of environmental protection intent. But fundamentally the diagram captures an enduring tension within Northern Ireland on the merits of concentration versus dispersal. Indeed that debate has been ongoing since the publication of the Belfast Regional Survey and Plan (the Matthew Plan) in 1964, which sought to contain the outward growth of the city through the imposition of a stopline and link this with the selective expansion of a number of urban centres. A key paragraph in the new strategy resonates loudly with the advocacy of that earlier prescription. Thus *Shaping Our Future* argues:

The key to achieving an optimum balance between over-concentration around the Belfast Metropolitan Area and excessive dispersal is to sustain a reinforced network of strong urban hubs, linked by an upgraded strategic transport network. This will provide accessible counter-magnet development opportunities to the metropolitan core, thus helping to ease development and transport pressures in and around Belfast. (DRD, 2001: 46)

The Matthew Plan by way of comparison suggests:

The prime object of the plan in this respect is, to a modest extent, simultaneously to demagnetize the centre and reinvigorate the many small towns in the region. This is a highly complex conception; both aspects (limitation and growth) must be complementary, not only on paper, but in fact in time and in balance. It implies a technique of planning and execution appropriate to administration at its highest levels (p18) ... The network of main roadways as now planned and partly under construction will in general link the growth centres to Belfast, but some modifications, mainly in the form of spurs will be necessary. (Matthew, 1964: 24)

Housing provision and land supply

At the Public Examination into the Draft Regional Strategic Framework, considerable time was taken to work through and refine the housing need forecasts for Northern Ireland. The Panel's report set out a suggested allocation between the Belfast Metropolitan Area with its hinterland and the rest of Northern Ireland. This division is retained within the new strategy which allocates 77,500 new dwellings to the former and 82,500 to the latter through to the year 2015. The strategy also identifies a set of District housing indicators which range from 1,400 additional residential units in Moyle by 2015 to 51,000 units in the six Districts of the Belfast Metropolitan Area (Figure 13.2). In the draft strategy the preliminary housing targets were further disaggegated to regional town and rural community components, but this task has now been left to the follow-on Area Plan process.

FIGURE 13.2 HOUSING INDICATORS BY DISTRICT COUNCIL AREA, 2015

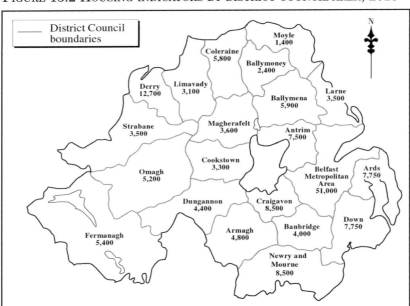

Source: Adapted from Department for Regional Development (2001), *Shaping Our Future*.

The new strategy, however, provides a number of very strong policy steers on how the interpretation of these indicators is to be worked through:

288

- primacy is to be given to main towns in order to support the achievement of 'critical mass'. The optimal housing balance between towns, villages and dispersed small settlements is predicated on ensuring that the growth potential of the principal urban centres for employment and services is not undermined;
- more use is to be made of recycled land and buildings thus reducing the need for greenfield development land. The strategy sets a regional target of 60 per cent of future residential development and associated job provision within existing urban limits through to the year 2010, which contrasts with the recent level of achievement of not more than 30 per cent;
- large-scale development proposals for the expansion of an existing settlement with a population of under 5,000, or for the creation of a 'new settlement' must be 'exceptional' in their intention to meet specific housing needs in the East of the region. Important criteria are set out in the document against which such proposals will be assessed and which shift the conventional developer-led interpretation of this scale of development more towards self-sufficiency of social and physical infrastructure, along with convenience to a commuter rail network.

The implementation of this regional scale allocative model of housing provision will, however, considerably test the durability of the new political and technical consensus, especially at local level when it comes to the matter of area plan preparation. Sub regional disaggregations are unlikely to be sufficiently sensitive in all situations to local building rate dynamics thus requiring comprehensive land supply monitoring along with speedy review and adjustment of development plans.

Belfast Metropolitan Area

The Belfast Metropolitan Area (BMA) currently has a population of around 600,000 people and takes in the administrative area of Belfast City Council along with the adjacent urban parts of the District Council areas of Carrickfergus, Castlereagh, Lisburn, Newtownabbey and North Down. Over 1 million people live within a thirty-mile radius of Belfast City Centre. The strategy notes that over the past three decades the inner city has experienced decline followed by an ongoing process of renewal. This has been matched over the same period by suburban expansion and overspill to Bangor, Carrickfergus and Lisburn. Given the seriousness of the congestion pressures on the city and the ready availability of appropriate investment locations in nearby centres, it is proposed firstly to enhance the development of Antrim, Banbridge, Craigavon, Downpatrick, Larne and Newtownards as counter-magnets to the BMA. The District housing indicators in Figure 13.2 above are illustrative of this preference. The second pillar of the urban strategy will be to secure the expansion of seven small towns around the BMA to help meet housing need generated by the latter. Thus Ballyclare, Ballynahinch, Carryduff, Comber, Crumlin, Dromore and Moira have been designated on the basis of their location on key transport corridors and infrastructure availability as an additional ring of overspill settlements. And finally, for the BMA itself the thrust of policy will continue to be urban revitalisation. What emerges for this core part of Northern Ireland, therefore, is a complex set of spatial interdependencies characterised by multi-dimensional patterns of living, working, shopping, education and recreation. Nevertheless, some 42,000 additional dwellings are estimated as representing the housing need within the BMA urban area. Notwithstanding the commitment, as noted above, to brownfield recycling, it is inevitable, therefore, that peripheral land release on greenfield sites will be required over the years ahead, thus widening the development footprint of Belfast. Green belt protection interest groups will continue to strongly contest these land releases, not least in connection with the forthcoming Belfast Metropolitan Area Plan.

Transportation is the glue that will hold together this emergent city-region geography. Within the new strategy, emphasis is placed on the creation of a Metropolitan Transport Corridor Network radiating out from Belfast City Centre and characterised by improved public transit services. The great danger, however, is that the disconnection between land use development and transportation solutions will deepen. There is every likelihood that the certainty of private sector-led new housing in accordance with the wider locational preferences of this strategy will generate increased car travel into and within the BMA. An uncertain and expenditure-constrained public sector thus faces immediate and longer-term challenges in responding adequately to these congestion realities. The strategy document is short on commitments to the contrary.

Rural Northern Ireland

In accordance with a recommendation from the Public Examination Panel, the new strategy contains a separate chapter on rural Northern Ireland. At the draft proposals stage the 'rural community' was defined as comprising the distinctive elements of small towns under 10,000 people, villages and small settlements, and open countryside, which in 1996 collectively totalled some 652,000 persons. Within the latest document, in contrast, the geography of rural Northern Ireland is described as consisting of main towns, small towns and villages, and open countryside with a total population of 1.012 million in 1998. The inclusion of main towns in this definition of rurality is significant and recognises the functional interdependence which exists across the settlement hierarchy throughout Northern Ireland. Using this broader definition of the rural, the regional development strategy estimates that just under 70,000 dwellings will be required in small towns, villages and open countryside through to 2015, with up to 40,000 dwellings located in the main towns. In short, some 44 per cent of new housing will be targeted outside the cities and main towns of Northern Ireland, which is broadly in line with the 41 per cent share of the existing Northern Ireland population within this territory.

The future distribution between small towns, villages and open countryside is footnoted in the strategy as a matter to be decided at the district level through the development plan process. Nevertheless, some insights into future policy practices

291

can be gleaned from the text of *Shaping Our Future*. In the first instance, there is welcome recognition of contrasting development pressures between the Belfast Travel to Work Area and the rest of the region which, in turn, require a differentiation of planning response. This translates to a raft of policies which are supportive of revitalisation in declining settlements as opposed to careful growth management in those small towns and villages that have been rapidly expanding. The tone of these measures and their related implementation go well beyond the sphere of land use planning. However, the muted response by government bodies to the regional strategy, linked to their unease about the degree to which the document is over-arching and binding, must cast doubt on its capacity to deliver on this front. Secondly, while there is positive policy expression to create and sustain a living countryside with a high quality of life for all its residents, concerns are equally noted about the perceived cumulative visual impact of inappropriate single house development. The strategy states:

> These growing pressures present a threat to the open countryside which is a vital resource for sustaining the genuine rural community. The cumulative impacts of this development include: loss of agricultural land and habitats; fields being sold off to house townspeople; increased traffic on rural roads; the risk of pollution from growing numbers of septic tanks; the increased visual impact of more structures in the landscape; unnecessary extension of infrastructure and services; and a weakening of towns and villages. (DRD, 2001: 89)

The strategy suggests that where adverse cumulative impacts are identified within rural Northern Ireland it will be necessary to take 'difficult decisions at the local level in relation to the control of individual properties' (105). The eventual publication of a Regional Planning Policy Statement on the Countryside is promised by the strategy to help refine a set of regulations connected to the implementation of the strategy in relation to rural Northern Ireland. While the regional strategy has been careful to avoid detailed policy prescription on this issue, it remains the case that single house development in the countryside will continue to run as a deeply contested feature of the planning policy arena. The possibility of stricter controls will no doubt be energetically resisted by local authority elected representatives and a well-organised coalition of over 500 rural community groups.

THE NORTHERN IRELAND REGIONAL STRATEGY:
A SOCIETY-WIDE HUG?

Planning frameworks at national and regional scales are much in vogue. In Ireland and Wales the completion of National Spatial Strategies are paralleled in England by the emphasis placed on Regional Planning Guidance. A possible move to regional spatial strategies, as canvassed in a Government Green Paper (Department of Transport, Local Government and the Regions, 2001), underlines the depth of the current quest to secure more effective linkages between strategic and local planning. This type of strategy at a generic level can perform a number of uses, which Harrison and Todes (2001) summarise as comprising:

- guidance for public sector investment in infrastructure and services;
- the spatial allocation of public sector support to reduce spatial inequalities;
- indicative guidance for private sector investment;
- public/private collaboration in development;
- rationalised resource allocations across space and within government policies and programmes;
- a level of certainty and consistency in decision making within and across sectors;
- spatial guidance for land use management.

In other words, strategic frameworks should seek to represent the visible expression of the much vaunted phrase 'joined up government'. Their ambition should be matched by a depth of possibilities which acknowledge that contemporary governance

293

is worked out through multiple stakeholders operating at different spatial scales. The history of regional planning in Northern Ireland is dominated by an authoritarian and allocative model of who gets what and where, and, as noted above, the content of *Shaping Our Future* continues with this tradition in relation to housing guidance. But in the wake of an unprecedented and welcome participatory effort to engage with multiple stakeholders outside government (Murray and Greer, 2000), the final form of *Shaping Our Future* demonstrates the reality of turf protection politics heavily camouflaged by large doses of Micawberesque rhetoric which is light on a 'how-to' commitment. A hard-won consensus has been purchased at the cost of strident optimism, generality and policy ambiguity. The upbeat language of inclusiveness weighs heavily in a narrative which adopts the comfortable metaphors of the 'family' of settlements, Belfast as the 'heart' of the region, and the conjoining of rural at every opportunity with 'community'. In contrast, the tone of the 'Implementation' section comes across as an urgency to create as much administrative space as possible between the parent authority, the Department for Regional Development, and its government siblings.

Rural planning and development in Northern Ireland has long had to deal with a suite of wicked dialectics which surface, for example, as West of the Bann versus East of the Bann, countryside development versus landscape protection, rural versus urban, and top down prescription versus bottom up involvement in the policy process. The deeper issues which these represent are about spatial and social equity, dealing with a divided society, how the rural is perceived, and the weight to be given to new alignments of participatory democracy. Each chapter in this book offers insights on these vexing questions. Thus the economic challenges in rural Northern Ireland across agriculture, business and tourism are matched by crises of place whose total collapse has been, at best, forestalled by an energetic civil society and some imaginative public sector intervention. It could be argued that the success of *Shaping Our Future* is its sophisticated combination of planning process and, at times, ambiguous language which have tackled head-on (and sometimes avoided) these wicked dialectics to produce a statement that can appeal to multiple interests. As has been observed in other circumstances, there is something for everyone, but everyone does not get everything that they have argued for. However, in its frequent retreat to land use management in general and development control in particular, *Shaping Our Future* falls short of providing the necessary leadership for truly transforming the rural. The strategy looks out to a time horizon of 2025 but its relevance for and acceptability in rural society will unquestionably fracture much earlier if its interpretation is dominated by quite narrow functional and bureaucratic concerns related to the determination of planning applications. Rethinking the future of the rural in Northern Ireland and its relationship with rural planning remains a pressing necessity for policy makers.

INTEGRATED RURAL DEVELOPMENT REVISITED

As noted above, the Regional Development Strategy, *Shaping Our Future*, represents the latest manifestation of a debate about the quantity and distribution of settlement in Northern Ireland that reaches back to the Matthew Plan in 1964 and the 1975–1995 Regional Physical Development Strategy. It is opportune, therefore, to resurface the principles of Integrated Rural Development since it was this concept that breathed life into the rural economy and society at a time when the urban-led approaches of Matthew and its later variations were perceived as being inimical to the well-being of rural communities.

While there have been many interpretations of Integrated Rural Development, its principal tenets, which have a particular resonance in the Northern Ireland context, may be outlined as:

1 a concern that funds for development from international, national or local sources are used efficiently, and that packages of measures are mutually reinforcing in their impact on problems rather than being dispersed or fragmented;

2   a multi-sectoral approach to development. While improve-
    ments to agriculture are a critical element in the overall
    process, measures to promote other sectors of the economy,
    to supplement or to promote an alternative to income from
    farming, are fundamental to the concept;
3   economic measures to be paralleled with initiatives in the
    social sphere, especially in education and training, together
    with improvements in infrastructure;
4   an attempt to concentrate effort on aiding poor areas
    and more specifically poor people living in such areas. As a
    corollary, development inputs are to be matched with the
    specific needs and aspirations of the target groups to which
    development programmes are addressed;
5   a requirement that local people become actively involved not
    only in identifying needs and opportunities for development,
    but also in the working through of projects;
6   a demand for institutional reform, expressed mainly as the
    devolution of powers from the national to the regional and
    local levels of administration.

All these principles have been applied within Northern Ireland
over the past twenty-five years, with their record of success and
setbacks being recounted in this volume of essays. Two issues
are worthy of particular mention. Firstly, attachment to place
and homeland has been reaffirmed again and again. This is
poignantly evident in the determination of the farming sector to
struggle on in the face of a litany of difficulties. At a more
general level the overall distribution of population throughout
Northern Ireland is testament to a sense of commitment to the
pays, as noted by Graham in the previous chapter. Had the
growth centre model of the 1960s and 1970s been pursued
with unswerving purpose, the result in terms of a rootless and
largely unfulfilled population can only be imagined. In this
respect the contribution of rural development to a lessening of
the misery of the Troubles is underplayed.

Secondly, the growth of an articulate, vibrant civil society,
supported by a mesh of active community groups and served by
a cadre of experts from central and local government, together

296

with independent organisations, is nothing less than remarkable. There have, of course, been reverses, as in the case of some economic projects, but this is only to cavil at the creation of a highly effective and valuable social phenomenon.

It is argued here that the last decade represented the great leap forward in terms of rural development, and in a very strict sense its driving forces are to be found in the *Shaping Our Future* document. And yet, at this moment of celebration there is cause for concern which goes well beyond the reaches of academic reservation. Thus, for example, the adoption of *Shaping Our Future* by the Northern Ireland Assembly propelled the advancement of a new plan for the Belfast Metropolitan Area. This is commendable in itself, but its broad-ranging and detailed inquiry across environmental, social and economic concerns in the Belfast complex runs the risk of relegating the rural to a state of limbo. The perceived boldness of endeavour connected to the Belfast Metropolitan Area Plan contrasts with the mechanistic formula being rolled out for rural areas in Northern Ireland by other Area Plans and where the allocative and hierarchical housing unit model is far removed from the warm rhetoric of *Shaping Our Future*.

The promise of the publication of a Regional Planning Statement on the Countryside does nothing to allay such concerns. If anything, it brings them into high relief since the erstwhile equation of the rural with countryside and landscape is seen to be re-worked and the compendium of policies and regulations as contained in the 1993 *Planning Strategy for Rural Northern Ireland* easily comes to mind. Rural planning and rural development, far from being integrated, face the unwelcome prospect of being at odds, one with the other.

This divergence is highlighted by the recently published *Northern Ireland Rural Development Programme Strategy 2001–2006* (Department of Agriculture and Rural Development, 2001). The strategy identifies five priority themes: capacity building, local regeneration projects and programmes, sectoral development projects and programmes, micro-business development, and natural resource rural tourism. These are set within a broader spatial context of North-South and East-West cooperation. The Minister, Bríd Rodgers, in the Foreword to the document, pledges that she will be chairing a Rural Proofing Forum to ensure that government policies take account of rural needs and that an Inter-departmental Rural Development Steering Group made up of senior officials from all government departments, first established in 1990, is to remain in place. This positive and confident approach, supportive of rural communities, is addressed to a broad, frontal assault on rural disadvantage and is quite clearly dependent upon the close cooperation of policy makers. Even when potential difficulties are envisaged, the document is up-front and heartening in tone, as in the case of the environment: 'An important challenge for the Rural Development Programme is to simultaneously make use of the economic potential of the natural environment, while also protecting it and the economic and social context that sustains it.' And again: 'It is, therefore, important that rural communities are helped to become actively involved in the management and improvement of the environment in their areas and take ownership of local environmental projects' (16–17). The important point here is that these sentiments are in marked contrast to the Northern Ireland Regional Development Strategy, which returns to the *ideé fixe* of rural physical planning in Northern Ireland, that of single house development in the countryside. This is a bleak repeat of the almost primeval antipathy to new single houses in the landscape, coupled with a wringing of the hands about the weakening of the towns and villages in predominantly rural areas. Perhaps this is where the gaping fault line between rural planning and rural development lies: planning looks for problems: development looks for solutions. The enduring frustration with rural planning in Northern Ireland derives from its tendency to desocialise the territories which it claims an affinity with: the pre-eminence of landscape protection policies on planning policy maps fosters a sense of rural space that, in short, is envisioned as being socially empty (after Harley, 1988).

At the wider scale of the island of Ireland, an uncannily similar gulf has been exposed. Just as the Northern Ireland Regional Development Strategy has been progressed, so too the

National Spatial Strategy for the Republic of Ireland has been a focus for the re-working of the regional planning studies of the 1960s. What emerges is a picture of two Irelands, each long embedded in history and comprising, firstly, a more urbanised, densely settled east coast corridor that stretches from Larne to Rosslare, and with some geographic licence through to Cork on the south coast, and secondly, a more rural, small town and village dominated area, roughly demarcated as being to the west of the Bann and the Shannon. In the Republic intense effort has been directed at exploring ways to reduce the growth of the Greater Dublin Area, which is projected, if untrammelled, to increase in population by more than 800,000 to almost 2.4 million people by 2020. At the same time a background paper for the National Spatial Strategy (Department of the Environment and Local Government, 2001) notes that over the past five years, one in three houses have been built as one-offs in the countryside, a total of 18,000 out of 50,000 in the year 2000, with the most notable occurrence being in the corridor from Galway to Leitrim, where the urban structure is weakest. Assessing the merits and drawbacks of single houses in the countryside has been one of the most constant features of physical planning in Ireland over the past thirty years, although the debate is never more than one-sided when it comes to planners assessing costs and benefits. It is as if single houses in the countryside are an affront to one of the central pillars of planning orthodoxy. The similarity in thinking between the approaches to the future spatial planning framework of Northern Ireland and the Republic of Ireland is myopic in the circumstances of rural areas in both jurisdictions, since it relies on the old, urban-driven approach, even if the language of growth centres has been replaced by a new European vernacular of gateways and hubs.

MOVING RURAL PLANNING AND DEVELOPMENT BEYOND *SHAPING OUR FUTURE*

A more radical approach to the future planning and development of rural Ireland is required, one that is more patently bottom up in its canons and committed to strong links between all levels of administration. This has been made much more possible of late by the burgeoning amount of small area data becoming available for analysis (see for example, McHugh, 2001) and the process of baselining key indices in rural areas. Lest this plea be dismissed as mere academic quibbling, the Northern Ireland Executive should publish a Rural White Paper, support the preparation of sub-regional integrated rural development strategies, and seek to deepen respect for pluralism in rural society through authentic dialogue. Taken together, these have the potential to move rural planning and development beyond the limited scope of *Shaping Our Future*.

(1) The publication of a White Paper for Rural Northern Ireland.

It is interesting to note that this received enthusiastic endorsement by the Panel which convened the Public Examination into *Shaping Our Future*, but has been quietly sidelined by government during the interim. Rural White Papers have been published for other parts of the UK, and in 1999 the Department of Agriculture and Food issued a comparable document for the Republic of Ireland. A major policy statement on rural Northern Ireland is, thus, significant by its absence. It is important that the terms of reference for the preparation of this White Paper are agreed by the Northern Ireland Assembly on a consensus basis with rural constituencies, and, accordingly, the following checklist adapted from the then UK Department of the Environment, Transport and the Regions (1999) statement on rural strategies is put forward to facilitate that conversation:

1 an analysis of the Northern Ireland economy should specifically consider rural areas and their distinctive features and include consideration of land and water based industries as well as countryside environmental assets;
2 rural needs should be considered using indicators which can properly assess such needs;
3 there should be consultation with key rural partners and other stakeholders concerned with all aspects of rural areas in Northern Ireland;

4 the White Paper should cover all rural areas in Northern Ireland — both those in need of regeneration and others;

5 the White Paper should consider the inter-relationships of the rural and urban components of Northern Ireland;

6 recognition should be given to the need to integrate social, economic and environmental considerations at the local level in rural areas;

7 the White Paper should identify approaches tailored to rural areas to meet the rural issues identified in the preceding analysis;

8 barriers to the development and delivery of programmes meeting rural needs, not least in relation to matters of inclusion and diversity, should be identified;

9 the White Paper should give encouragement to the preparation and local delivery of sub-regional strategies which take forward rural objectives;

10 the roles of rural partners in the implementation of the White Paper should be clearly set out and it should give specific encouragement to local government and rural community involvement in decision making and delivery;

11 government should demonstrate that it is organised in a way which will help with the identification of future rural issues and the effective delivery of rural programmes;

12 the White Paper should set out a fair and defensible basis for the allocation of resources between rural and urban areas;

13 methodologies should be identified to monitor and evaluate rural programmes in terms of outcomes and impact in rural areas;

14 the White Paper should commit government to an ongoing scrutiny of rural policies and initiatives in order to promote flexible responses to changing circumstances.

It is within this context that two particular proposals can be located which could contribute to bridging the gap between rural planning and rural development. Firstly, as demonstrated by Sterrett (Chapter 5), house design is a notable feature of contestation in rural areas. But design considerations have wider application across other types of built development and deserve equal attention. A design advice unit should be established under the auspices of the Rural Development Council to assist prospective developers to negotiate the physical planning process. With a modicum of carefully crafted design input, the Northern Ireland landscape could absorb much larger quantities of development. Secondly, the CRISP initiative (discussed by McSorley and McKane in Chapter 10), deserves to be re-launched on a more comprehensive inter-agency basis in order to support the continued regeneration of small towns and villages, especially in relation to environmental improvements. This layer of settlement geography is crucial to the future well-being of rural society and thus it is vital that commitments are also made to support a programme of infrastructural improvements, not least those related to adequate waste water treatment facilities which profoundly determine prospects for small settlement growth.

(2) The preparation of new sub-regional integrated rural development strategies.

One of the limitations of *Shaping Our Future* is the portrayal of rural areas as a monolithic 'rural resource'. On the other hand, at local level there is a plethora of planning activity which runs the gamut of Department of the Environment Area Plans, District Council Local Agenda 21 strategies and area-based partnership strategies, LEADER + strategies, and community-led strategies and plans. Government departments, agencies and other public bodies also have their corporate strategies, development programmes and shorter-term plans. Within the border corridor between Northern Ireland and the Republic of Ireland there is a further suite of strategies and plans sponsored by local authority clusters. In short, there is a crowded arena of planning activity which urgently requires streamlining and greater coherence. A move towards the preparation of sub-regional development strategies in Northern Ireland is timely.

At the same time it is important to recognise the obligations of legal process and operational accountability in that endeavour.

The former gives an enduring procedural distinctiveness to statutory development plans, while the latter places greater emphasis on the performance and results of public bodies over a shorter time span. The merging of statutory land use planning with broader social and economic strategic planning is thus ruled out. But quite clearly it is important that there is close coordination and complementarity of objectives between each approach. Rural development, for example, should not be frustrated by inappropriate planning control policies.

There are substantial economies of scale benefits which can accrue from having new sub-regional integrated rural development strategies in place:

- First, they recognise that the territories of most existing District Council areas are small in size and that for many industrial activities and occupational groups the labour markets are much larger. Certainly it is the case in Northern Ireland that few areas may be considered as local labour markets except perhaps in respect to unskilled and low paid work.

- Second, the goods and services produced (and withdrawn) by the private, community/voluntary and public sectors within the territory of a single District Council are likely to be aimed at a much wider catchment area and thus have a bearing on the employment and quality of life of a much larger number of residents.

- Third, it makes it possible to introduce into our definition of rural areas a new time–space dynamic based on advanced telecommunications where the friction of distance is less significant and the urban and the rural are appreciated as being truly interdependent (for example, in regard to training and third-level education).

- Fourth, it enlarges the scope for enhancing networked relationships among multiple stakeholders (for example, firms, chambers of commerce, enterprise support organisations) and diverse initiatives (for example, Territorial Employment Pacts, or the social economy), thus adding momentum to the territorial clustering of social capital.

- Fifth, it provides an opportunity for local areas to be focused developmentally on what they can do best and do differently, rather than seek to do everything as identified on a menu of funding opportunity. Local behaviour can change from competition and duplication to complementarity within a sub-regional development framework.
- Sixth, in a world where production and consumption increasingly focus on images and symbols, the larger territorial focus provides scope for the construction of new place identities which can reinforce the marketing of everything from regional foods to tourism products and craft goods.

Local government, in collaboration with the Department for Regional Development, should be charged with taking the lead role in coordinating the preparation of new sub-regional integrated rural development strategies. These should have a spatial representation and become the vehicle through which initiatives and programmes are brought forward in consultation with rural people. Moreover, the operation of the local authority cross-border networks (discussed in Chapter 11 by Greer) provides an important mechanism to unlock the potential of the border corridor territory in both jurisdictions, not least in relation to the provision of and access to services. The Northern Ireland Regional Development Strategy is patently uncomfortable with this dimension, as exemplified by its muted identification of 'Transnational Development Linkages and Opportunities' (Figure 13.1), a sensitivity which hopefully will be avoided by the National Spatial Strategy for the Republic of Ireland.

(3) Deepening respect for pluralism in rural society through authentic dialogue.

The next decade is a crucial period for the future of rural society, as Northern Ireland continues to adapt to the provisions of the Good Friday Agreement of 1998, the countryside moves deeper into a post-productivist agricultural regime, and the transfer of substantial EU assistance declines beyond 2006. The retention of rural development as a priority of public policy and greater responsiveness by physical planning require the continuity of participatory dialogues at regional, sub-regional and local scales on the basis that these narratives of individual and collective effort to bring about change can influence the way that rural places, communities and identities are interpreted. The value of dialogue at a conceptual level can be summarised as follows:

- it can better connect the top down and bottom up perspectives on development by facilitating new understandings;
- dialogue can change the views of participants;
- dialogue works on the basis that many people have pieces of the desired way forward;
- dialogue does not require that conclusions are reached on everything, but rather is an ongoing process linked to a capacity to develop new ideas;
- authentic dialogue is built around a respect for fairness, appreciation of diversity, and quality relationships.

But these interlocking dimensions also have relevance for a deeper transformation of the rural in Northern Ireland. Within the region a complex support infrastructure has been established to facilitate dialogue in line with the view that extensive participation can contribute to democratic renewal. A very wide range of training and educational materials related to participation have also been published and, specifically within the sphere of rural planning and development, include advice on consultative processes (Rural Community Network, 2001), learning communities (Rural Development Council, 2001) and village strategies (Murray and Greer, 2001). A key challenge ahead is thus one of continuing to animate and then sustaining a multiplicity of rural voices. It is argued here that this can best be advanced, in terms of coherence, by seeking a commitment at all levels in society to the principles of equity, diversity and interdependence.

These principles have long been championed by the Community Relations Council and the International Fund for Ireland as a new way to build respect in a society with multiple divisions (Murray and Murtagh, 2002). They depend on dialogue to promote equality of access to resources, structures and decision-making processes and for the adoption of actions to secure and maintain these objectives. These conversations must in turn be set against an ever-changing variety of community and individual experiences. Thus respect for diversity affirms the value which can be derived from the existence, recognition, understanding and tolerance of difference, whether expressed through religious, ethnic, political or gender background (Community Relations Council, 1998). Diversity, accordingly, is about being free to shape and articulate multiple identities. Finally, interdependence requires a recognition by different interest or identity groupings of their obligations and commitments to others and of the interconnectedness of individual/community experiences and ambitions, leading to the development of a society which is at once cohesive and diverse; interdependence is thus about quality of relationships.

The Introduction to this book makes the point that the urban is so often the departure point for analysis and prescription relating to the rural. A respectful dialogue conducted on the basis of equity, diversity and interdependence can remove the rural from that residual location. Moreover, it can interweave those public policy-making processes connected to rural planning and development with a more complete understanding of the changes required to meet multiple needs set within the economic, social and cultural identities deployed by individuals in different circumstances. Understanding better the nature of and interaction between individual and collective identities within rural Northern Ireland, their linkages with local territories and their relationships with service organisations will provide that much-needed new awareness of how rural Northern Ireland is itself being redefined from within and without.

In conclusion, the rural in Northern Ireland matters. A reconsidered, bottom up, radical and interpretative agenda is necessary, not least at a time when the old certainties of urban-based concentrations of investment on their own are appreciated as inadequate. Sustainability is a contemporary buzz-word, and in rethinking rural planning and development, as outlined above, it will be possible to reinvigorate this concept, so often used to question the viability of an assumed monolithic rural society, into one which celebrates its diversity, persistence, achievements and legacy.

REFERENCES

Community Relations Council (1998), *Into the Mainstream: Strategic Plan 1998–2001*, Belfast.

Department of Agriculture and Rural Development (2001), *The Northern Ireland Rural Development Programme Strategy 2001–2006*, Belfast: HMSO.

Department of the Environment and Local Government (2001), *The National Spatial Strategy: Implications for Housing*, Dublin.

Department for Regional Development (2001), *Shaping our Future — Regional Development Strategy for Northern Ireland 2025*, Holywood: Corporate Document Services.

Department of Transport, Local Government and the Regions (2001), *Planning: Delivering a Fundamental Change*, London: HMSO.

Harley, J.B. (1988), 'Maps, Knowledge and Power', in D. Cosgrove and S. Daniels (eds), *The Iconography of Landscape*, Cambridge University Press.

Harrison, P. and A. Todes (2001), 'The Use of Spatial Frameworks in Regional Development in South Africa', *Regional Studies*, vol. 35, no. 1: 65–72.

Matthew, R. (1964), *Belfast Regional Survey and Plan, 1962*, Belfast: HMSO.

McHugh, C. (2001), *A Spatial Analysis of Socio-economic Adjustments in Rural Ireland 1986–1996*, unpublished PhD thesis, Department of Geography, NUI Maynooth.

Murray, M. and J. Greer (2000), *The Northern Ireland Regional Strategic Framework and Its Public Examination Process: Towards a New Model of Participatory Planning? A Research Monograph*, Belfast: Rural Innovation and Research Partnership.

Murray, M. and J. Greer (2001), *Participatory Village Planning – Practice Guidelines Workbook*, Belfast: Rural Innovation and Research Partnership.

Murray, M. and B. Murtagh (2002), *Reconnecting Rural People Through Authentic Dialogue: Equity, Diversity and Interdependence in the Northern Ireland Rural Development Arena*, Cookstown: Rural Community Network.

Rural Community Network (2001), *Consultation Practice Guidelines*, Cookstown.

Rural Development Council (2001), *Learning Communities: A Workbook*, Cookstown.

INDEX